Demystifying Tibet

Demystifying Tibet

UNLOCKING THE SECRETS
OF THE LAND OF THE SNOWS

Lee Feigon

ELEPHANT PAPERBACKS
Ivan R. Dee, Publisher, Chicago

DEMYSTIFYING TIBET. Copyright © 1996 by Lee Feigon. All rights
reserved. This book was first published in 1996 by Ivan R. Dee.

First ELEPHANT PAPERBACK edition published 1998 by Ivan R. Dee,
Publisher, 1332 North Halsted Street, Chicago 60622. Manufactured in the
United States of America and printed on acid-free paper.

Maps by Victor Thompson

Library of Congress Cataloging-in-Publication Data:
Feigon, Lee, 1945–
Demystifying Tibet : unlocking the secrets of the land of the
snows / Lee Feigon. — 1st elephant pbk. ed.
p.   cm.
Originally published: 1996.
Includes bibliographical references and index.
ISBN 1-56663-196-3 (pbk.: alk. paper)
1.   Tibet (China)—History.   I.   Title.
DS785.F34   1998
951'.5—dc21   98-9475

For my children, Maia, Brooke, and Gera

Contents

Foreword

Long before I was to journey to Tibet, I gained indirect access to its culture and history by hearing of the experiences of Dr. William McGovern. My father had taken one of McGovern's courses at Northwestern University in the late 1930s and had come away with indelible memories of the professor's colorful tales.[1] McGovern had lectured my father's class about his travails in Tibet and his struggle to cross rugged mountain passes in midwinter dressed as a Sikkimese servant. He had stained his body and even his eyes dark to avoid detection and had become the first Westerner to enter the Tibetan capital, Lhasa, in almost two decades. It was an exciting story, one that awakened my interest in Asia, especially Tibet. But it was not until I was writing this book that I finally read McGovern's romantic and suspenseful true-life adventure, *To Lhasa in Disguise*.

McGovern was a Tibetan scholar with an excellent command of the language and of cultural and social distinctions, and his book makes for interesting and entertaining reading. But like virtually every other Western writer who has gone to Tibet, from the eighteenth-century Scotsman George Bogle to the authors of the *Lonely Planet* tourist guide to the region, McGovern regarded his visit to Tibet as an adventure with a land outside of time and history. In this he reflects a Western attitude toward Tibet that is no less riddled with patronizing stereotypes than the view currently displayed by the Chinese.

Westerners can at least blame their remoteness from the country for their perpetuation of stereotypes and weird travelers' tales about Tibet. The Chinese have no such excuse for their insistence that Tibet has long been part of the "Middle Kingdom." They continue to perpetuate an even stranger and more patronizing image of Tibet than do most Westerners.

In this book I examine the country behind the myths to locate the origins of today's Tibet and to sort out its controversial relationship with China. In penetrating the veil of myths that have been written about Tibet, one discovers how long and distinguished is its history and how recent is the Chinese idea that Tibet is part of China. As late as the early twentieth century, Chinese nationalists who tried to stretch the territory of the Chinese state to claim that Greater China should encompass Vietnam, Korea, and even Japan still rejected the idea that Tibet could be part of China. It was not until well into this century that the notion began to take hold—almost accidentally.

The fact is that culturally, linguistically, and religiously the Tibetans are distinct from the Chinese. Although the two peoples obviously share characteristics as a result of their long association with each other, their differences far outweigh their similarities. The Tibetans have far more in common with their nomadic central Asian neighbors than with the sedentary, rice-eating Chinese.

One of the most compelling reasons for studying the Tibetans is to demolish myths not only about Tibet but also about China, especially the notion that China has always been the *zhongguo* or "Central Kingdom" to the various cultures and peoples in the region. Before the emergence of the modern nation states, for hundreds, probably thousands of years, Chinese and Tibetans as well as Mongols, Manchus, and other peoples intermingled with one another in border areas, often changing identities and even nationalities almost at will. Present-day Chinese claims to Tibet are based on an assumption of Han superiority and an assertion that the other cultures and civilizations of the region gradually and inexorably have been absorbed into the Chinese nexus. In fact, this has not been the case. Not only did the Chinese often become Tibetans—as well as Mongols and Manchus— but the cultures of these peoples were by no means subsets of that of China, either in the past or in the present. The history of the Tibetan-Chinese relationship thus sheds light not only on the formation of Tibetan identity but also in part on the creation of Chinese national identity.

In the writing of this book my wife Leanne again provided valuable editorial assistance. I am grateful to Alex Day, a former student who, even after his graduation, has continued to offer invaluable research ideas and suggestions. I refer to his real-life experiences in this book. I also thank the students who came on the Colby College trip to Tibet with me, especially Christopher Bennechi and Sarah Steindel Blood, who made a video of the experience.

My thanks to Ed Gargan for graciously putting up with me in India, and to Morris Rossabi who read an earlier version of this manuscript with phenomenal speed and promptness as well as his usual insightfulness. I am grateful to the Dalai Lama for meeting with me and permitting an interview.

Librarians and archivists throughout the world, from Lhasa to Dharamsala, and from Chicago to Waterville, Maine, have my gratitude. But I especially wish to thank Sonny Pomerleau for the great number of interlibrary loan resources she secured for me.

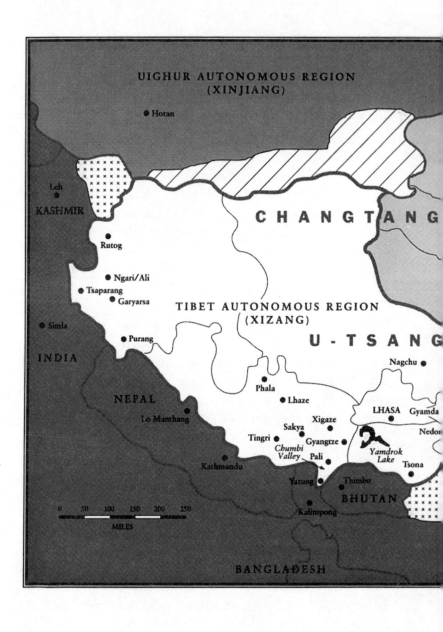

UIGHUR AUTONOMOUS REGION
(XINJIANG)

Hotan

KASHMIR

Leh

CHANGTANG

Rutog

Ngari/Ali

Tsaparang

Garyarsa

TIBET AUTONOMOUS REGION
(XIZANG)

Simla

U - TSANG

Purang

Nagchu

INDIA

Phala

NEPAL

Lhaze

LHASA   Gyamda

Lo Manthang

Xigaze

Nedor

Sakya

Tingri

Gyangtze

Chumbi
Valley   Pali

Yamdrok
Lake   Tsona

Kathmandu

Yatung   Thimbu

BHUTAN

0   50   100   150   200   250

Kalimpong

MILES

BANGLADESH

INNER MONGOLIA

Dunhuang

Jiayuguan

Zhangye

M D O

NINGXIA

Delingha

Qinghai Lake
(Kokonor)

Parig

Golmud

Xining
Kumbum

Lanzhou

Chabtsa
(Gonghe)

Rekong
(Tongren)

GANSU

INGHAI

Machen

Labrang

Tewo

Jyekundo
(Yushu)

Sershu

Zogye

Ngaba (Aba)

Songzhou
(Songpan)

Nangchen

Derge

Kanze
(Garzè)

Barkam

SICHUAN

Riwoche

Chamdo

Yarlang
Tsangpo

Gonjo

Nyarong

Tawu

Draya

Chengdu

vi
Nyingtri

Bowo

Batang

Litang

Kangding/
Tachienlu

Markam

Chongqing

Daoba

Jiulong

Dzayül

Dechen
Gyaltang

Muli

BURMA

GUIZHOU

YUNNAN

Tibet
Autonomous
Region (TAR)
or Western
Tibet

Areas with Tibetan
autonomous
status under
Qinghai, Gansu,
Sichuan and
Yunnan provinces

Territory
claimed by
the Tibetan
Government
in exile

Disputed
territories
between India
and China

Demystifying Tibet

ONE

❧

Images and Realities

For centuries Tibet has cast its spell over the Western world: from early explorers who risked their lives in Himalayan mountain passes, to Victorian armchair travelers who merely dreamed of the region's glories, to modern jet-setters chalking off yet another exotic locale. Western images of Tibet have piled up like snow, each layer loosely following the contours below but the whole mass entirely obscuring the detail underneath. The general drift has been that Tibet is seen as a snowy Shangri-la inhabited by a spiritual, peace-loving, yet simple people in splendid isolation from the rest of the world.

Not only are these stereotypes inaccurate, but most are secondhand at that. They derive from earlier stereotypes about Asia, and especially China, developed at a time when few Westerners traveled outside their own borders. For them Asia was a fantasy onto which they projected both the hopes and nightmares of their own lives. Over time, as Westerners came into closer contact with China and the reality of the country intruded on their fantasy, the focus of many myths about Asia shifted to Tibet.[1] Thus misconceptions about Tibet were the compilation of even broader errors.

Like many fantasies, the image of Tibet contains elements of reality. The real Tibet, though far less ethereal, is no less picturesque than most Westerners have imagined. It is indeed a stunningly beautiful land nestled in the Himalayas, where turquoise lakes reflect snow-capped peaks. Herds of lumbering yaks graze in the valleys while the mountains teem with rare black-necked cranes, snow leopards, and hundreds of other exotic species. In Lhasa, the capital, a colorful ethnic assortment of pilgrims winds through the architectural wonders of the Potala Palace.

And yet none of these marvels is quite as it seems. Even the topography is deceptive. Nicknamed "the rooftop of the world" and "the land of the snows," the Tibetan region, with an average elevation of 13,120 feet above sea level, is indeed the highest inhabited area in the world. But it is neither as cold nor as snow-covered as outsiders expect it to be. This is because the most heavily populated areas of present-day Tibet, despite their high elevations, lie at distinctly southern latitudes. Although at 11,700 feet Lhasa is more than twice as high as Denver, it is at the same latitude as Saudi Arabia or Orlando, Florida. The high altitude makes for cold nights; still, the average temperature in the Tibetan capital in January is 32 degrees Fahrenheit, and summer temperatures are much higher. It does snow occasionally in November and December, but in spite of the country's reputation much less accumulates than might be imagined. As the days lengthen in January, most of the little snow that has fallen the previous month melts.

The melting is aided by one of the sunniest climates on earth. On average the sun warms Tibet for more than 3,400 hours each year.[2] This is roughly comparable to the desert area of the American Southwest, said to enjoy more sunshine than any other region in the world. In the thin atmosphere of the high Tibetan altitudes the sun is unfiltered. (Indeed, the high levels of ultraviolet radiation may be responsible for Tibet's having one of the highest incidents of cataracts in the world.[3]) The rays penetrate with such strength that even in the dead of winter, after the temperature has plunged well below zero during the night, days warm into the upper fifties or higher in Lhasa.

But Tibet ranges beyond Lhasa. In the southeast it dips down to touch Burma and Southeast Asia. In the west it borders India and Nepal. Today the northwestern frontier marks the beginning of Chinese Turkestan, but at one time Tibet butted up against Persia and the Middle East. To the east and north is China.

On paper Tibet appears most accessible from western China. There are no great mountains to cross before entering Tibet from this easterly direction. But this too is deceiving. The populated heartland where Lhasa is located is much closer to Nepal and the rest of the Indian subcontinent than to China. The inhabitants of the region have traversed the Himalayan passes connecting the two regions for centuries. Similarly, the occupants of northern Tibet have moved back and forth to Mongolia and central Asia. Thus even the seemingly simple task of identifying Tibet's closest neighbors is not an easy one.

Some of the mystery concerning the country is due to the fact that there are four different ways of defining Tibetan territory.[4] *Historical* Tibet was a vast dominion once stretching across much of Asia. The achievements of this dominion are often overlooked and belie the image of the Tibetans as an isolated and simple people. Yet even today, *cultural* Tibet is almost as big as its historical dominion. Tibetan populations still live in much of western China, Burma, eastern India, and Pakistan as well as Nepal, Bhutan, and Sikkim. Fewer than a hundred years ago, vast parts of present-day India as well as Pakistan still considered themselves under at least nominal Tibetan rule.

Geographic Tibet is smaller but still vast, about the same size as the whole of Western Europe. All told, the Tibetan highlands occupy approximately one-fifth of the total land mass of China, extending over 750,000 square miles through the Asian heartland. Most Tibetans consider all of geographic Tibet, and some of the lower-lying areas of western China as well, as part of their country.

Administrative Tibet is the Tibetan Autonomous Region. A unit of the People's Republic of China, it is the political remnant of the Tibetan state. In modern times the Chinese have created much of the confusion about Tibet, claiming that Tibet has long been a part of China. This is a recent historical fiction, though one to which many Chinese ardently cling. In any case, the Tibet they have created is a shrunken version of the original. It does not include the bulk of two of the three major regions of Tibet. Much of what was once called Kham is now in Sichuan, and virtually all of Amdo has been formed into Qinghai province. Even so, this area is enormous. It encompasses more than 470,000 square miles, considerably more than one-eighth the land area of all of China, which is roughly the size of the United States. This stripped-down version of Tibet is still about the size of all of Eastern Europe exclusive of what before 1991 was the Soviet Union.

But barren rocks and deserts cover much of this region. The temperature extremes further limit the country's agricultural production. In spite of relatively mild temperatures in the main populated areas of the southwest near Lhasa, the country as a whole averages fewer than fifty frost-free days each year. Under five people per square mile live in administrative Tibet. Its huge size notwithstanding, its two million people account for less than two-tenths of 1 percent of the total population of the People's Republic of China.

The Tibetan region was not always this desolate. What is now Tibet was once a coastal flatland. Then, some 45 million years ago, the Indian peninsula slammed into the Eurasian mainland. The resulting collision shoved the country skyward, in the process creating the Himalayas, the newest and tallest mountain range in the world, a range that is still growing. Geologists estimate that the Indian subcontinent has continued to penetrate the Eurasian mainland at a rate of about four centimeters per year. As India slides beneath Tibet, the soil that erodes from the Himalayas flows through the Ganges delta to replenish the subcontinent.

Geography here has created a superb political metaphor. For as India and China have coupled together, Tibet, stuck between them, has gradually contracted.⁵ If one believes in the dire symbolism of all this, there is new cause for hope. A recent geological survey has found that the Tibetan plateau has stopped contracting and that India, instead of sliding beneath the country, is now sliding off to the side.⁶

As the Tibetan coastal plains have collapsed, they have also moved closer to the heavens. A series of variously named mountain ranges rings and traverses Tibet. Like those of most of central Asia, they are simply extensions of the great Himalayan range. These subsidiary ranges include the jagged peaks of the Karakoram range, which straddles Tibet's western border. In the north they encompass the scraggy mountain tops of the Changtang, a rocky plateau almost eight hundred miles wide, booby-trapped with quicksand, swampy marshes, and glaciers. The great salt flats and brackish lakes of the Changtang are remnants of the Tethys Sea, which bordered Tibet before the great continental collision. Ringing the plateau on the north are the Kunlun and Tanggala mountains. Farther to the north the country drops off into the Qaidam Basin, a respectable nine thousand feet above sea level despite being dwarfed by its surroundings.

For centuries natives and foreigners regarded these Ti-

betan mountains as exercising a special magic. Today geologists believe they may in fact hold the key to shifts in the
world climate.[7] For one thing, the rapid and continuing lifting of the Himalayas and their associated ranges are said to
affect the trajectory of the jet streams, which control the general climatic patterns over North America and Eurasia.

Meteorologists believe the runoff from the Tibetan highlands may have an even greater effect on the global climate.
This is because all the major rivers of Asia originate in Tibet.
The great Indian rivers—the Ganges, the Sutlej, the Karnali,
and the Indus—begin in the Tibetan Kailas. The mighty Yarlong Zangpo, or Brahmaputra River (known in Bangladesh
as the Jamuna), first flows through the lowland valleys of
Tibet, separating the Himalayas from the Kailas Mountains
before turning into India's Assam Valley and ultimately join-
ing the Ganges and dumping its waters into the Bay of Bengal. The famous Southeast Asian rivers, the Mekong and the
Salween, start in central Tibet. And the headwaters of the
two great rivers of China, the Yangzi and the Yellow, are on
the northeastern part of the Tibetan plateau in what is now
China's Qinghai province. The confluence of all these rivers
in one place means that the runoff from the mountains of
Tibet affects the vegetation and agriculture of one of the
most fertile and populated areas of the world, home to half
the human race. Even minor ecological change in Tibet can
therefore have a major impact on vast portions of humanity.

For millions of years the runoff from the mountains of
Tibet at various times may have altered the amount of carbon dioxide in the atmosphere and radically affected the climate of the globe. Newly risen mountains exposed to the
elements the chemical substances contained in their rocks. As
a result, during periods when the Himalayas rose rapidly, the
rate of chemical erosion increased. Rain and melting snow
carried these chemicals into the streams and rivers that flow
through the fertile Asian agricultural heartland before exit-

ing into some of the world's great oceans. These chemicals changed the alkalinity of the oceans, especially in coastal waters. Giant algae blooms resulted. Because plants absorb carbon dioxide and emit oxygen, this huge increase in phytoplankton growth sucked carbon dioxide out of the atmosphere, diminishing what is now called the greenhouse effect and causing the earth to cool.

Carbon dioxide from the earth's atmosphere is also absorbed into rain. When rain hit newly exposed rocks in the Himalayas, the carbon dioxide combined with the stones' calcium deposits. According to scientists, as much as one-quarter of all the rock sediment released into the world's oceans has come from the Tibetan Himalayas, though they make up only 5 percent of the earth's surface. These minerals eventually formed the limestone that coats the ocean floor and is processed by marine life into shells. As this limestone increased, the amount of carbon dioxide decreased, causing the earth's atmosphere to cool further.[8]

Scientists still argue about whether most of this cooling occurred suddenly when the Tibetan plains first rose fifty million years ago, or if it is happening gradually. Some have argued that during periods of rapid uplift in Tibet—and by "rapid" geologists mean periods of millions of years—the carbon dioxide in the atmosphere diminished, which in turn increased cooling and glaciation. According to this theory, changes in the Tibetan mountains (as well as those of South America) produced the Glacier Age. Only when these mountains stopped rising rapidly did chemical erosion ease. Then the composition of the earth's waters returned to normal and the glaciers receded.[9]

Some scientists have further speculated about other effects on world and regional climate of geological and ecological change in Tibet. A recent study, for instance, has found that the duration of the snow cover in the Tibetan Himalayas directly and immediately affects the date of withdrawal of the summer monsoon from northwest India,[10] which in turn has a major impact on crops and industry in that region.

The denuding of Tibetan forests and grasslands that has occurred under Chinese occupation may drastically affect the world's climate and well-being. Some scientists fear that because of Tibet's high altitude, the carbon dioxide discharges from its forests and fields transfer more rapidly into the jet stream and thus affect not only the agricultural well-being of China and Southeast Asia but the weather in other parts of the globe as well. They are even more alarmed about nuclear wastes the Chinese have been dumping on the Tibetan plateau and the nuclear weapons they have stationed there.

The dramatic topography of Tibet provides a fitting backdrop for its peoples and monuments. Tibet's elevated inhabitants constitute one of the most eclectic populations on earth, one at odds with many popular depictions.

From eastern Tibet come Khampas, a tall, strikingly handsome people with angular features. Swords at their sides, the men enjoy their reputation as bandits, sometimes boasting to visitors about the number of Chinese they have beheaded. They bear little resemblance to the idealized vision of peaceful souls in Shangri-la. From central and northern Tibet come nomads in dreadlocks. The women, their plaited hair polished with yak butter, wear much of their families' wealth in the form of elaborate, gem-studded silver headdresses and earrings, making it readily available for aggressive trading. Goloks come from what is now administered as China's Qinghai province but which the Tibetans consider the Amdo region of their country. Fierce-looking Golok men, once feared for their banditry, wear yakhide boots and sheepskin jackets, sometimes topped incongruously by felt bowler hats that provide protection from the intense sun.[11]

Sherpas, Mongols, Muslims, solidly built peasants from southeastern Tibet, and elegantly dressed urbanites round out the riotous mixture of Tibetan types that can be found on a typical winter's day in Lhasa. Outlanders crowd the town, walking, playing, touring, and occasionally squatting by the edge of the roadway engaged in business of a less-than-public nature.

Cleanliness and sanitation rank low on the Tibetan scale of priorities. At the Jokhang temple, the so-called cathedral of Tibetan Buddhism, the rancid smell of yak butter, smeared on hair, skin, and clothing, and fueling thousands of candles, overpowers all other odors. Outside in the bazaar that surrounds the temple, the scene is far from idyllic, as spiritual supplications mix with spirited trading. But for the most part everyone remains good-natured. Even as they bargain and thrust merchandise on would-be buyers, the Tibetans joke and kibitz, seemingly ever willing to make fun of themselves.

Their marital customs strike outsiders as bizarre. Tibetans have traditionally practiced both polygamy—the custom of one man having more than one wife—and polyandry, the custom of one woman taking more than one husband. Among the common folk of central Tibet, polyandry seems to have been much more common than polygamy, and it is exemplified in the relative independence of Tibetan women.

Uniting this mix of peoples and races are language and religion. Despite differences in dialects, Tibetan is considered to be one distinct language, part of the Tibeto-Burman grouping of the Sino-Tibetan language family, though some now argue that its relationship to Chinese is tenuous at best and probably insupportable.[12] All agree that Tibetan is most closely related to Burmese and to the various tongues spoken by a few small groups of Himalayan and Southeast Asian peoples. But in the eclectic nature of Tibet, the written script, which is adopted from Indian writing, comes from the other side of the Himalayas.

In the winter, pilgrims from every part of ethnic and political Tibet crowd into Lhasa, forming long lines at the major shrines such as the Potala Palace and the Jokhang temple.

Tibetan religion is also eclectic. It combines the iconography of Indian Hinayana Buddhism with the doctrines of Chinese Mahayana Buddhism. It has also been influenced by the native shamanist Tibetan Bon religion, which still has its own school of adherents, as well as by Persian and central Asian beliefs. The resulting Buddhism has sprouted even more schools than the Tibetan language has dialects. All these schools revere their principal leaders as reincarnations of the leading deities of the Buddhist pantheon. In modern times the various schools have all considered the best known of these leaders, the Dalai Lama, as the supreme religious and political figure in the country. All Tibetans try to make periodic pilgrimages to Lhasa to show their devotion to the Dalai Lama and the shrines he once inhabited. In the winter they crowd the streets of the capital as well as those of other monastery towns.

Even more numerous than the chatting pilgrims crowding the temples and marketplaces are the dogs. As devout

Frank Lloyd Wright hung a photograph of the Potala Palace in his studio—the only building displayed there that the famous architect did not design. The palace is often called the world's largest wooden skyscraper.

Buddhists, Tibetans believe that canines are part of the cycle of rebirth, so no one can disturb them. These are not the majestic mastiffs of the countryside or the aristocratic Lhasa Apsos found in the homes of the elite; rather they are mangy mutts. Everywhere they can be seen scrounging for food, begging for scraps, and dozing on sidewalks and along roads. They roam the streets and monasteries of the country, copulating at will and sometimes sinking their teeth into unwary travelers.

As annoying as these dogs appear to the modern-day visitor, they must have been worse in earlier times. The British East India Company representative George Bogle, who visited Tibet in 1774, complained: "There is no walking out after it is dark, on account of the number of dogs which are then let loose; they are of the shepherd breed, the same kind with those called Nepal dogs, large size, often shagged like a lion, and extremely fierce."[13]

Cows and sheep also wander the sidewalks of Lhasa, grazing on bits of vegetation. It is not unusual to see Tibetans walking prized rams on leashes and even bringing them into restaurant kitchens while they eat or drink. Nor is it remarkable that sheep graze in the courtyard of the Lhasa Hotel, where they are quite sensibly used to keep down the grass.

As simple as Tibetan life appears to the outsider, Tibet is the seat of one of the most intriguing cultures in the world. Perhaps the most striking expression of this culture is in the great Tibetan monuments, which stand in sharp contrast to the country's backward urban and rural image.

Lhasa is home to the towering Potala Palace, one of the most beautiful and complex structures in the world, often referred to as the world's largest wooden skyscraper. Amazingly the Tibetans built the Potala in the seventeenth century without the use of the wheel. Believing that the circular shape of their prayer wheels was a sacred form, the Tibetans at that time chose not to deploy anything shaped like a circle for transportation or cartage. Instead, Tibetan laborers dragged the beams and other material for the construction of this massive, thirteen-story structure with a thousand rooms and more than ten thousand shrines from the surrounding valleys to Lhasa and then pulled them up the hill overlooking the city. The Potala's design and proportions still amaze builders. Frank Lloyd Wright kept a picture of the Potala in his studio—the only structure displayed there not designed by Wright himself.[14]

Clearly Tibet has sufficient oddities and incongruities to make it an interesting puzzle to any visitor. For centuries these paradoxes have tempted outsiders to claim they have solved the mysteries of the region. In spite of or perhaps because of this, even the origins of the Tibetan people have been obscured by rumor.

Western writers have speculated wildly on this subject. In the mid-nineteenth century, for instance, Joseph Wolff, an eccentric British explorer and missionary born the son of a Bavarian rabbi, popularized the idea of a long-lost population of Jews in the Himalayas.[15] In the early twentieth century Thomas Torrance, a Christian missionary, attracted considerable attention with his arguments that the Qiang (a proto-Tibetan tribe most scholars consider to be the main ancestors of the Tibetans) "show Semitic features" and that "many of their customs, too, indicate a close affinity to those of the Hebrews." The Qiang is, he concluded, "a Jew among our West China peoples. You can scarcely hide him even when his blood has been mingled with a strain of Chinese."[16] Most scholars long since have abandoned this notion, but in recent years the same argument has again been advanced by Rabbi E. Avichail, who operates Amishav, an institute in Jerusalem dedicated to finding and bringing back to the fold the ten lost tribes of Israel.[17]

The Nazis also developed a fascination with Tibet. In the late 1930s Hitler and Himmler went so far as to send an expedition into Tibet to measure Tibetan head sizes and ascertain that the Tibetans were not Jews but true Aryans.[18] Hitler even is reputed to have brought a group of monks back to Germany, instructing them to perform special chants to alter weather patterns in preparation for his ill-fated Russian invasion.

Others still believe the Tibetans to be descendants of a forgotten Christian kingdom. This idea, which began in the Middle Ages, shows how Western images of China later have been transferred to Tibet. In the twelfth century, stories circulated in Europe of a rich and powerful Christian kingdom in Asia ruled by a priest-king known as Prestor John. A short time later Marco Polo described a land called Tendruk that was part of Chinggis (or Genghis) Khan's empire and was, he claimed, ruled by a descendant of Prestor John who "is both a Christian and a priest; the greater part of the inhabitants being also Christians."[19] Marco Polo did not make much of

Tendruk because the bulk of his book focused on China (or Cathay as he called it), which he depicted as an advanced civilization possessed of wealth and commerce beyond anything imagined in Europe. But throughout the late Middle Ages the idea of a Christian kingdom in China loomed large in the imaginations of missionaries, who preferred to believe that ultimately the whole world would see things their way. It fascinated rulers as well as traders. Many traveled east or sent expeditions in that direction, hoping to open a second front behind the hostile lines of the Muslim and Mongol worlds.

Actual travelers to the region, however, soon turned their attention from the Chinese to the saffron-robed monks and the monasteries that characterize the Buddhism of Tibet, and which at least outwardly resemble Christian trappings. As early as the thirteenth century, the unofficial liaison of the king of France to the Mongol khan, Friar William Rubruck, described one such monastery as a Catholic sect whose practices had, as his chronicler John MacGregor puts it, simply "atrophied with time or isolation."[20] Given these similarities it may not be surprising that after the Jesuit Mateo Ricci reached China in the late 1500s and found no large Christian presence there, efforts to discover a lost Christian kingdom in Asia began to center on Tibet. The Jesuit Father Antonio de Andrade, who established a mission in Xigaze in 1620, believed, as MacGregor writes, that "Lamaism is but a degenerate form of Christianity, corrupted by its years of isolation. . . . He saw in Tibetan worship a recognition of the Trinity of God. . . . The tunics and mitres worn by Tibetan lamas could, with some imagination, be compared with the robes of Christian priests, and elements of baptism, confession, and communion seemed to have been present in Lamaism."[21]

This story took on a new twist in the nineteenth century when a Russian wrote an account in French of an Indian

Water plays an important role in Tibetan Buddhism, and different water vessels are often used for washing, rituals, and offerings. The water in this vase, which has a cover of bright multicolored silk, is poured into the hand and drunk during ceremonies. *(Land of the Lamas)*

story which claims that "Jesus in his youth went towards the East, down the silk caravan route, and spent several years in India, Kashmir, Ladakh, and maybe Tibet."[22] The Russian and several more recent travelers claim to have seen in Ladakh (which is also known as Little Tibet) a Tibetan version of the Gospels in which it is written that Jesus "was not killed because of Jewish activity or High Priests, but because the Romans feared he would lead a revolution."[23]

Tibetan Buddhism is not, of course, an isolated form of Christianity, and by the nineteenth century, as most missionaries were forced to accept this truth, the country took on a new image. Legends, however, persisted. Many Westerners perceived Tibet as China's alter ego.[24] The Manchus, a non-

Han group with ties to the Tibetans, then ruled China, and by the nineteenth century they also had begun to exercise a loose control over Tibetan foreign relations. Their efforts helped associate the region with China in Western eyes. As a result, Tibet became the new Asian fantasy land, an area that remained closed well after China opened itself to foreign contact. Tibet even took on the same dualism with which China had traditionally been viewed—alternately either the wealthy, virtuous land that gave birth to much of what we today consider civilization, or a country of heathen barbarians.[25]

By the mid- to late nineteenth century, as Peter Bishop observes, Tibet

> seemed to contain a strange mixture of opposites: the religion appeared rational yet thoroughly superstitious; to combine a high level of morality with rampant demonology and occultism. As a system it seemed exemplary in terms of its organization and its attainments in diplomacy and manners; yet dirt, idleness and mindless uniformity were conspicuous on a daily level; the leadership of the high lamas was, on every account, singularly inspiring yet carried with it dark overtones of spiritual and political absolutism; on the surface the country seemed naively content, but radiating out from Lhasa was a web of political and religious intrigue.
>
> Whilst apparently closed off and isolated from the mainstream of the world, Tibet seemed to exert an extraordinarily far-reaching spiritual influence. Even the landscape was at one and the same time exhilarating and boring. There always seemed to be more of Tibet—more of it geographically, and more of it in terms of its contradictions.[26]

This was a time of major geopolitical shifts. The Chinese, Nepalese, British, and even the Russians threatened Tibetan sovereignty. At the same time pressure from the West beleaguered other Asian countries, including China and Japan. Both nations responded by limiting their foreign contacts. Tibet eventually acted similarly, though even after Westerners were officially banned, foreigners continued to visit Tibet. But the image of a closed Asian society—first China, then Japan, and finally Tibet—became fixed in the Western imagination.

The mountains reinforced this view of Tibet as an isolated society. The mountains limited British imperial expansion in India, marking the boundary between the Asia Britain was able to conquer and the Asia whose ancient empire eluded it. The Western idea of mountains as sacred territory endowed with special qualities amplified this image. By the nineteenth century the Tibetan Himalayas were acknowledged to be the world's highest mountains, taller even than the Andes. Mount Everest, the tallest mountain in the world, was viewed with mystical awe.

Reports that flourished throughout the nineteenth and twentieth centuries of great deposits of gold in Tibet added even more glitter to Tibet's image and gave cynics an explanation for the Tibetan policy of consistently and successfully preventing foreigners from entering their country. The association of Tibet with gold had been made since the time of Herotodus, who spoke of great ants in the desert north of India who threw up sandheaps filled with gold.[27] Travelers' accounts appeared to confirm these rumors. In 1730 the leader of the Capuchin friars in Lhasa, Horace Della Penna, commented on "the many gold mines" in the country.[28] About fifty years later the Scot George Bogle noted that "extraordinary quantities of gold" went to the emperor of China.[29] By 1800 the British East India Company envoy to Katmandu noted that "the territories of Bootan and Tibet are said to abound with Gold and silver mines. . . ."[30] These stories grew throughout the nineteenth century, creating an aura of wealth, mystery, and magic around the image of Tibet, especially the country's capital, Lhasa, and its greatest monument, the Potala.

By the turn of the twentieth century, Tibet had arrived in the Western imagination. As Peter Bishop wrote:

> Tibet was not just *any* place, not just *one* among many within the Western global imagination. For a few years at the turn of the century it became *the* place. It was for the fin de siècle what Tahiti and China had been for the eighteenth century, what the Arctic was for the early-to-mid-nineteenth century and the source of the Nile for the late nineteenth century. The acclaim given to explorers of Tibet and Central Asia was exceptional; it was as if Tibet touched some fundamental surface of the era's imagination.[31]

Western writers reflected this image of Tibet in their literature. After Arthur Conan Doyle killed off Sherlock Holmes in a plunge from a cliff with his arch-rival Moriarty, Doyle resurrected Holmes who explained to Watson that rather than dying he had escaped from the precipice at the last minute and then had "traveled for two years in Tibet . . . visiting Lhassa, and spending some days with the head lama."[32] In creating this excuse for Holmes, Doyle took advantage of the popular Western image of Tibet as a land of levitating monks and spiritually wise lamas.

But while writers treated Tibet as home of the spirit, British diplomats around the turn of the century saw it as one of the last battlegrounds of imperialism. The weakening of the Chinese empire and Russian expansion into central Asia had brought tsarist forces to the doorstep of Tibet. Thus began the so-called "Great Game." In 1904 the British under Colonel Francis Younghusband invaded Tibet to force trading relations on the country and thereby forestall the Russians. But, realizing the difficulty of maintaining their military presence in Tibet and fearing the Russians would retaliate in other areas, the British backed off this attempt to force the Tibetans into their orbit. Once they had gained their own trading rights and a minimalist presence in the area, the British allowed the continuation of Tibet's ties with the Qing dynasty in China and the resumption of the country's isolated and nonaligned state with the rest of the world.

The result reinforced the image of the country to travelers as a last frontier—one whose isolation buttressed the hope that it offered wisdom, gold, and spiritual riches. As war and conflict cut off the country throughout the early twentieth century, so the image grew of Tibet as the last citadel for the dreams of the adventurer. As Bishop has observed, by mid-century Tibet "held out the promise of hope and guidance for many Westerners alienated from their own culture. The passionless beauty and geometric perfection of the mountain which dominated James Hilton's Shangri-la was an apt symbol of this benevolent but aloof wisdom."[33]

The Chinese were seen as despoiling this image when they invaded the Land of the Snows in 1950. In 1959, when the Dalai Lama fled Tibet, he declared that "forced labor and compulsory extractions, and systematic persecution of the people, plunder and confiscation of property, and the execution of certain leading men in Tibet are the glorious achievements of the Chinese rule in Tibet."[34] Cold war views of communism joined old stereotypes of Asia. The Tibetans were once again seen as a simple spiritual people threatened by a new version (communism) of the old Russian plague that the British (in the Great Game) had attempted to thwart.

Once again the image of Tibet was formed by attitudes toward China, but now it was directed toward Chinese Communists. This view of Tibet did not change even after U.S. relations with China improved in the 1970s and the

1980s. Tibet remained China's alter ego, the country where the evils of communism still showed themselves at the same time that capitalism was believed to be sweeping Beijing. After all, the Chinese still oppressed and isolated Tibet even as they allowed Canton to be flooded with Coca-Cola and video games.

As China became an essential stop on any grand tour for prosperous Europeans and Americans, Tibet took on China's old role as Asia's most exotic and difficult-to-reach tourist destination. Westerners sympathized with its inhabitants as they did with the oppressed of any third-world country. Westerners applauded the peaceful image of the Dalai Lama, mostly because they contrasted it with the materialism of their own lives and with their belief in the intolerance of Islam, the inferiority of Hinduism, or even the gross atheism of the Chinese Communists. Tibet, then, became the quintessential Asia of the Western imagination, the poor oppressed land with an ancient culture and spirit.

In 1989, after the brutal military suppression of Chinese students during the Tiananmen demonstrations in Beijing, world attention focused on human rights abuses in Tibet. The world came to understand that the same Chinese military that had oppressed the sophisticated young democratic stalwarts in Beijing also exploited the Tibetans.

Unfortunately this sympathy for Tibetans strengthened the world's view of them as the purveyors of a kind of humble goodness, symbolized by the image of the Dalai Lama as one of the world's true figures of peace and wisdom. Although this image is meant to glorify the Tibetans, it really obscures them. It perpetuates a stereotype of Asians who are either all good or all evil, never real people. It contrasts the evil Chinese against the good Tibetans and accomplishes almost the opposite of what it seeks to promote. Instead of treating the Tibetans as a separate people, it casts them again into the shadow of China.

In truth, for thousands of years Tibet's history has both been intertwined with China's and separate from it. But in spite of what the Chinese claim today, Tibet historically has not been dependent on China or—before 1950—been a part of China. It is true that in the thirteenth century, when the Mongols ruled China, and again from the eighteenth to the early twentieth century when the Manchus ruled that country, Tibet was loosely associated with China. But in all other periods Tibet's history has been politically and culturally totally independent of China's. Even during the times of the loose association, the Chinese exercised no control over their neighbor's internal affairs. The Chinese themselves did not argue that Tibet was part of their country until the twentieth century. Indeed, most early Chinese nationalists wanted nothing to do with Tibet.

The history of Tibet as an independent state and the complicated story of how the Chinese came to believe that Tibet has long been a part of their country have both been poorly understood. The bright, unfiltered light that strikes the Tibetan peaks lays bare a unique culture and history. It is time to focus this light onto our stereotypes so that the history of Tibet can shine forth from the recesses of the Western imagination and the clutches of its Chinese neighbor.

TWO

❦

The First
Tibetan Dominion

Entering Xigaze, northeast of Lhasa, in the early 1920s, the eminent anthropologist William McGovern was immediately confronted by "the Chinese graveyard." It was, he notes, "an apt symbol of the extinct suzerainty* of China over Tibet" and of the vast cultural and national differences between the two societies. Even lower-class Chinese did not wish to be buried among Tibetans. Upper-class Chinese, as McGovern notes, did not wish to be buried in Tibet at all. Instead their families paid to have their bodies transported back to China to be buried in their native land.[1]

The distaste which the Chinese and Tibetans today feel toward each other stems in part from their long political rivalry but also from cultural traditions, such as burial rites, so

---

*The word suzerainty is itself an example of the arcane and easily misunderstood language with which scholars discuss and obscure Tibet. Not even the most ardent Sinophiles argue that in historical times Tibet was actually a complete part of China. Instead they maintain that at times China had suzerainty over Tibet, a legal term that implies a system of government by which one independent state somehow has political control over another state.

vastly different that they are often mutually repugnant. The Chinese go to elaborate extremes to see that their bones are interred in the gravesite. Today the Chinese still consign large amounts of precious land to entomb the departed. Tibetans, on the other hand, generally do not bury their dead; sometimes they cremate them. McGovern notes that "In certain instances the flesh is fed to the pigs and dogs."[2] Most Tibetans, however, prefer "a sky funeral," believing it is the only way to ensure a proper rebirth. Specially trained monks hack the body to pieces, grinding the bones up and mixing them with the flesh, which they feed to the vultures bit by bit, all the while carefully warding off four-legged carnivores.

Differences such as these burial customs indicate the separate historical traditions of the two countries. Yet in an effort to demonstrate Tibet's links to China, the Chinese deny Tibet's long independent historical tradition. Every middle-school child learns the story of Chinese Princess Wencheng and her marriage to the famous Tibetan king, Songtsen Gampo, more than a thousand years ago. The princess, according to the patronizing lesson, brought culture and civilization to the Tibetans, and ever since the land has been closely tied to China.

The story of the Chinese princess bride is offered to Chinese children as proof that Tibet has long been under China's domination and influence. But the story really exposes the cultural defensiveness and half-truths which the Chinese use to justify their occupation of Tibet. As those Chinese students who pay close attention to the story understand, if Tibet had really been a tributary state looking to China for culture and civilization, the seventh-century Tang emperor would not have sent his daughter to marry the Tibetan king. He did so only because he correctly understood the strength and power of his Tibetan neighbors and preferred to make peace rather than war.

In talking with Chinese schoolchildren, I have noticed that this story often makes Chinese children uneasy. The implicit though obviously unintended assumption in the tale is that the Tibetan state was on an equal footing with the great Tang dynasty. This belies Chinese ideas about the supposed superiority of their culture to that of their neighbors. Chinese children weep over the idea of the beautiful princess spending her life among the strange and difficult Tibetans. They know she didn't really sinicize her husband and his subjects. Indeed, although the account of the Chinese princess bride is still taught to schoolchildren, most Chinese historians now acknowledge that in her time Tibet was an independent country completely separate from China. The overwhelming majority of Chinese see the Tibetans as a people different from themselves, and believe that any Chinese, especially a beautiful young woman, forced to live in Tibet among the Tibetans is in effect being consigned to a living hell.

In times past, an independent Tibet ruled vast portions of China, India, Nepal, central Asia, and even the Middle East, forcing the rulers of these countries to send their precious goods and even their princesses to Tibet. Reams have been written about smaller rival states, but no other great dominion is as little known as the one the first Tibetan kings forged high in the Himalayas. The lack of knowledge about the Tibetan states has allowed the Chinese to create their misleading history of the relations between the two cultures.

The Tibetan state first rose to prominence around the sixth or seventh century. It was a time when powerful new states formed throughout Eurasia—in China, Korea, Japan, northern India, the Middle East, and even Europe. These states came together after Turkish-speaking tribes captured the fabled Silk Road city of Samarkand and unified the central Asian trade routes in the middle of the sixth century. Their conquest linked the European and Asian continents.[3]

Traders soon developed a thriving commerce among the great Eurasian cultures.[4] Technology and ideas flowed throughout much of the civilized world, stimulating industrial and political innovations.[5]

Tibetan goods that now seem bizarre became prized throughout Eurasia. Yak tails from Tibet, for instance, were popular all along the Silk Road. The Indians set these tails into expensive handles and used the *chowries,* as they were called, as brushes to keep the flies off people, horses, and elephants. The Chinese sewed them into their hats. Musk harvested from the special deer of Tibet was made into perfume in Europe, China, and India. Tibetan craftspeople perfected gold and silver ornaments prized by wealthy merchants in the Chinese capital.

Until recently few historians paid much attention to the Tibetan accounts of their past triumphs.[6] Those who did assumed that many of the individuals described in these tales were not real people but mythical heroes or composite figures. Tibetan histories diminished into fable and became no more substantial than the murky legends and entertaining stories that assert that the mating of a monkey and a she-devil produced the first Tibetan.

Monkey gods are a standard part of religious folklore in India, Tibet, and other parts of the Buddhist world, including China. But the Chinese also often use the image of a hairy monkey as a way to insult the intelligence and culture of people they despise as inferior. The Tibetan claim of descent from this animal is almost incomprehensible to the Chinese and is an example of the vast intellectual and attitudinal differences between the two cultures.

The Chinese assume these contrasts verify their own superiority. They believe that Tibetans must have looked to them for civilization. Western historians, influenced by their own stereotypes of Tibetan isolation and primitivism, have blindly accepted these interpretations.[7] They would have done a lot better had they paid attention to the Chinese children who read the story of Princess Wencheng. The attitudes of these schoolchildren indicate a sense of separateness from the Tibetans. Historians should know that the idea that the Chinese and Tibetan nations are one is a relatively recent construct. At the beginning of this century, most Chinese nationalists were still arguing that Tibet was not really a part of China.

Despite ample evidence, most Westerners are still ignorant of the great Tibetan states of the past. In 1907 explorers stumbled upon piles of old Buddhist records in an annex to a cave temple in the central Asian city of Dunhuang, now part of China's Gansu province. The area once served as an archive for the Tibetan regional government in the area, and it contained reams of Tibetan court documents concealed in a fashion similar to the Dead Sea Scrolls. These documents proved to be a treasure trove of material on early Tibet.[8] As they gradually have been translated, they have enhanced our understanding of the size and sophistication of the early Tibetan dominion and motivated scholars to search out Arab and Chinese accounts of Tibetan military victories and trading missions.

Chinese accounts relate that Tibetans descended from the Qiang, a proto-Tibetan group of nomadic shepherds (still in existence in parts of China today) who first appeared in western China sometime before 1000 B.C.E. (The Qiang are mentioned in Chapter One as the group which the Christian missionary Thomas Torrance thought were Jews and whom the Israeli Rabbi E. Avichail still believes to be one of the ten lost tribes.) From the third to the sixth centuries C.E., the Qiang controlled large parts of north China. Although it is all but certain that the Qiang were never Jewish, there was no doubt some mixture between Qiang and Chinese groups.[9] But from the start the Chinese thought of the Qiang as a different and barbarian culture and race.

The Qiang groups who wandered into Tibet intermingled with other groups: the aboriginal populations of the highlands,[10] nomadic steppe tribes from the north, as well as Persian and Indian groups to the south and west. The resultant mix created the variety of cultural and physical types that make up the Tibetan population. It also helps account for the many stories of the development of Tibetan civilization, including the claim that its first ruling house descended from an Indian prince who showed his subjects how to construct houses.

By about the fifth or sixth century the Tibetan builders had established a number of walled cities and castles along the Yarlong Zangpo, or Brahmaputra River, in the area of southern Tibet now considered the heartland of Tibetan culture. Around 570 C.E., Tibet's warrior-king Namri Songtsen united the nomadic traders, wealthy peasants, and craftspeople of the Yarlong Valley into a military dominion that bordered China in the south and central Asia in the west. Namri's soldiers wore Tibetan chain-mail armor so fine that his enemies complained that bows and even swords could not pierce it. The Tibetans apparently copied the form of their armor from the Persians, but Tibetan workmanship was unequaled.[11] The armor completely covered the soldiers' bodies, leaving only two slots exposed for their eyes. The Tibetans even forged armor for their horses, making their cavalry almost impervious in battle. Tibetan craftsmen were famous throughout Eurasia. Tibetan goldsmiths manufactured fine mechanical gold objects, greatly coveted in the Chinese capital and along the Silk Road.[12]

When Namri Songtsen died, probably from poisoning, Songtsen Gampo, Tibet's greatest king and Namri's son, succeeded him. Today Tibetans everywhere revere Songtsen Gampo. His likeness adorns Tibetan shrines and monasteries, and he is treated as a holy religious hero. But he was no saint. Even more than his father, Songtsen Gampo was a

Machiavellian politician and visionary. He knew how to exploit the power of his position, and he wasted no time in stamping his mark on Tibet. He consolidated his hold over the Tibetan throne and then in 635 joined the newly established Chinese Tang dynasty (618–907) in attacking and defeating the Tuyuhun, a Mongol group that had occupied the northern part of the Tibetan plain.

The Tuyuhun had controlled the area above and below Lake Kokonor (Qinghai Lake). The Kokonor region borders the Gansu corridor where the caravan trails of the Silk Road linking Europe with China and Tibet begin. In the Gansu corridor Mongolia, Turkestan, China, and Tibet come together. Here the Middle East connects with China. As their share of the spoils, the Tang took the Gansu corridor and attempted for the first time to project Chinese power onto vast portions of central Asia. But Songtsen Gampo kept the highlands. In one fell swoop he became the supreme figure of power on the Tibetan plateau.

This land on the northwestern part of the Tibetan plateau, where the Tuyuhun once lived, is Amdo. It is a cold, bleak area with the most extreme temperature fluctuations in all of Tibet. It alternates between the grasslands and deserts of the Changtang and the reasonably fertile and populated districts around Lake Kokonor. Today it has been claimed by China as Qinghai province. It is now home to the Chinese gulag and serves as the reservoir for much of China's nuclear wastes, frightening environmentalists who are concerned about the fragile ecosystem of this sensitive and influential region. China's claim to the region is vehemently disputed by the Amdowas, a fierce and independent group which historically has been in conflict with central Tibet as much as they have been in alliance with it.

The Amdowas have been responsible for some of the

most important cultural and political innovations in Tibetan history. In modern times they count the present-day Dalai Lama as one of their own. They also include the rugged and lawless Golok nomads, feared among both Chinese and Tibetans for their banditry.

But the Amdowas were never in sole possession of the land they call Amdo. Then as now, the territory was inhabited by a mixture of ethnic groups, all of which have at various times claimed the area as their own. In many respects this border region has been a kind of Tibetan Yugoslavia in which groups that have lived side by side for hundreds, probably thousands of years nonetheless have clung fiercely to their own ethnicity and nursed a dislike for one another. Only in recent years has massive Chinese immigration begun to change the character of this part of the Tibetan plateau, perhaps irrevocably.

Songtsen Gampo was the first Tibetan leader to amalgamate the mixed Mongol, Turkish, and Tibetan populations of the region into Tibet. He claimed all of geographic Tibet, and by so doing he threatened the just established Chinese positions in Gansu and central Asia. He wasted little time in taking advantage of his situation.

He demanded that the Chinese emperor present him with a princess bride. Royal weddings accompanied by imperial dowries were a common feature of the diplomacy of the period, but in this case the Chinese supposedly rebuffed Songtsen Gampo. In retaliation, in 638, his forces raided the Chinese border town of Songzhou, currently the Sichuan provincial town of Songpan.

This area well to the south of the Qinghai-Gansu region was made part of China after 1950, but the Tibetans have long considered it part of eastern Tibet or Kham. Kham is one of the most spectacular parts of a dramatic and striking land. The Himalayas extend north to south rather than east to west through Kham, obstructing the main routes between

Tibet and China. The land is further disrupted by the valleys and gorges cut by the three great rivers that run through the area—the Salween, Mekong, and Yangzi. A relatively mild climate and heavy rainfall give the region a population greater than all the rest of Tibet, and heavy forestation. In recent years the cutting of these forests, home to the giant panda and many other endangered species, has become one of the most controversial charges against the Chinese government.

Even in modern times it is hard to consider the rugged people who live in Kham as victims. The fierce yet jovial Khampas are often described as a race of giants. The men are tall, often over six feet, with angular features. They braid red cloth into their hair and carry swords at their sides. The Chinese Communists speak of them as " 'cavaliers, wild, undisciplined, and accustomed to living by loot.' The Dalai Lama admits: 'The Khampa's most precious possession is a gun'; even the reserved Scotsman Hugh Richardson, one-time British resident in Lhasa, calls them in his History of Tibet, 'a wild, war-like feuding sort of people.' "[13] Though much of their territory has today been merged into China's most populated province, Sichuan, the Khampas bear little resemblance to their Chinese neighbors, and the two groups have long fought over various pieces of land. It was the Khampas who began the 1959 Tibetan rebellion against China.

The first official battle over the eastern edge of Kham took place in the seventh century. In this fight the Tibetans drove the Chinese out of the city of Songzhou. A few months later, however, the Chinese returned and chased out the Tibetan troops. A truce followed. The Chinese emperor presented Songtsen Gampo with a Chinese princess bride, and the Tibetans sent a tributary mission to the Chinese court.[14]

The Chinese have long claimed that Songtsen Gampo's acceptance of this bride proves that Tibet became a Chinese

The Jokhang temple was built to house this famous statue of Sakyamuni brought to Tibet by Princess Wencheng, Songtsen Gampo's Chinese wife. Cast from an alloy of gold, silver, copper, zinc, and iron mixed with jewels, it is Tibet's most sacred image. Note the variety of butter lamps burning beneath it, the white Tibetan ceremonial scarf draped over it as an offering, and the picture of the current Dalai Lama placed reverently to the side.

tributary state. What most Chinese accounts fail to mention is that Songtsen Gampo took a number of different wives in his efforts to reinforce his position and create new political alliances. He married at least one daughter of a potential rival within the Tibetan ruling class and one from the Tangut tribes he had earlier conquered. Later Tibetan accounts point out that the Tibetan ruler had previously conquered Nepal and had also taken a Nepalese princess for his wife, though the failure of earlier records to mention this wife has caused recent historians to question whether this marriage ever took place.[15] The Chinese also fail to explain that tributary missions in those days (and later) were often simply trading missions between equal powers. The fact that the Chinese called another state a tributary power proves nothing at all about the real relationship between the two countries.

In fact, Songtsen Gampo shuffled his military alliances back and forth like his marital ones. In 648 he invaded northern India to help rescue an envoy of his Chinese ally (an event the Chinese accounts are always quick to point to as evidence of his tributary status), but a few decades later the Tibetans were once again fighting the Chinese.

Songtsen Gampo was not a simple military chieftain. He was a clever, imaginative ruler able to foresee the complex needs of his new state and to understand the political and cultural structures necessary to build a fresh civilization. He proved as eclectic in his pursuit of institutions to further the power of his government as he had been in his choice of wives. He sent one of his nobles to India to bring back a script for the writing of the Tibetan language. (A recent scholar has argued that Tibet had a writing system in place by this time, and that Songtsen Gampo simply improved it.[16]) Soon scribes were churning out government memos and documents in the new language. Songtsen Gampo even supervised the drafting of the Six Codices Tibetan constitution, which set forth the basic laws and political and administrative structure of the new regime. This document regularized business practices and gave the country a unified system of weights and measures as well as guidelines for proper social conduct.

To make writing easier, Songtsen Gampo encouraged the introduction of paper from China. At the same time he presided over a flurry of other innovations. Tea and alcoholic beverages came to Tibet from China. Chinese, Indian, and even Middle Eastern architectural, religious, and political forms flourished.

Tea, especially, caught on. By the time of the next ruler, Songtsen Gampo's grandson, tea had become the national beverage of Tibet. That the Tibetans adopted the Chinese

Ingredients for making tea: On the table are two brass teapots next to wooden and ceramic bowls and a brick of tea. Below is a copper pot and kettle, a tsamba bag, a wooden butter box, a tea churn, and a tea strainer. *(Land of the Lamas)*

habit of tea drinking might be thought to show the cultural affinity of the two civilizations. But Tibetan tea is not brewed from the delicate loose leaves preferred by the Chinese of today. Rather, Tibetans import tea dried and compressed into hard bricks.[17] Packed like this it lasts forever and is often extensively traded before finally being consumed. It is the kind of product suited for tough caravan rides into the Himalayas and the harsh climate of the Tibetan plateau.

The differences in their tea-drinking practices are a clear indication of the vast distinctions between Chinese and Tibetan culture and help explain why the Chinese feel so uncomfortable around Tibetans. The Chinese carefully brew their leaves in special pots. They have an elaborate literature that discusses the subtle variations in flavor that may be created by slight shifts in the leaves, the brewing methods, or even the texture of the teapot or the cup into which tea is poured. They mix nothing into the drink itself; rather they sip it unadulterated.

Tibetans, on the other hand, blend salt, yak butter, and sometimes yak dung into their tea, practices that horrify the Chinese and have shocked Western visitors. When Tibetans add yak dung, they do it to hold together the small tea-leaf particles that are chipped off the bricks. A little bit of moist yak dung acts as a kind of adhesive, holding the pieces in place and preventing loose particles from clogging the drinker's mouth. Even without the dung, the yak butter imparts a strong flavor to the tea, making it an acquired taste.

Some foreigners do like it. The British consular official F. Spencer Chapman waxed almost poetic when he observed the colorful way the tea was made at a high-class house he visited. He described the way the bits of leaves were boiled for several hours, "then the infusion is poured into a section of hollow bamboo, where it is churned up with a plunger,"[18] and the butter and salt added. He called the result "a purplish liquid of unusual taste for tea, but as soup excellent. The great thing is to blow aside the floating scum of butter before you drink." Spencer also claimed that "any good Tibetan drinks fifty or sixty cups of tea every day of his life."[19] This is probably an exaggeration, though the cups are small and it is a fact that Tibetan tea is a major source of both nourishment and fluid for many Tibetans. In the high altitude large amounts of fluid are necessary.

Still, even outsiders who do not mind the gamy taste of the yak butter and dung have a hard time with the salt. Tibet is far inland. Tibetan salt comes from the saline encrustations surrounding the brackish lakes of the Changtang. These lakes are the remains of the Tethys Sea which once bordered Tibet before the Asian and south Asian mainlands crashed together and created the Himalayas, lifting Tibet toward the heavens and draining its ocean boundaries. The salt is acrid tasting and is often contaminated with grains of crystal compounds other than sodium chloride.

Even Tibetan alcohol is unusual. Although alcoholic beverages supposedly were also introduced into Tibet from China during Songtsen Gampo's reign, Tibetan libations are quite unlike any their neighbors to the east imbibe. The Chinese drink a number of sorghum- and rice-based liquors, some, such as mao tai, as high as 140 proof. Upper-class Tibetans occasionally imbibe a kind of *arak,* which is also very strong. But they mostly drink *chang,* a yeasty, barley-based, pallid-looking beer they can consume in huge quantities.

The changes wrought by the Tibetans of Songtsen Gampo's time in a practice as seemingly simple as tea-drinking illustrate that whatever stories the Chinese tell, even in the seventh century Chinese and Tibetans were two different cultures with different manners. In the settlements they developed along the Yarlongpo River, Tibetans cultivated barley, a grain the Chinese generally despise and that varies from the rice, wheat, and sorghum that the Chinese grew in their lowland settlements.

To this day, their cooking styles are also dissimilar. The Chinese steam rice or bread and eat it with sauteed or stir-fried vegetables, bean curd, and sometimes bits of meat. Tibetans lightly roast their barley (and sometimes simply parch it without really cooking it), then grind it into very fine flour called *tsampa.* It is either eaten dry, moistened slowly in the mouth with saliva, or mixed with a little tea. After mixing it with tea, Tibetans knead it into doughboys and somehow manage to eat these starch balls without choking.

The way the people in the two societies eat contrasts sharply. The Chinese abhor eating with their fingers and look with disgust at Tibetans who use their typically unwashed hands to pour barley flour into their mouths.

But the Chinese react even more strongly to other Tibetan practices, particularly the eating of raw meat. The Chinese always cook their meat. Though the eating of raw meat may be *au courant* in trendy social circles in the West, the idea is abhorrent to the Chinese, who associate it with barbarism. The Chinese generally eat meat only in small portions, cutting it into little pieces and mixing it with other ingredients. They maintain that the cutting of meat, like the butchery of animals, is something to be done in the kitchen, well away from the table.

The Tibetans by contrast often not only eat large portions of meat but eat it uncooked. McGovern commented that the two daily meals of Tibetan peasants "consist almost invariably of the same food, viz., meat, barley, and tea."

> The meat eaten in Tibet is either mutton or yak's flesh. A haunch is left outside to freeze, and this preserves it to a certain extent for several months, though the recurrent heat of the day causes it to thaw sufficiently to become putrescent. At night it freezes again, a process which repeats itself as long as the meat lasts. The Tibetans do not object to the semi-putrescence, as they consider that the taste is in this way improved. Occasionally the meat is cooked, but for the most part the peasants prefer to eat it raw. Hacking off small pieces with their great knives, they eat it with their fingers.[20]

Tibetans do eat *momos,* a kind of meat dumpling similar to its Chinese equivalent, and *tukpa,* boiled millet noodles with meat, similar to Chinese *mian* (or *lo mein* as it is often called in the West). But as McGovern observes with just a little exaggeration, "fish and fowl are considered too filthy to be eaten. Vegetables are unknown."[21]

Today, when Tibetans worry that their country is being overwhelmed by many new influences from China, it is instructive to note how the many changes brought into the area by Songtsen Gampo and his successors were adapted in a uniquely Tibetan manner. Before Songtsen Gampo's death, Tibetans had developed many of the eclectic features that still distinguish their culture today.

Many Tibetans today argue that the most significant change Songtsen Gampo wrought on Tibetan society was in laying the foundation for the development of Buddhism in Tibet. Songtsen Gampo himself was probably not a Buddhist. Yet he is said to have designed his palace and built temples for his queens to serve the new creed. The palace buildings were large, magnificent constructs filled with numerous texts. They were the centerpieces of the walled capital he constructed on the same hilltop that features the Potala in what is today Lhasa. The thick exteriors and hilltop position of the capital could be easily defended against hostile military forces. Songtsen Gampo enhanced the image of the capital's imperial power by commissioning large, awe-inspiring Buddhist statues to be placed in these buildings. The supposedly magical effects of the statuary reinforced the temporal strength of the state.

Like rulers in Korea, Japan, and other places at about the same time, Songtsen Gampo apparently introduced Buddhism to enhance the aura of the state and attract skilled workers to serve it. When he built temples or simple chapels, he induced literate clerics of Chinese or Indian origin to staff them. He put them to work as artisans and bureaucrats serving his kingdom. The monks helped Songtsen Gampo impose on the Tibetan dominion the orderly bureaucratic style the Sui and Tang had perfected in China. The mark of the bureaucrat, the written memorandum, proliferated, an impor-

tant acquisition in a state just developing a writing system.
The monks and the religious edifices they occupied projected
the image of the newly centralized Tibetan dominion
throughout the realm. Songtsen Gampo's monks and soldiers
occupied the same buildings and worked side by side to extend his position throughout his dominion.

Buddhism also provided the government with a unifying
ideology. Buddhism's emphasis on the equality of all men
placed competing groups on an equal footing.

In China too the spread of Buddhism initially helped
bolster state institutions and reinforce state doctrines. But in
Tibet, unlike in China, Buddhism eventually became a central feature of the state. It is ironic that even though the Tang
dynasty is renowned for purging Buddhism from the Chinese
state, one of China's greatest influences on Tibet was purportedly the Princess Wencheng's efforts to promote Buddhism there. Among other achievements, she is credited with
the construction of one of the most famous monasteries in
Tibet's history.

In fact her influence has probably been overblown. Buddhism was not yet widespread during this early period, and
much of what existed came from India and central Asia.
Thus the resulting mixture was not a triumph of Chinese culture but an example of the way that Tibetan Buddhism, like
virtually every other aspect of Tibetan culture, assumed its
own distinct style.

Songtsen Gampo died in 649. In spite of the religious
aura he gained in later centuries for his role in introducing
Buddhism to Tibet, it is unlikely that Songtsen Gampo
would have been concerned that his successor showed little
interest in the foreign religion, and that most Buddhist influences quickly disappeared. Songtsen Gampo's main concern
had been strengthening and expanding the dominion he and
his father had created.

*   *   *

In 670, twenty-one years after Songtsen Gampo's death, Tibetan forces routed the Tang from the Tarim basin in what is now Xinjiang province, or Chinese Turkestan, and gradually extended the Tibetan dominion along the Silk Road. Tibet finally controlled the trade routes that linked the Eurasian continent. As a contemporary Tibetan historian has written, "Along these caravan routes Chinese silk and Indian ivory, spices and gems flowed west, while bronze and glassware from the Byzantine Dominion traveled east. Kucha was famous for gold, felt, and perfumes, Khotan for jade and carpets, Ferghana for horses and armor."[22]

Historians of the Tang dynasty, usually considered the strongest and most militarily aggressive of Chinese dynasties, admiringly described the Tibetan dominion as more than "10,000 li (3000 miles)," extending from "the land of the p'-lo-men' (Brahmins) in the south and the prefectures of Liang-chou, Sung-chou, Mao-chou, and Sui-chou (along the Min river) in the eastern borderlands."[23] By the late seventh century, the Tibetan dominion stretched from upper Burma and Nepal through eastern central Asia.

Even at its zenith fifty years later, the Tibetan state was vastly different from its Chinese rival. The Tang was a great empire with a sophisticated bureaucracy, a long literary tradition, and a large, stable agricultural population. The Tang stretched further into central Asia than any Chinese state before or after. It had a greater ethnic mix than its Chinese successor states. Yet it was centered on the peasants who settled and toiled in the rice paddies and millet fields of the Chinese plains and river valleys as well as the merchants, artisans, and literati-bureaucrats of the great cities of central and north China. These comprised an enormous population of sixty million people.

The Tibetan state, in contrast, extended over an even larger territory than did its Chinese rival, and its armies were more than a match for those of the Tang. But its population of nomadic traders and craftsmen was far less disciplined, more varied, and probably less than one-tenth the size of China's. It was a central Asian–style kingdom more than an empire, one whose accomplishments nevertheless were astonishing.

Tibet's achievements are even greater when it is understood that not only did this dominion extend over a huge territory of great ethnic and cultural variety, it was broken into numerous geographical and climatic units and separated by some of the tallest mountains in the world. These divisions have given the Tibetan terrain its rugged beauty, but they also have perpetuated tribal independence and impeded unity. Local leaders, especially in Kham and Amdo, were naturally hostile to the idea of a centralized state with heavy taxes. Only a high degree of organization and a promise of lucrative trading concessions held this dominion together.

This state structure weakened after Songtsen Gampo's death, but by the middle of the eighth century it had regained its strength. In 755 the great king Trisong Detsen (755–797) assumed the Tibetan throne. As the Tang reeled from internal dissension, Trisong Detsen sent his forces deep into China. By 760 he had conquered much of Sichuan and had begun to demand that the Chinese send him annual tribute payments of fifty thousand rolls of silk, a huge sum at the time.

When the payment was late in 763, the Tibetans attacked and captured the Tang capital at Changan (near present-day Xian), installing on the throne the brother of the former Tibetan king's Chinese wife. It was a halfhearted effort on the part of the Tibetans, and the Chinese drove them from Changan a few weeks later. Yet for later generations of Tibetans, this seemingly fleeting victory has become a matter of great pride. Some still gloat that Tibetan troops remained in the countryside near the city for several years, and Tibetan forces continued to dominate much of western China for almost half a century.

But Tibet was less interested in China than in the lucrative trade routes of central Asia. At last in 790 Trisong Detsen reconquered all the old Tibetan positions along the Silk Road. By the time of his death in 797, Tibet controlled vast portions of central Asia, large parts of China and Burma, and all of Nepal, Bhutan, and Sikkim, as well as most of present-day Bangladesh, Pakistan, and a fair amount of northern India including the state of West Bengal. It is said that under Trisong Detsen the Bay of Bengal became known to Islamic writers as the Tibetan Sea.[24]

In another way Trisong Detsen's reign was a defining moment in Tibetan history. Unlike Songtsen Gampo, Trisong Detsen's personal piousness is beyond dispute. In 779 he made Buddhism the official state religion and routed from the court those rivals who adhered to the native animistic Bon doctrine. Bon, the original Tibetan religion, was a shamanistic cult in which priests used magic rituals and hexes to control mountain, forest, and water demons. Followers worshiped the spirits of local mountaintops and lakes. Bon divided the world into three parts—heaven, earth, and the underworld. Even today in Tibet it still has many adherents. But its decentralized nature made it inappropriate to the needs of a large centralized state.

It was an opportune moment for Tibet to have a committed Buddhist on the throne. Judaism, Manicheism, Christianity, and Islam were all inspiring their own political movements. As the king of a Buddhist state, Trisong Detsen won an autonomy of action and metaphysical justification for his state that allowed his political organization to compete with those inspired by these other religious doctrines.

It is said that when Trisong Detsen made Buddhism the official religion of Tibet, he held a two-year debate between Chinese and Indian monks over which form of Buddhism

Tibet should adopt. Religious debates were common during this period. The Khazars, a central Asian people who converted to Judaism in the 740s, are said to have chosen their new religion only after first hearing a debate among Christian, Islamic, and Jewish proponents. Debates such as these illustrate the importance that rulers of the time placed on the need for religious legitimization. For Trisong Detsen the debate had geopolitical as well as religious significance. Given the antipathy between China and Tibet, Indian Buddhist influences naturally were declared the ultimate winner, though in fact Tibetan Buddhism has developed its own unique characteristics and contains both Chinese and Tibetan elements.

The monks held their debate at the Samye monastery about fifty miles southeast of Lhasa. This was Tibet's first monastery, built by Trisong Detsen probably in 767.[25] Damaged many times by fire, the huge complex still stands, a testimony both to its construction and to the reverence it inspires among Tibetans. Trisong Detsen's builders modeled the monastery along the same lines as the Otantapuri monastery in India. The main part of the complex consists of a large temple surrounded by four small ones. The configuration simulates the cosmos. The large central building portrays Mount Sumeru, the core of the universe in Buddhist belief. The four surrounding pagodas represent the four worlds that are said to encircle this great mountain.

This depiction of the cosmos using concrete forms or diagrams is what is known as a *mandala* or sacred circle, the visual map Buddhists use during meditation to guide them in integrating their being with the Absolute. Hindus use a similarly structured image called a *yaanta*. The Buddhist development of the *mandala*, which obviously derived from its Hindu counterpart, followed the shift in Buddhist doctrine from an emphasis on the central figure of Sakyamuni, the Buddha, to the idea that Buddhahood was something that could be obtained by all. Instead of just one Buddha, new Buddhist ideas stressed a multitude of Buddha forms. Each of the five buildings that form the core of the Samye monastery symbolizes a Buddha. The sacred circle is formed by the four lesser Buddhas (the four smaller temples) encircling the central Buddha (the large temple structure). The contemplation of this image of the cosmos is supposed to lead the devout to nirvana.

The imagery has a special significance for Tibetans. The structure of the *mandala* and hence of the Samye monastery is based on a Tibetan geographical fact. In Tibet the four great rivers of the Indian subcontinent—the Indus, Sutlej, Ganges (technically the Karnali, one of the major tributaries of the Ganges system), and Brahmaputra—all originate at the base of the great Mount Kailas. In imitation of this natural marvel, ancient religious thinkers throughout Asia are thought to have drawn the cosmos as a great towering form surrounded by four lesser ones.

Even before Trisong Detsen's time, Mount Kailas had become the most sacred peak in all of Asia. As Charles Allen notes, "This mountain was said to be the navel of the earth and the axis of the universe, and from its summit flowed a mighty river that fell into a lake and then divided to form four of the great rivers of Asia. It was the holiest of all mountains, revered by many millions of Hindus, Buddhists, and Jains as the home of their gods."[26] The awe with which this mountain is regarded has helped give Tibet its mystical and religious aura.

Travelers are mesmerized by the sight of the mountain. The Japanese explorer and monk Ekai Kawaguchi commented, "I shall never forget, so exquisitely grand was the scenery. . . . Verily, verily, it was a natural mandala."[27] Located in northwest Tibet, Mount Kailas presents a spectacular sight. Each of its four faces has been likened to a jewel, crystal in the east, ruby in the west, sapphire in the south,

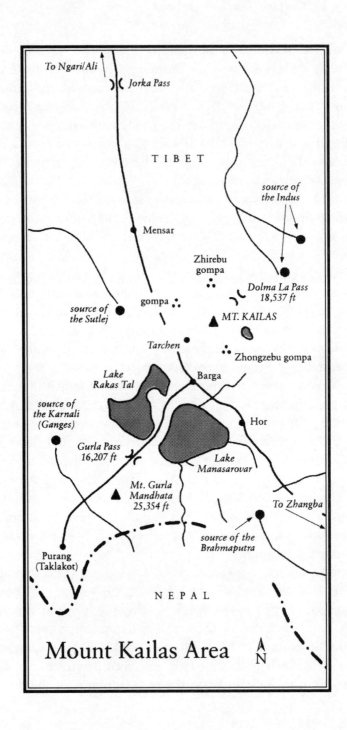

Mount Kailas Area

and gold in the north.[28] At its bottom are the turquoise waters of Lake Manasarovar.

Hindus believe this lake was created by the gods as a place for the sons of Brahma to bathe, and that the top of the mountain is the home of the great god Shiva. Every year scores of Hindus make the difficult pilgrimage to Mount Kailas, believing that "when the earth of Manasarovar touches anyone's body or when anyone bathes therein, he shall go to the paradise of Brahma, and he who drinks its waters shall go to the heaven of Shiva and shall be released from the sins of a hundred births."[29] Moreover, Kailas is not just "the Olympus of Hinduism and Buddhism; it is also the home of the 'black belief,' the old shamanistic religion of Bon-Po that flourished in Tibet long before the arrival of Buddhism."[30]

In constructing Samye as an impressive center for his Buddhist national creed, Trisong Detsen cleverly created a structure that both built on existing native mythology and took advantage of the status the country's topography enjoyed in the eyes of millions of Buddhists, Hindus, and other south and east Asians. With Samye, Trisong Detsen put into tangible form the Tibetans' growing sense of themselves and of their land as a kind of religious focal point.

Never mind that nineteenth- and twentieth-century explorers have discovered that the four great rivers of south Asia do not in fact all emanate from the same lake as the legends have claimed. They start close enough to one another that we can understand why ancient peoples thought they came from a single source. There may in fact be underground aquifers that do link them all together and will eventually prove native mythology correct.

Even before the construction of Samye, the culture, economy, military might, and topography of Tibet had given the people of the land a special identity and feeling of self-importance. With Samye, Trisong Detsen solidified and enhanced Tibetan consciousness and ethnocentrism. While the Chinese thought of themselves as the political and cultural *zhongguo* or Central Kingdom of the world, the Tibetans after Trisong Detsen began to view themselves as the center of the universe. The ideologies of the two neighbors grew far apart. The Chinese developed their poetic and bureaucratic skills, but Tibetans drew inspiration from their nearness to Mount Kailas and cultivated the powerful and magical religious aura that has given birth to legends of Shangri-la, the valley in Tibet where no one ages.

Architects designed Samye so that the building gave material expression to the various cultural influences at work in Tibet. They built each of the three floors of the large central building in a different style, one Chinese, one Indian, and one Tibetan. The design graphically represents the different forces that influenced and composed the Tibetan dominion as well as the varied origins of the artisans who labored on the project. The work of these Chinese and South Asian builders soon attracted others of their countrymen. When the project was finished, many foreign clerics and workers came to live at Samye. Their presence in turn helped bring scores of young Tibetans to the monastery to be educated and trained.

As Christopher Beckwith has pointed out, contrary to popular conceptions about the Middle Ages, this was a time when literacy was expanding throughout Eurasia and the old classics were being retranslated into new languages. Like his contemporaries in the Arab world who sponsored translations of ancient Greek works into Latin, or those in Europe who helped revive and popularize Latin, Trisong Detsen authorized the translation of huge numbers of Sanskrit, Chinese, and central Asian texts into Tibetan. These created a Tibetan Buddhist literature used to educate the young men who flocked into Samye and other Buddhist complexes.[31] Little by little, Tibet became a major center of Buddhist ideas and influence. The Tibetan translations broadened the spiritual possibilities of a society that geography already had infused with religiosity.[32]

This educated elite also became available to staff Trisong Detsen's newly expanded dominion and began to forge the uniquely Tibetan forms of Buddhism. In China, government officials were scrupulously nonreligious; in Tibet, officials were increasingly Buddhists.

These Buddhist officials were not doctrinaire in their beliefs. Trisong Detsen's new clergy emphasized "worldly Buddhist rites." Just as he had incorporated the Bon attachment to Mount Kailas into his new Buddhist symbolism, so Trisong Detsen's Buddhists embraced Bon rituals used to attain practical goals such as accumulating wealth or destroying enemies. Tibetan Buddhists engaged in activities abhorrent to members of their faith in other countries. For instance, Buddhists are not supposed to take a life, even an animal's life. This precept usually is observed in Tibet only in the most technical way. On his travels, McGovern noted that because of Tibetan sensibilities, he was at one point forced to do the dirty work of dispatching a wounded horse. But the same men who had refused to kill the beast thought nothing of sharing with him the "raw and still quivering flesh."[33]

In fact, as befits a largely nomadic group that raises great herds of sheep, goats, and yaks, most Tibetan Buddhists consume a great deal of meat in their diet. In urban areas, Muslim butchers do the slaughtering. In rural areas, Tibetan herders often resort to subterfuges such as stuffing the mouths and nostrils of their animals with mud and leaving them to suffocate. When the Tibetans come back a few hours later to find their dead yak, the herders apparently have little difficulty in persuading themselves they might as well eat the carcasses rather than let them go to waste.

In earlier times, Tibetans had even fewer scruples. During the ceremonies for the Chinese peace treaty of 782, which took place after Buddhism had become the official religion of Tibet, some Tibetans (without protest from the Buddhists among them) sacrificed animals and smeared their lips with animal's blood. Even in the treaty of 821, the participants evoked not only Buddhist deities but also non-Buddhist ones such as the "sun, moon, and stars."[34]

In spite of this occasional amiability, the struggle between Buddhism and Bon continued. Power was at stake. Bon had legitimized the old nobility. To adherents of Bon, preserving the faith was not just a matter of religious conviction but of survival against political upstarts. Bon supporters disputed the Buddhists bitterly at court. This fight grew more intense after Trisong Detsen died in 797, possibly poisoned by his wife. His son, Muni Tsenpo, succeeded him. But the old Bon nobility, which included his mother and her family, opposed the new ruler.

According to most accounts, in 799 Muni Tsenpo's mother poisoned him and placed another son on the throne. But nothing about this story, even the dates of Muni Tsenpo's rule, is clear. Nor is it certain if she killed him because of political and religious motives, if she did indeed kill him. One version of the story holds that she murdered him because she was jealous of his beautiful young wife, a former consort of her husband. The king is said to have given his consort to his son to protect her from the clutches of the queen.

Whatever the case, the court suffered this dissension from within just as new enemies prepared to attack the dominion from without. For by now the Tibetan dominion had expanded across the Pamir Mountains into the present central Asian republic of Tadzhikistan and had reached the borders of Persia. This Tibetan expansion worried Arab strategists. In 801 the Arab leader Harun ar-Rashid (r. 786–809), the caliph of Baghdad made famous in the *Tales of the Thousand and One Nights,* joined forces with China against Tibet.

Then in 838 several members of the old Bon nobility attacked the reigning king and strangled him. Lang Darma, the king's brother, who had instigated the plot, ascended the throne and began to persecute Buddhists. Lang Darma almost succeeded in destroying Buddhism in central Tibet. Many Tibetan historians claim that Buddhism was saved in 842 when a wrathful Buddhist monk named Lhalung Palgye Dorje shot an arrow through Lang Darma and ended the first Tibetan dynasty.

The killing of the king is said to have both destroyed the state that had made Tibet great and saved the religion that has given the country much of its unique flavor and culture. After the assassination, Tibet was never again as powerful, but following the death of Lang Darma the country continued to develop the Buddhist aura for which it is still famous. Over time, the great Tibetan kings such as Songtsen Gampo and Trisong Detsen began to be seen more as religious founders than as mighty conquerors. It is no wonder that the tale of Lang Darma's murder has resonated with Tibetans for hundreds of years.

So important is this story that the murder is ritually reenacted in an annual dance. An actor in a black hat plays the monk who attracted the attention of the king and then shot him. His dance is usually featured as the crowning event of the long New Year's celebration, highlighting its central importance in Tibetan history.

In the story the assassin wore a black hat and robes and rode a horse whose white mane he had blackened with soot. After the killing he fled, turning his robes inside out and splashing his horse in a river to wash off the soot, and he made clean his getaway.

In the dance, the actor wears a hat and robes bedecked with skulls, images of thunderbolts, and peacock feathers.

He is surrounded by monks who dance amid clouds of smoke from burning incense. They are laden with props of swords, axes, and drums made from human skulls. In mock battles, blood and guts appear to flow all over the dance floor. But in spite of its goriness, the dance has a magical resonance. Even a jaded British observer such as F. Spencer Chapman claimed that at the end of the dance, "All at once, as if the devils that have accumulated in the Old Year are indeed destroyed, the sky is miraculously cleared, the wind drops, and the evening sun shines through once more."[35]

Lang Darma was the last king descended from Songtsen Gampo. With his death Tibet once again disintegrated into a number of small principalities scattered in the valleys and on the plateaus, some ruled by families claiming to be descendants of the old kings. In 866 the Tibetan government ceased to exist altogether. By the beginning of the tenth century few traces of the Tibetan dominion remained. Its governmental archives had been sealed or burned, its former political structure forgotten, and its military and economic might replaced by new central Asian dynasties.

Tibet's fate was similar to that of most of the other large states of the period. The 843 Treaty of Verdun split Charlemagne's dominion among his three grandsons, and in the succeeding century the Viking invasions exacerbated the divisions. Arab invasion followed by revolutionary internal change a few decades later tore apart the Byzantine dominion in the middle of the ninth century. The Tang dynasty collapsed about fifty years later. For the next several hundred years, China was militarily weak and often divided into several competing states.[36]

During this time Tibet increasingly turned back toward the Buddhist legacy of Songtsen Gampo and Trisong Detsen. It was an age of intellectual fermentation throughout the world. Great works of religion, literature, and philosophy were written in China, Japan, and the Middle East. In Europe and Tibet, political fragmentation helped spur the return to monastic life and the birth of important new religious ideas. Tibet, the home of Mount Kailas, emerged as a place where, as Chapman puts it, "religion always comes first, and God, says a Tibetan proverb, can only be approached through a lama. The monasteries are therefore the chief influence in the country."[37]

The monastic system began to develop in the wake of the ninth-century collapse of the Tibetan dominion. Deprived of state support, devoted Buddhist followers held on in isolated communities, particularly in Amdo and western Tibet. Over time they gained adherents by emphasizing magic rites and erotic public dances. Such displays may not sound particularly dignified or Buddhist, but they contributed toward the growth of Buddhist centers as major hubs of stability and learning. Trade gravitated to these Buddhist centers, and individual monks again became major political players.[38]

As one scholar has written, "The extent to which Buddhism came to influence the social, cultural, and political life of Tibet was unparalleled elsewhere in Asia."[39] Given the past religious aura of the country, this is not surprising. Scores of Buddhist institutions developed throughout the country, each gradually articulating its own characters.

The Indian teacher Atisha played a prominent role. He was lured to Tibet by the worldly promise of vast sums of gold, arriving at the Toling monastery in western Tibet in 1142. While China employed Buddhist metaphysical concepts to enliven Confucian doctrines and to bolster a more autocratic state bureaucracy, Atisha helped Tibet strengthen the monastic Buddhist system that gradually became the base of Tibetan society and politics.

Atisha purged the dissolute and sometimes explosive

local charlatans who often aroused the masses against the local authorities. He toned down the Buddhist erotic rites and public displays. This is not to say that Buddhist imagery in Tibet became subtle. Anyone who has ever seen a Tibetan monastery knows, as Chapman observes, that the "Lamaists are great connoisseurs of hells. They recognize thousands, of which there are sixteen specially select abodes, eight of which are hot and eight cold. These hells, whose varied forms of entertainment bear a close resemblance to the torments of Dante's inferno, are carefully graded."[40]

Atisha helped begin the process of bringing into the monastery the magic and mystery that Tibetans love. Ultimately the frescoes in monasteries became so detailed that they depicted specific punishments for highly specialized groups of people. Some monastery walls, for instance, portray the "hell for doctors who kill their patients through incompetence; in this the victims are scarified and clumsily dissected, only to be reunited and revived so that the process can continue indefinitely." In others, "men who grumble against the weather or obstruct watercourses (an obscure connection!) have molten iron poured down their throats."[41]

Atisha also created a distinct monastic order that separated the clergy from the lay public and instituted strict monastic discipline. Monasteries in Tibet became independent political and religious centers which exercised a powerful pull on the surrounding countryside. This decentralization radically distinguished the Tibetan political tradition from the rationalist, nonreligious central bureaucratic apparatus then being honed in China.

Over time the monastic influence increased. Tibetan rulers routinely began to exempt Buddhist monastic lands and property from secular taxes. The Buddhist orders in turn gave local princes and nobles new allies and provided them religious justification for escaping Bon circumscriptions on their authority. Gradually monastic holdings grew. Powerful

Captain Hamilton Bower, a nineteenth-century English visitor to Tibet, referred to the famous Cham dances as "one of the quaintest and weirdest sights I have ever seen." Other Victorian visitors dismissed them more harshly as devil dances. Characters include the skeleton-appearing Lord of the Cemeteries and the stag-head messenger of the Lord of Death. *(Northwestern University Archives)*

monastic orders became major players in the fragmented local power structure. Feudal leaders sent their sons into Buddhist institutions as a way of ensuring the maintenance of family authority. These local noble families became an increasingly strong force in the monasteries. Often the position of abbot was no longer chosen from among the monks but was passed down within families from uncle to nephew.

By the thirteenth century, monastic dynasties controlled much of Tibet. Buddhism had become an ingrained and distinctive part of Tibetan life, affecting many of the features of the society's politics and culture. Unlike its Chinese neighbor, the Tibetan state had always depended heavily on a religious aura, one that took much of its power from the mystical inclination of its people and their unique geographical position astride the Himalayas. Over time, as China refined its civil bureaucracy and the neo-Confucian ideology used to rationalize it, Tibet created the decentralized monastic system that made religion the key political as well as cultural institution in Tibetan society. By the thirteenth century, Chinese and Tibetans differed so radically from each other that it would be hard to imagine that later anyone would seriously claim they were part of the same nation.

THREE

❦

Tibetans, Mongols, and Manchus

On my way to Tibet in 1991, I passed through Beijing. Walking down Wangfujing, the busy shopping street at the center of the city, I fell in behind several American tourists and a Chinese friend taking them on a tour of the city.

"Look over there," the Chinese host told the Americans. "Those strange-looking people wearing knives at their sides are Mongols."

The people to whom he pointed were Tibetans. I witnessed the conversation without comment, but later that day when I encountered these same tourists as they walked into a hotel dangling shopping bags at their sides, I could not restrain myself.

"You know, those men with daggers on their belts that your Chinese friend was calling Mongols were really Tibetans."

"But he should know!" they replied in disbelief. "He's Chinese!"

In fact, Chinese often cannot tell the difference between Mongols and Tibetans. Men from both groups typically hang a pouch on the right side of their belts to hold a small

knife and a pair of chopsticks. Many Chinese see all non-
Han ethnic groups as equally foreign and alien, and readily
mistake the ethnic origin of minorities, especially those carrying daggers.

The real problem, though, is that the Chinese have been
confused by the long and close association between Mongols
and Tibetans, an association that has often pitted the two
groups against the Chinese. Recently Chinese scholars have
tried to clarify this confusion, insisting that Tibet became
part of China in the thirteenth century after the Mongols
conquered both China and Tibet.

Yet the logic of the claim is shaky. During the thirteenth
century the Mongols did conquer and for a while control
both China and Tibet, but they also occupied most of central
Asia, the Middle East, and even eastern Europe. If the Mongol conquests made Tibet and China part of the same country, it could also be argued that eastern Europe and Korea
belong to China. Unlike Tibet, Korea was ruled as a Chinese
province by the Mongols. China's claim to Tibet is made especially preposterous by China's recognition of Mongolia as
an independent country separate from China. In any case,
the test of past conquest and rule by another nation would
make Taiwan part of Japan, for Japan occupied the island
for more than fifty years, in the process radically altering
Taiwan's political, social, and economic structure.

The Tibetan-Mongol relationship was not simply that of
conquered and conqueror. The two neighboring groups have
long had an important association, one which highlights
their mutual differences from the Chinese. During the Han
dynasty (206 B.C.E.–220 C.E.), Chinese strategists warned of
the dangers to their country from a combination of the
Qiang (or Tibetans) and the Xiongnu (the Mongols). Four
hundred years later, Songtsen Gampo began the first Tibetan
dominion with his conquest and absorption of the Tuyuhun,
a Mongol people living at the northeastern edge of the Ti-

betan plateau. In 1209 Chinggis Khan embarked on his world conquest only after he had first absorbed the Xixia, a Tibetan kingdom that controlled much of Amdo and northwest China.[1]

In 1240[2] one of Chinggis's grandsons successfully invaded central Tibet. The grandson made Kunga Gyaltsen, the head of the Sakya monastery, his personal Buddhist tutor and the supreme master of Tibet.[3] This appointment marked the beginning of the mixed religious-civil rule that has uniquely characterized the Tibetan political system. Kunga Gyaltsen assured his countrymen that the prince had told him "that if we Tibetans help the Mongols in matters of religion, they in turn will support us in temporal matters. In this way, we will be able to spread our religion far and wide."[4] This statement turned out to be prophetic.

Sakya, where Kunga Gyaltsen's monastery is located, is a drowsy little town, fewer than a hundred miles from Xigaze and a little bit off the main track connecting Lhasa with Nepal, not far from the road that leads up Mount Everest. It is somewhat ironic that the Chinese claim Tibet became a part of their country when the country was dominated by a religious group that lived so close to and were obviously greatly influenced by Nepal and the rest of south Asia. The central Sakya monastery that Kunga Gyaltsen helped establish remains, but most of the ring of smaller monasteries that once dotted the hills around Sakya were destroyed during China's Cultural Revolution. Even the once impressive northern monastery is now gone. Piles of broken bricks and rubbish on a hillside behind the town are all that is left of it.

In the 1990s the Chinese attempted to turn the still magnificent central monastery in Sakya into a tourist attraction. Millions of dollars, most of it raised by Tibetans, were lavished on the renovation of its airy, elegant prayer hall. The Chinese went to great pains to promote the temple's thousand-year-old Buddhist scriptures, valuable porcelains, and vivid murals.

The Chinese may intend to bolster the leadership of the Sakyapas (as proponents of the Sakya school are called) as an alternative to that of the Dalai Lama. But they have failed to note that the Sakyapas' lead monastery is based no longer in the town of Sakya. Several hundred years ago it moved to Dege, a town in northern Kham that is now part of Sichuan province. The lamasery in Dege is the site of one of the most famous Tibetan printing presses. The scriptures produced here are so highly regarded that visitors can observe the faithful wash themselves with and even drink the inky water used to clean the printing blocks.

Today, as in Chinggis's time, the Sakyapas are a free-wheeling group. They permit their monks to marry and drink alcohol. Many specialize in magic. In the 1960s respondents told scholars that their leader could bring forth springs from rocks. The Sakyapas claimed that he reversed the flow of a stream when it blocked his path while traveling in Nepal.[5] In the thirteenth century the Sakya monks' reputation as sorcerers appealed to the Mongols, who wanted to hex their enemies or obtain potions said to prolong life and induce sexual ecstasy.

The Sakya leadership is hereditary, and the relationship between the Mongols and Tibetans was cemented by Phags-pa (1235–1280), the nephew and heir of Kunga Gyaltsen. The boy grew up in the care of the Mongols and ingratiated himself with the great Mongol leader and conqueror of China, Khubilai Khan.[6] When Khubilai became the supreme khan in 1260, he made Phags-pa state preceptor *(guoshi)* and a few months later put him in charge of all Buddhist clergy. Phags-pa created new Buddhist court ceremonies for the Mongols and, according to David Morgan, provided Khubilai and his heirs "with a pseudo-historical legitimation in Buddhist terms by incorporating them into the line of

Buddhist universal emperors, the Chakravartin kings, and he produced a Buddhist religio-political theory of world rule."[7]

Khubilai used Phags-pa to restrain Chinese cultural influences on his court. Phags-pa invented a new script, adapted from the Tibetan alphabet, for the writing of both Mongolian and Chinese. For a brief time this Tibetan writing system was the official language of the realm. Khubilai was proud of it and saw it as a way to unify the various cultures in his dominion. As a symbol of the bond between Tibetans and Mongols, Khubilai presented Phags-pa with the giant white conch shell still kept in the central monastery in Sakya. Sakyapas believe this shell to be the remains of Buddha "from one of his previous lives as a mollusk."[8]

Khubilai went so far as to send the last boy emperor of the Song dynasty to the Sakya temple to be trained as a monk.[9] Historians believe that Khubilai schemed to make this emperor, "who after the dethronement still commanded the adoration of Song Loyalists," into "a spiritual leader to serve the new Son of Heaven from the other land, and to confirm the latter's authority!"[10] But the Mongols were no more successful in making people believe the emperor was now a Tibetan monk than the Communists have been in making the Tibetans feel like Chinese. Four years after the emperor finally was ordained in 1296, the Mongols ordered him to commit suicide.[11] Nor did the writing system that Phags-pa established for Khubilai last long. During Khubilai's lifetime, the Chinese and even most Mongols ignored it.[12] After the death of Khubilai, the Mongols returned to the Uyghur script and the Chinese returned to the characters that they use today.[13] The Chinese could no more adapt to Tibetan and Mongol practices than could the two groups adjust to Chinese ones.

Marriage and religion linked the Tibetans to the Mongol ruling family.[14] Tibetans became important officials during the Yuan dynasty in China. The Tibetan statesman and fi-

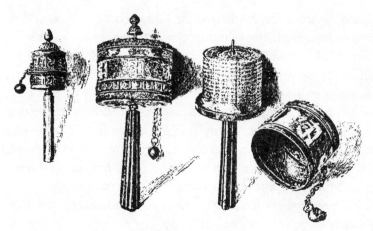

These hand-held copper and silver prayer wheels come in various sizes and can be turned by hand, hot air, wind, or water. Just as the pilgrim must circumambulate sacred shrines in a clockwise direction, so these instruments, which are special to Tibetan Buddhism, must be spun clockwise. The scrolls (shown in the opened prayer wheel at the right) release prayers and invocations that bring merit to the user. *(Land of the Lamas)*

nancier Sangko, for instance,[15] at one point became the virtual head of the Yuan government and the author of some of its most innovative policies.[16] But the Yuan never integrated Tibet into its Chinese empire. The Mongols considered Tibet an autonomous region and gave local elites tremendous latitude. Indigenous lamas continued to hold on to the levers of government in Tibet with nominal instruction from Phags-pa and his successors who remained in Beijing. The Tibetan borderlands in Kham and Amdo were under the supervision of various Mongol imperial princes and thus altogether outside the bounds of the regular Mongol civil bureaucracy in China.[17]

It was a matter of topography as much as ethnicity. The Mongols could conquer Tibet, but the logistics of maintaining military forces and sending bureaucratic messengers there were almost impossible. With each mission, fresh troops would have to climb what the famous Swedish explorer Sved Hedin later described as "the gigantic wall which Nature has built up like a bulwark to guard the secrets of Tibet on the north."[18]

In the thirteenth century there was no road between China and Tibet. Although the Chinese have recently built an artery, a contemporary guidebook warns its readers about the rugged terrain from Sichuan province into Tibet, suggesting: "Due to landslide, mud slides, snow, washouts, and even glacial blockages, the route is best not attempted in winter (September to February). . . ." Even in August this modern feat of engineering is often washed out and at best extremely difficult to navigate.[19] Nor would the Mongols have done much better if they had tried to send troops and supplies into Tibet from the north. The recently constructed Qinghai-Tibet highway is "the world's highest road." The guidebook notes that "Until recently, this route was one of the roughest rides in the world."[20] Moreover, travelers cannot even access the highway until they reach Qinghai, on the Tibetan peninsula, an arduous hike in its own right. And the northwestern route from Xinjiang, built by the Chinese in 1957, crosses the Kunlun Mountains through one of the most inhospitable and sparsely populated areas of the world. The guidebook claims that today the rugged truck drivers who ply the road carry rifles which they use to shoot game along the way.[21]

Unable to maintain control of or communicate closely with Tibet, the Mongols could only mount periodic attacks against the country when it seemed to go astray. These ended in 1358, when Changchub Gyaltsen of the Thel monastery rallied several rival monasteries and successfully rebelled against the Mongols and Sakya. Tibet again became a completely separate country. The main legacy of Mongol rule was a religious government.

When the Ming government was established in China in 1368, it did sometimes label its trade with Tibet as tribute. But as Hugh Richardson, the last British ambassador to

Tibet, has noted, the Ming's classification of Tibet as a tributary state was as meaningless as the subsequent Qing dynasty's similar classification of the Vatican.[22] The Ming
typically called all foreign trade "tribute" as a way of bol-
stering imperial prestige and helping the emperor retain lucrative trade monopolies.

Far from being a subject of the Ming, Changchub Gyaltsen modeled himself after Songtsen Gampo, and again extended Tibetan power into Kham, Amdo, Nepal, Burma, and
Bangladesh. Some of the massive hilltop forts he built for his
officials still exist. On his trip to Tibet in the 1920s, William
McGovern compared them to medieval castles.[23] Early in this
century, the British considered the fort at Gyangtze, Tibet's
fourth-largest city, to be the strongest in central Asia. When
the Younghusband expedition attacked it in 1904, the lightly
armed Tibetans repelled the British for several weeks until
they brought up cannon to blast through its walls.

Today the giant stone fort still looms over the roughneck
town of Gyangtze, reminding visitors that this is one place
where the Chinese have not yet expunged the native Tibetan
spirit. In winter, herdsmen ride their yaks and horses into
town, check their swords at the doors of local saloons, and
drink and gamble away their days and nights.

Today the Shalu monastery near Gyangtze shelters the
only major remaining example of Sakyapa art. Because of
the Sakya-Mongol alliance, donations for the building of
new religious centers poured into Sakya during the period of
Yuan domination. The Sakyapas hired a great number of
artists from nearby Nepal who helped create the intricate detail that characterizes Sakyapa designs. Often they depicted
various members of the Buddhist pantheon enclosed in elaborate shrines. Today the Shalu monastery is virtually a mu-
seum of these paintings, which greatly influenced Buddhist
art throughout Tibet and the rest of east and central Asia.

Changchub Gyaltsen and his followers strengthened the

cultural ties between Tibet and Nepal that had developed because of the Sakyapas' closeness to the other side of the Himalayas. Changchub encouraged monks and translators from Nepal (and other nearby countries) to immigrate, and new editions of Indian, Chinese, and central Asian religious discourses, or *sutras,* began to circulate.

New religious schools emerged. In the original Tibetan Bon religion, practitioners commonly sacrificed animals and even humans. Followers worshiped the spirits of local mountaintops and lakes. The fifth-century Tibetan poem *Kesar* describes the gore of early Bon rituals: "There is continual talk of eyes being torn out, of blood being drunk from skulls, of tortured enemies, of trophies consisting of parts of the human anatomy offered as gifts to victorious kings, and so on." When a spy is captured, King Kesar, who is celebrated as a kind of Tibetan god of war, "gloats over the tortures he is about to inflict on him."

> The blood of the liver will escape from the mouth,
> Though we do not injure the skin,
> We will take out all the entrails through the mouth,
> The man will be alive, though his heart will come to his mouth.[24]

Gradually Buddhism helped pacify the violent nature of Bon. Bon believers assumed many of the teachings and even the lamaseries of the Buddhists. Tibetan Buddhist schools inherited from Bon an emphasis on magic and ritual. The late-nineteenth-century American explorer W. W. Rockhill noted: "The ordinary Tibetan will assure you that the only difference between a Bonbo and a lama is that, in walking around a sacred building or monument, the Bonbo keeps it on his left while the latter keeps it on his right. The Bonbo sacrifice living animals, especially fowls, to their gods, and this is an abomination in the eyes of the lamas."[25] Even into the 1990s, travelers could still find Bon ghost traps over the doors of some houses. As Chapman noted in the 1930s: "These, a relic of the old Pon [sic] religion, are to avert devils from the inmates of the house. The lower part is the skull of a ram with the horns attached; over this are several flat pieces of wood on which there are paintings rather resembling the court cards in a pack; these are effigies of the people in the house and are meant to divert evil from their originals; above and beyond these a web of colored wool is arranged in geometric patterns."[26]

The sensual and gory Bon practices that seeped into Tibetan Buddhist schools such as the Sakyapas have from time to time attracted the scrutiny of Buddhist reformers. This happened in the fourteenth century following Changchub Gyaltsen's ascension, when Tibetan Buddhists again came into contact with foreign Buddhists and renewed their interest in their doctrine's original texts.

The most famous reformer was Lobzang Trakpa Tsongkhapa (1357–1419), whose Gelugpa school today predominates in Tibet. He insisted on a return to celibacy, abstention from alcohol, and vegetarianism. Some scholars refer to Tsongkhapa as the "Luther of Tibet." But as Hugh Richardson observes, Tsongkhapa, unlike Luther, "had no wish himself to interfere with the ways of others outside his monastery, and even if others were jealous of his successes, there is no sign of any open hostility between his community and others during his lifetime."[27] He better resembled his contemporary, Jan Hus (1372–1415), in his learned disavowal of what he considered to be the flawed practices of his own church.

Tsongkhapa came from the district of Tsongkha in Amdo near Lake Kokonor. His name means literally "the man from the land of the onions." This area, the heart of the province the Chinese today call Qinghai, is not far from the birthplace of the current Dalai Lama and the recently de-

Tibetan art is almost always religious in inspiration. Here Tsongkhapa (1357–1419), founder of the Gelugpa order, is pictured with the Dalai Lama under his right arm and the Panchen Lama under his left. *(from a Tibetan painting)*

ceased Panchen Lama. Because settlers lately have poured into the region, its population is now overwhelmingly Han. But the area has long been one of mixed population, and Chinese scholars have claimed Tsongkhapa was really a Mongol by birth, which Tibetans adamantly deny.[28]

Tsongkhapa gained followers after he moved to the Lhasa area. Changchub Gyaltsen had just established his dynasty in the nearby town of Nedong. Tsongkhapa glorified

Lhasa, Songtsen Gampo's ancient city and the site of the Jokhang, the ancient cathedral of Tibetan Buddhism. He established the *Monlam,* or peace prayer festival, a three-week event that took place in Lhasa at the Tibetan New Year. It has since become the largest annual Tibetan festival.

The ostensible aim of the festival is to hasten the coming of the reign of the "Buddha of Conquering Love." Tens of thousands of monks crowd into Lhasa from all over Tibet and sometimes take control of the city. They have often used the festival as an opportunity to even scores against civil officials; recently they have used it to protest Chinese rule.

Many of these monks normally sequester themselves in one of the great monasteries built by Tsongkhapa and his followers near Lhasa—Ganden, founded in 1409; Drepung, constructed in 1416; and Sera, erected in 1419. Although in Tsongkhapa's day each of the three monasteries probably housed only a few hundred inhabitants, within about a century Drepung alone held more than ten thousand monks, making it the largest monastery in the world. Sera eventually housed almost as many monks as Drepung. Ganden, which suffered very heavy damage during the Cultural Revolution, came to harbor about four thousand of the devout. These giant Gelugpa monasteries formed their own armies and independent governments. Their monks wore yellow head coverings rather than the red ones favored by their best-known rivals. As a result, Gelugpa monks have become popularly known in China and the West as the Yellow Hats.

The Dalai Lamas lived at Drepung before the reconstruction of the Potala Palace. Drepung is so large that from a distance it "resembles a large fortified city."[29] The climb to the top of the monastery is grueling and is made worse by the packs of wild dogs that today roam its steps. Unlike the Chinese who consider stewed dog a winter delicacy, the Tibetans protect the animals, believing them to be incarnations of deceased people. They are allowed to roam free throughout much of Tibet. Their presence overwhelms Drepung, as dogs of all shapes and sizes defecate, copulate, and fight for scraps from the monastery's huge kitchens.

The outer commotion created by the scrabbling dogs at Drepung is echoed by the often divisive internal factions of the organization. The monastery is divided into four colleges, each with its own abbot. At one time each of these colleges was favored by monks from a different locality —Kham, Mongolia, and so forth—further aggravating and yet at the same time representing the differences within Tibetan society.

The Sera, almost as large as the Drepung, is similarly structured and is one of the best-preserved monasteries in Tibet. The destruction of the Cultural Revolution inexplicably missed this institution once known for its anti-Chinese stance and its band of fighting monks. Today the visitor can often see red-robed monks sitting in the yard in groups of ten or fifteen, practicing what they call debating. One monk stands in the center of each group, lecturing loudly and thumping on his side or clapping his hands in the faces of the others for emphasis.

Such tactics honed the beliefs of the faithful and helped the new doctrine gain followers during the turmoil that swirled through the country after 1432. In that year a succession crisis brought down Changchub Gyaltsen's Pogmatra dynasty. Tension erupted between the two main districts of central Tibet—Tsang, where Sakya is located, and U, the area that surrounds Lhasa, Nedong, and Samye and features the tombs of the first Tibetan kings.[30] Today the authorities of the two areas cannot even agree on the date to celebrate the Tibetan New Year. On a trip to Xigaze in the winter of 1991, our Lhasa guide seemed astonished to discover that the town was closed to visitors because its religious authorities had proclaimed that the New Year festival there started several weeks before it did in neighboring Lhasa.

In 1445 Tsongkhapa's successor, Gedun Truppa (1391–1474), took advantage of the crisis and expanded the Gelugpa influence from U into Tsang by building a new monastery near Xigaze, the major city in this region where the rival Karmapa school (whose monks are known as the Red Hats) had dominated. The new monastery, Tashilhunpo, is now the headquarters of the Panchen Lama, the person second in command in the hierarchy of Tibetan Buddhism.

Xigaze lies in a fertile river plain on the road from Lhasa to Nepal and close to the route to Amdo. It has become a drab, Chinese-looking city as Tibetan houses have been replaced by the square, gray cement apartment blocks typical of major Chinese towns. As in Lhasa, recent Chinese immigrants outnumber the native Tibetan population. Xigaze's fort was largely dismantled in the Cultural Revolution. The stone outcropping on which it stood looms over the city, desolate and shorn.

But the Tashilhunpo monastery still towers forcefully above Xigaze, boasting a twenty-six-foot-high gilded bronze Buddha crafted in 1914. In the past, the monastery was known for its size and for the importance of its leaders; until the 1950s its abbot was still the titular king of Tibet. Today, now that the inhabitants of Drepung and Sera have been greatly diminished, Tashilhunpo is probably the largest and most vibrant monastery in Tibet. One observer has suggested that it is "the only one that does justice to the term 'monastic city.' "[31]

Gedun Truppa, who built Tashilhunpo, wisely instituted the idea that his successor should be a reincarnated lama. When the old lama died, his spirit would enter the body of a young child who would become the new lama. Of course, the identity of this child would not be obvious: Gelugpa authorities would be entrusted with finding him and acting as his regent. This ensured that their own power continued and possibly increased. Because these authorities were in charge

Young monks train in debate at the Sera monastery. One monk stands over the others, gesturing and gesticulating loudly.

of educating the child into the faith, they made sure that the young lama developed the proper loyalties.

This tradition of succession proved beneficial to the Gelugpas. From the fall of the Pogmatra dynasty in 1432 until 1498, when lay princes from the Tsang town of Rimpung conquered Lhasa, strife swept the country's political and religious establishment. Their method of succession kept Gelugpa leaders from being pitted against secular families and made the group appear to be an oasis of stability. The school's leaders decided whether they wanted to turn to an ordinary family without influence or a wealthy well-connected clan that would support the sect. As scholars have noted: "Despite the mystique with which some Westerners like to regard the whole practice of reincarnating lamas, the custom was clearly adopted and maintained primarily for reasons of statecraft."[32]

After the death of Gedun Truppa, his spirit passed to Gedun Gyatso (1475–1542), posthumously considered the Second Dalai Lama, and then from him to Sonam Gyatso (1543–1588). Yet by this time the school's fortunes had begun to decline. Desperate to keep the Gelugpa school alive, in 1578 Sonam Gyatso accepted the invitation of the Mongol leader Altan Khan to visit his headquarters in Mongolia and to instruct him in Tibetan lamaism as the first Sakyapa had instructed Khubilai Khan.

Altan Khan created the position of Dalai Lama (a Mongolian translation of his Buddhist ordination name Gyatso or "great ocean") for Sonam Gyatso. Sonam, who respectfully and retroactively claimed that his two predecessors had also been Dalai Lamas, officially became known as the Third Dalai Lama.

The Third (really the First) Dalai Lama never returned to central Tibet. He spent the rest of his time in Kham, Amdo, and Mongolia, where he persuaded Altan Khan to forbid blood sacrifices and the worship of ancestral images. Sonam Gyatso gave Altan Khan the title of "Religious King, Brahma of the Gods," and "prophesied that within eighty years the descendants of the Khan would become the rulers of all Mongolia and China."[33] Buddhist monasteries soon covered Mongolia, many peopled by their own living Buddhas. Sonam's work assured that the Mongols and Tibetans would remain linked and share a common religious faith.

The Third Dalai Lama's followers cemented this alliance with the Mongols when they chose a successor after his death in 1588. The child reincarnation they happened to identify as the Fourth Dalai Lama was Altan Khan's great-grandson. If the Third Dalai Lama's decision to accept Altan Khan's invitation to visit Mongolia was a difficult and desperate attempt, the Tibetans' decision to pick the khan's descendant as their Dalai Lama was an easy and deliberate choice.

By the time the Fourth Dalai Lama was enthroned in Tibet, Mongol military might was no longer as powerful as it had once been. So the Dalai Lama had to employ personal persuasion rather than Mongol power to reach out to his potential followers in Tsang. He did this by giving the title of Panchen Lama, or "Great Scholar," to Lozang Chosgyan, the abbot of the Tashilhunpo monastery in Xigaze. Thus the two major regions of central Tibet each had its own influential Gelugpa political and religious leader.

The Dalai Lama traditionally has been considered the more important of the two figures. But in formal Buddhist terms, the Dalai Lama gave the Panchen Lama a position higher than his own. For the Dalai Lama is considered the incarnation of Buddha's body, while the Panchen is the incarnation of Buddha's mind. Because the mind is superior to the body in the Buddhist pantheon, the Panchen Lama should rank higher than the Dalai Lama. Tibetans, however, have typically ignored this technicality.

In the late 1500s and early 1600s, neither the Dalai Lama nor the Panchen Lama were held in the kind of awe they today inspire. This veneration resulted from the efforts of the man known as the Great Fifth. After becoming Dalai Lama in 1622, the Great Fifth allied himself with yet another Mongol leader, Gushri Khan. In 1637, after years of fighting, Gushri Khan established the Great Fifth as the supreme temporal as well as religious leader in Tibet. The Great Fifth in

turn granted Gushri Khan the title of Religious King and
Holder of the Buddhist faith.

In 1642 the Dalai made Lhasa the new capital of Tibet.
It was here that the Great Fifth laid the foundation for the
Potala Palace. He built the structure on the same hill as
Songtsen Gampo's seventh-century palace and apparently
along similar architectural lines, selecting a site equidistant
from the Sera and Drepung monasteries. When he moved
out of Drepung, the Dalai Lama became a truly national figure with a palace to match his ambitions.

The magnificent thirteen-story Potala is still the official
residence of the Dalai Lama (not to be confused with the
Norbulingka or Summer Palace on the outskirts of the city).
Billed as the largest wooden skyscraper, the Potala towers
over Lhasa. It is, as one witness has commented, "one of the
most astonishing buildings in the world, whether it is seen
from afar perched on the summit of the eminence which rises
from the level plain of Lhasa, with the sun striking flame
from the golden pavilions of its roof, or whenever, riding out
before dawn, you see the moonlight thrown back with un-
earthly brilliance from the whitewashed wall of the immense
southern face."[34]

Almost all observers have marveled at this building, and
would agree with Kawaguchi when he notes that: "The
palace is so splendid that even its picture looks beautiful."[35]
The building possesses such power and has such a mystical
aura that the seasoned explorer and cynic Chapman observes
that "the Potala represents the very essence of the Tibetan
people. It has a certain untamed dignity in perfect harmony
with the surrounding rugged country."[36]

The name Potala was taken from that of a rock in southern India said to be the abode of the God of Mercy, who is
incarnate in the Dalai Lama. The palace measures 440 feet
high and 900 feet in length, and seems much larger because
it is built on top of a mountain. As Chapman notes: "The

Potala gives the impression not of having been built by man but of having grown there, yet this apparent aimlessness is focused, first by the red central block and then by the golden pavilions on the roof, so that the eye is naturally led from the less important to the essential, both visually and spiritually; for in so much as the gilded roofs over the mortal remains of the Dalai Lamas are the dominant features of the architecture, so is the incarnate spirit of these rulers the very soul of Tibet."[37]

The palace is filled with a fascinating mix of religious and cultural items, including such relics as drums made from human skulls (to symbolize the impermanence of life) and thick gold *chortens* (tiered shrines) containing the remains of deceased Dalai Lamas. The complex includes thirty-five chapels and several meeting halls, meditation chambers, and mausoleums. In the basement are prisons and torture chambers, now closed to the public, and at the top are the former residences of the Dalai Lama. The view from the large middle courtyard conveys a sense of the overall size and shape of the palace and its relationship to the city below it.

Although the scene from the courtyard is stunning and the religious artifacts in the various halls outstanding, much of the inside of the Potala is dark and dismal. The rooms are damp, cold, and putrid-smelling. Hordes of monks and pilgrims shuffle through the building every morning, burning and dripping yak butter in every room and in front of every shrine. Some visitors carry candles made from the butter while others tote large jars or cans of the foul-smelling stuff, scooping it into burning vessels that stand in the rooms. Occasionally pilgrims carry yak oil which they rub into their hair along with the ashes supposedly of dead lamas that they cull from little holes in the floors. Palace monks sometimes dispense yak oil to the faithful, who swallow it straight, a sight sure to make even the most hardy foreigner gag. The dirt, smoke, and odors of the Potala cling to visitors for days. Moreover, the candles threaten to enflame the clothing of jostling onlookers as well as the vast wooden structure itself. At the least, the closeness of the crowds, the long waits in line, and the smell make foreigners, already dizzy from the high altitude, feel faint.

The numerous rooms of the palace appear to be haphazardly laid out and the staircases that zigzag through the thirteen floors are difficult to climb and poorly placed. Though the original Potala consists of a central red palace and two white palaces (actually wings) completed about fifty years later, visitors can easily lose their bearings.

In the 1990s the Chinese completed a much-needed but highly controversial remodeling of the Potala. The Chinese claim to have relied extensively on indigenous Tibetan architects for most of the renovations. Foreign critics claim that the changes have destroyed some of the unique aspects of the structure. Particularly alarming to historical preservationists are Chinese plans to reduce the number of yak-butter lamps and to install electric lights to make the building more attractive to tourists.

The palace was the central structure of a vast monastic empire created by the Great Fifth. He steadily increased Gelugpa power, purging many of the Red Hat monasteries and establishing new monasteries and nunneries loyal to the principles of his school and to him personally. The Great Fifth made the monastery the central feature of the Tibetan community and the mainstay of the new political order. He allowed the larger monasteries to draft serfs to work for them, to conscript new monks from their serfs, and to maintain monopolies over major staples of the Tibetan economy such as barley, butter, and tea. The Great Fifth also established throughout his domain a special tithe to fund prayer services, which served to support the monasteries. More than any other leader, he firmly established the principle of rule by a religious theocracy in Tibet.

Before the 1950s at least 2,500 monasteries dotted Tibet, and by some estimates as many as one of every four adults was a monk or a nun. Because these monks and nuns were supposed to remain celibate, their presence was a tremendous check on population growth, though Tibetans generally tolerated their religious leaders' sexual liaisons more than their European counterparts did. Today, in the wake of the destruction of the Cultural Revolution, probably less than 10 percent of the monasteries remain, and most have suffered enormous damage. And although the number of boys and girls entering monasteries and nunneries grew rapidly in the 1980s, that number remains an insignificant percentage of Tibet's population.

The Great Fifth not only helped develop the religious theocracy that the Communists later destroyed, but also tried to unify his country by establishing a national costume. He ranked his officials by their various articles of dress. And well into the twentieth century visitors observed: "Seasons as far as man is concerned are directed by government decree in Tibet and high officials regulate their dress by law. The 25th of the tenth month (the last of November), inaugurated by the Tsongkhapa butter festival, is the beginning of winter and wearing of heavy clothing dates from that period."[38] During his stay in the 1940s, Heinrich Harrier reported that he "continually used to hear complaints that the changeover had come too soon or too late and that people were stifling or half-frozen."[39]

Most Tibetans wear a sheepskin cloak during winter. Harrier reported that the one for which he was measured in Lhasa in the 1940s was made from sixty skins.[40] Chinese-made clothes have lately become popular, but common people still often wear the *nambu*, a wool sash about eight inches wide. Poor people usually wear white belts while the wealthy wear more expensive colorful ones.

Thirty years after assuming his title, the Great Fifth be-

Tibetan boots rise almost to the knee with a slit in back and a colored garter to tie them at the top. They are soled with yak hide, though the colorful, often red tops may be made from felt, cloth, or leather. *(Land of the Lamas)*

came the first Dalai Lama to visit China. In 1644 a Mongol-related people, the Manchus, had conquered China and established the Qing dynasty (1644–1911). In 1652 the Dalai Lama accepted their invitation to visit Beijing.

His visit might be seen as a minor historical footnote except that contemporary Chinese nationalists assert that the Dalai Lama's trip was a tribute mission to the Chinese capital and therefore shows that Tibet has long been a dependency of China. Tibetan historians argue that the Manchu emperor sought the Dalai Lama's aid in deterring attacks by various Mongol tribes.[41] Tibetans have also claimed that, "According to Tibetan tradition, the reason why the Manchu emperor repeatedly extended invitations to the Dalai Lama was the prophecy the third Dalai Lama made in 1578 that the descendants of Altan Khan would become supreme rulers of Mongolia and China in eighty years' time. Since Tibetans consider the Manchus to be closely related to the Mongols, the truth of the prophecy seemed to be confirmed."[42] Tibetan scholars also emphasize that the emperor purportedly walked up to the Dalai Lama and grasped his hand, an unprecedented greeting appropriate only for an equal. Yet they acknowledge that the Great Fifth later returned the gesture by kneeling before the emperor.

However historians interpret the visit, none question the fact that after the death in 1654 of Gushri Khan, Tibet's greatest Dalai Lama ruled a powerful independent empire whose geographical expanse rivaled that of the Qing. In battle after battle, the Great Fifth and his armies captured territory from Ladakh in present-day India to the Burmese border and beyond. In places such as Yunnan he even fought the Manchus. Moreover the Great Fifth established a cultural uniformity that prevailed throughout his domain through the twentieth century.

In 1679 the Great Fifth dispelled the trappings of Mongol power and appointed as regent Sangye Gyatso, his spiritual—and some say his natural—son. The Great Fifth died three years later, and Sangye Gyatso concealed the news from the Tibetan people for fifteen years in order to maintain his power. He continued his patron's construction projects and in 1690 laid the foundation for the Red Palace, the most recent and in some ways the most impressive wing of the Potala.

Sangye Gyatso's power is depicted in a famous mural that hangs in Lhasa's Jokhang Cathedral, Tibet's most sacred temple. In the painting he is being offered tribute by the Mongol patron of the Great Fifth, Gushri Khan. Sangye's actual turn at power was, however, not smooth. He did carry out a search for a new Dalai Lama but kept the boy hidden in the palace.

The Sixth Dalai Lama grew up discontent and ill at ease with his prospective position. After he reached adulthood, the Sixth Dalai Lama (1683–1706) was the only Dalai Lama who refused to become a monk. Though the office of Dalai Lama is that of a priest-king, no rule requires him to become a priest. Even today, all who join a monastery must master three stages of learning and testing to become a lama. Many in the monastery never complete the process. The Sixth Dalai Lama pushed this point to the extreme. He wrote romantic verses and songs, drank, and caroused with women. In fact, as Hugh Richardson observes, he was "the only writer of lyrical verse that Tibet has produced."[43]

Left to run the government by himself, Sangye Gyatso tried to promote an alliance with the powerful Mongol forces that threatened the Qing empire in central Asia.[44] The Manchus defeated this new Mongol threat (at least in part by persuading the Russians to stop selling guns to the Mongols.[45]) In turn the Manchus urged their own Mongol allies to invade Tibet. These Mongols were Lajang Khan (a descendant of the Great Fifth's former protector, Gushri Khan) and his soldier wife, Jerinrasi. In 1705 Lajang and Jerinrasi fought their way separately to Lhasa. Lajang promised to spare Sangye Gyatso's life, but Jerinrasi despised the regent and had him killed.[46]

The role Jerinrasi played in this invasion illustrates the striking difference between Mongol and Tibetan women and their much daintier Chinese counterparts. For generations Chinese women have perfected their makeup and dress to enhance their appearance. Until well into the twentieth century, Chinese women habitually bound the feet of young girls so they would remain small and supposedly pretty, despite the fact that this practice severely inhibited the girls' movements as they grew older. In Mongolia and Tibet, however, women have been expected to live a rugged nomadic life.

As Sir Charles Bell, one of the keenest observers of Tibetan life, has noted: "When a traveler enters Tibet from the neighboring nations in China or India, few things impress him more vigorously or more deeply than the position of the Tibetan women."[47] Foreign observers such as McGovern joke about the Tibetan practice of polyandry. Several times in his narrative, McGovern expressed fear that he or one of his men would be carried off by an aggressive Tibetan

The chief ornament worn by Tibetan women is their headdress. Because much of a family's wealth is often worn in the hair, married wealthier women generally wear more ornaments than unmarried women. The traditional headdress of central Tibet consists of a wood framework covered with coral, pearls, amber, and turquoise. The curved headdress here is typical of the province of Tsang; women from U wear a straighter, lower style. *(Northwestern University Archives)*

woman looking for another husband to add to her collection.[48] Chapman more subtly reported that he was somewhat shocked by the "complete promiscuity" in the country.[49] In recent years Chinese soldiers have been surprised by the Tibetan women fighters who have led some of the most famous revolts against Chinese rule.

Tibetan women, like their Chinese counterparts, do wear makeup and jewelry. Harrier noted that upper-class women spent considerable time fussing over their dress.[50] But some of this ornamentation differs markedly from that of the Chinese. Nomadic Tibetan women smear black ointment over their faces to protect their skin from the harsh climate. Nomad women carry their families' wealth on their persons in the form of expensive bangles and bracelets. Urbanites also wear enormous amounts of jewelry, traditionally received as gifts from their husbands upon their promotions as government officials. Both groups also don gorgeous headdresses decorated with coral, turquoise, and pearls; rings of various sizes; necklaces; hip chains; and earrings so huge that the holes through their earlobes must be enlarged to a diameter of an eighth of an inch.

After Lajang and Jerinrasi captured Lhasa at the behest of the Qing emperor, they declared the Sixth Dalai Lama illegitimate and ordered him sent to the Chinese capital.[51] But the Dalai Lama never reached China. He was taken to Amdo and then probably murdered. In 1707 Lajang installed a new Dalai Lama said to be his son. This inflamed Tibetans and sparked the overthrow of Lajang.

Tibetan rule grew so chaotic that in 1720 the Qing finally sent their own force to Lhasa. The Manchus helped install a new Dalai Lama, selected from an old Tibetan aristocratic family, and reorganized the Tibetan government to give the Dalai Lama more power. Today in Lhasa a tablet still commemorates this Manchu victory over the Mongols. During the Cultural Revolution, the Chinese moved the tablet from the grounds of the Potala Palace to a nearby park. Commissioned by the Qing and inscribed in Manchu, Chinese, Mongolian, and Tibetan, the tablet indicates a Qing attempt after 1720 to play an increasingly active role in Tibet.

But the presence of two thousand Manchu soldiers strained Lhasa's resources and created an inflationary spiral that local residents resented. In 1723 a new Qing emperor withdrew the garrison from Lhasa and abandoned the country's administration to Tibetan officials.

The fact that only two thousand people could significantly deplete the resources of the Tibetan capital indicates the fragility of the ecostructure of central Tibet. In the 1950s Chinese Communists created a similar inflationary spiral when their troops occupied Lhasa. They built roads and airports to bring in more foreign goods, but this further taxed

Tibet's fragile ecostructure. Minute changes in the Tibetan environment can radically affect the agriculture and even the climate of much of Asia and beyond. (See Chapter One.) Chinese actions in Tibet during the past several decades have caused controversy among environmentalists worldwide. The worst Chinese damage to the Tibetan plateau continues to occur in the outer territories of Greater Tibet, where the Manchus exerted a strong presence even after they abandoned central Tibet. It is here that in recent years the Chinese have cut the great forests and dumped nuclear wastes.

In Kham the Qing incorporated all territory east of the Yangzi River into Sichuan province. After Mongol disturbances in the Lake Kokonor region in 1724, the Manchus also formally annexed much of Amdo.

The Qing imported horses and rhubarb from eastern Tibet. Today almost no one would travel to this remote region just to obtain unremarkable rhubarb plants. But rhubarb was one of the first, and for centuries one of the most important, central Asian medicinal exports to Europe. Westerners considered it both a purgative and a tonic and believed it could help cure constipation, indigestion, diarrhea, dysentery, and certain skin diseases.

For centuries Europeans assumed that the medicinal variety of rhubarb was unique. Intrepid explorers searched the mountainsides of Asia for seeds that could be grown in the West. It has since been shown that several varieties produce medicinal effects, but to be potent the plants must be raised in the cold mountainous areas of China, Tibet, and Mongolia and harvested only after six years. Scientists speculate that the medicinal effectiveness of the plant stems from cultivation at the high altitudes (above ten thousand feet) and in the particular climate and soil of Kham and Amdo where rhubarb has historically flourished.[52]

From the sixteenth through the eighteenth centuries, rhubarb was one of the most expensive products on the mar-

ket. "In 1542 it was sold in France for ten times the price of
cinnamon and four times that of saffron, and in an English
price list bearing the date of 1657 it is quoted at 16s. per lb.,
opium being at that time only 6s. and scammony 12s. per
lb."[53] Westerners called it Turkish rhubarb because prior to
the development of the route across Eurasia from Manchuria
through Russia, it came across central Asia through Persia
into Turkey.

By the late 1600s profits from the rhubarb trade had
grown so huge that in 1657, not long after the Qing dynasty
formed, tsarist Russia established a monopoly supervised by
its ministry of war. By the end of the seventeenth century
Russia had secured most of the rhubarb market. As a result,
trade between Russia and China expanded tenfold, from
837,066 rubles in 1755 to 8,383,846 rubles in 1800.[54]

Although the Manchus tried to incorporate vast parts of
the Tibetan rhubarb-growing territory into their empire,
they failed to wrest control of this area from the Tibetans.
The Qing authorized hereditary native chiefs to rule the eastern districts of Kham under the authority of the governor
general of Sichuan. Yet through the nineteenth century
the Tibetans in this area continued to pay the Dalai Lama
five thousand taels in taxes. Moreover the Dalai Lama continued to receive recognition from many religious and lay
leaders in the areas of Kham that the Qing supposedly administered.

In Amdo the situation was even more complicated.
Legally the area became a superintendency of China's Gansu
province. But practically speaking, as the historian Joseph
Fletcher has explained it: "The indigenous peoples were ruled
by their own local chiefs under the supervision of an imperial
controller-general at Sining, who also had supervision over
the district of Ning-chen, even though from a Tibetan point
of view Ning-chen was part of Kham. Notwithstanding the
Ch'ing empire's direct jurisdiction, the Dalai Lama had a

commissioner in Amdo who supervised trade and controlled the local monasteries, and there is evidence that at least some people were paying taxes to Lhasa."[55]

This contradiction between the legality and reality of government highlights one of the major causes of the present acrimony between Chinese and Tibetans. Even when the two groups lived in the same or adjacent areas, they had little to do with each other. And both believed they controlled the same territory.

Another present point of contention is that of Chinese settlement on the Tibetan plateau. Originally the Chinese immigrated due to changes in trade, not because of deliberate government policy (which actually discouraged it). The introduction into China of New World crops such as corn, sweet potatoes, and peanuts created a population explosion that propelled the Chinese into Kham and especially Amdo.

But the Tibetans did not surrender control of even their most outlying areas to the Chinese. Traveling through Kham and Amdo in the 1880s, the American diplomat W. W. Rockhill found that in the farthest reaches of Tibet, where Chinese presence was strongest, Qing political authority still appeared weak. The remoteness of the area and the independence of the groups in the region made it impossible for the Qing to exert its authority there.[56]

As Rockhill's account makes clear, the Manchus dispatched various officials into Tibet, and the Chinese merchants and settlers who sometimes followed tried to take advantage of Qing authority (mostly by independent shows of force). But the Manchus never integrated even eastern Tibet into China. Traveling in some of the same territory just a few years after Rockhill, the British explorer Hamilton Bower constantly noted that the few Qing officials and soldiers he met at the farthest edge of Kham feared the Tibetans over whom they had no control. Arriving in the Sichuan border town of Dajianlu, Bower found that here too "the Tibetans have shown their commercial capabilities by almost completely ousting" the Chinese.[57]

The Tibetans not only ignored supposed Manchu rule in their outer territories; they completely dominated the Mongols in their midst. The American traveler Rockhill found the Mongols in Amdo to be living "in constant dread of their Tibetan neighbors, who rob and bully them in the most shameful way."[58] Historically it is clear that the Tibetans never felt dominated. Recently, however, that situation has drastically changed.

But even as they were losing political authority in the Outer Tibetan territories, and long after they had recalled their troops from central Tibet, the Manchus were drawn back there. In 1728, when another civil war broke out near the Tibetan capital, both sides appealed to the Manchus for support. Worried that the Mongols might again enter the fray, the emperor ordered a large force to Lhasa.[59] This time he also delegated two officials known as *ambans* to reside there permanently.

The *ambans* remained in Tibet through the twentieth century. Chinese nationalists can claim with some justification that the presence of the Qing *ambans* proves a long-standing Chinese presence in Tibet. Yet it would be a gross exaggeration to say that the Qing controlled Tibet and an even greater one to say that the dynasty had integrated Tibet into its Chinese empire.

Until the last few years of Qing rule, the emperor always took care to station Manchus, not Chinese, in Lhasa. The *ambans* were the emperor's personal representatives and military chiefs. Even the title of *amban* is a Manchu one, roughly equivalent to the Chinese *dachen* (minister of state) or imperial controller general.

To the Tibetans, this was an important decision. As Manchus, the *ambans* had a different relationship with the Tibetans than Chinese officials would have had. (After all, the Tibetans had long tolerated the presence of Mongols such as Gushri Khan's descendants, who retained titles claiming they were the kings of Tibet, though they lacked authority.) The Manchu nobility[60] had strong matrimonial ties to the Mongols. And, like the Mongols, they sincerely respected the Dalai Lama and the Tibetan Buddhist system. Instead of considering them as outsiders, Tibetans regarded the Manchus as representatives of the Tibetan diaspora community interested in preserving its traditions.

Moreover, although the *ambans* had broad authority within the Qing political structure, those in Tibet did not have much power even in areas the dynasty claimed to have integrated into its empire. Visiting Xining, the chief city in so-called Chinese Amdo, Rockhill was amazed at how little work the official had. According to Rockhill:

> The Amban himself hardly ever crosses the frontier. He occasionally visits the great sanctuaries and lamaseries situated within easy reach of Hsi-ning, and once a year he receives the Mongol princes at Tankar. He then distributes to them in the name of the emperor, and in quantities fixed by regulations, satin, embroidered pouches, knives, etc., and exhorts them to obedience. The chieftains do obeisance, kowtowing in the direction of Peking, in a hall reserved for such functions, and also partake of a banquet. Every three years these chiefs go to Peking, to carry tribute to the emperor and renew their oaths of allegiance. The former ceremony is known as the "little tribute," the latter as the "great tribute."[61]

Rockhill suggests that the only real business conducted by the *amban*'s office was his secretaries' extortion of semi-legal tariffs from Chinese merchants wishing to trade with the Tibetans and Mongols in the area.[62] Surprisingly these taxes were levied in Kham and Amdo, areas which the Qing

claimed to have annexed. In central Tibet, whose independent status the Qing acknowledged more clearly, the power
of the *amban* was even weaker. When Bower, for instance,
passed near Lhasa in the 1890s, Tibetan officials openly
stated that the *amban* was simply a goodwill ambassador
whose presence they tolerated.[63]

After 1728 the Manchus supported Pholhanas, a Tibetan military and political leader who long had been allied
with the Qing.[64] For almost twenty years he dominated the
civil government of Tibet. He persuaded the Qing to reduce
its garrison from five thousand troops to five hundred, and
established Tibet's own tribute areas of Ladakh, Sikkim, and
Bhutan. These Tibetan dependencies continued to pay tribute to the Dalai Lama until well into the nineteenth century,
when the British claimed them as both British and Tibetan
protectorates. Today these areas are all controlled by India.

When Pholhanas died in 1747, he was succeeded by his
son, Dalai Batur Gyhumey Namgyhal. Dalai Batur was a
forceful ruler. He killed his brother and plotted against his
nephews. He also impelled the emperor to reduce his garrison to one hundred soldiers, and began to form a Tibetan
military guard to take over the garrison duties from the remaining Qing forces. Dalai Batur tried to reassert Tibetan influence in those areas under direct Chinese supervision. At
the same time he attempted to develop an alliance with the
unsettled Zungar Mongols in the northwest.

The Manchus paid little heed to Dalai Batur until he
began to stir up the Mongols once again. The *ambans* understood that to protect themselves they needed to prevent a
new Tibetan-Mongol alliance. Because they could not take
action through the Tibetan government, they instead took
personal action against Dalai Batur. In 1750 they invited him
to their office and killed him. In retaliation, a Tibetan mob
stormed the garrison and slaughtered the two *ambans* as
well as one hundred Chinese and Manchu soldiers and civil-

ians. Thanks to the intervention of the Dalai Lama, the rest of the garrison was spared.

The outraged Qing sent yet another garrison of five thousand soldiers to Lhasa. They reinstalled the *ambans* and abolished the secular leaders in Tibetan government. In 1751, for the first time since the Great Fifth, the Qing also recognized the Dalai Lama as the official and undisputed ruler of Tibet.

Yet while the Seventh Dalai Lama subsequently ruled Tibet, the Qing emperor continually intervened to influence the political situation. Joseph Fletcher, the most authoritative scholar of this period, describes their relationship in this way: "From the Ch'ing point of view, the emperor was merely the Lama's secular patron. This meant that in Tibetan eyes the Dalai Lama's position was superior to that of the Ch'ing emperor, because in Tibet, whereas it was the duty of the laity to provide material support for the monastic community, the monastic community . . . was the ruling body, and lay persons, no matter how rich or powerful, were thus in a subordinate position."[65]

This explanation may underestimate the extent to which the Tibetans came to depend on Qing military power. In any case, ambiguities in the relationship that seem apparent today troubled neither the Tibetans nor the Manchus at the time.

The Manchus themselves were an ambiguous mixture of ethnicities. Jurcheds, Chinese, Koreans, and Mongols all came to call themselves Manchus after the group was formed in 1685.[66] Present Chinese claims to Tibet are based on an assumption of Han superiority and an assertion that the other cultures of the region have been absorbed gradually and inexorably into the Chinese nexus. In fact, this has not been the case. Bower, for instance, noted in the 1890s that Chinese men who had been sent to Tibet often married Tibetan women, and that their children grew up speaking Tibetan

with little if any knowledge of their Chinese heritage.[67] Not
only did the descendants of the Chinese sometimes become
Tibetans—as well as Mongols and Manchus—but they also
adopted cultures distinct from that of the Chinese.

The Manchu tie to the Tibetans was based on the
Manchu connection to the Mongols. No matter what their
putative racial heritage, the Manchus saw themselves as the
heirs of the Mongols, from whom many of them descended.
Like the Mongol rulers of the Yuan, the early Manchu emperors considered themselves Buddhist universal kings.[68]
They fostered the patron-priest bond that had existed in the
past between Mongol warriors and the leaders of the Tibetan
religious and secular hierarchy, especially the Dalai Lama.
The Manchus relied on this relationship to prevent their
Mongol brethren from uniting against the Qing empire.[69]

The system of government established in Lhasa during
the Qing dynasty was not a clearly delineated one by modern
standards, but it was one in which Tibetans still controlled
their own affairs and thought of themselves as an independent state. The Tibetan capital had become the Vatican (or
perhaps the Jerusalem) to a vast central and east Asian diaspora. During the Qing, the Manchus used this situation to
their advantage. They established a position in Lhasa and a
degree of control over the outer areas of Tibet. In the latter
half of the twentieth century, China's rulers have attempted
to distort this relationship to give historical legitimacy to
their efforts to integrate Tibet into China.

F O U R

⚘

The Closing
of Tibet

In the late 1980s, as demonstrations protesting Chinese rule erupted in Lhasa and emotions ran high, a British tourist in the Tibetan capital wore a T-shirt decorated with the image of the late American comedian Phil Silvers. As she strolled into a crowded shopping area, a passing Chinese soldier mistook the portrait of the balding actor (who once played Sergeant Bilko in a television comedy) for Tibet's holiest figure. When the soldier accosted the woman and tried to rip off her shirt, a mob of Tibetans surrounded her, pointing at her chest and shouting, "Dalai Lama! Dalai Lama!"

The absurdity of this incident illustrates the misunderstandings and suspicions Western visitors and the Chinese share in Tibet. Westerners relate the story to cast a farcical light on the stupidity and awkwardness of Chinese rule there and to mock the lack of worldliness of both the Chinese and the Tibetans.

The Chinese prickle at the patronization they detect in this tale. Such scorn from outsiders heightens their xenophobia. And granted, the Chinese have historical justification for their sensitivity. In the past, Tibet was a pivot point in the so-called Great Game the Qing played against Britain and Russia in inner Asia. As inheritors of the major portion of the Qing empire, the Chinese came to fear that the Western powers would use Tibet as a stepping-stone to China, and have learned to suspect foreign interest in the region.

Western designs on Tibet began to be drawn in the eighteenth century. In 1757, when the Seventh Dalai Lama died, the Qing eliminated the Zungar Mongol state in what is now the northwestern Chinese province of Xinjiang. Simultaneously the British defeated the French at the Battle of Plassey, consolidating their hold over India. Thus the growing British empire in India faced off against the Qing dynasty in the west and the burgeoning tsarist empire in the north. These expanding giants squeezed Tibet between them.

Even earlier, European adventurers had made their way into the country. Marco Polo is thought to have crossed over the Tibetan frontier in the late thirteenth century. Friar Odoric of Pordenone claimed (though few believe him) to have traveled to Lhasa in 1328. In the 1620s the Jesuits set up a mission at Xigaze, then abandoned it a few years later. In the eighteenth century, Capuchin priests bought land and built a church in Lhasa near the Jokhang temple, the so-called Vatican of Tibetan Buddhism. By this time "there was also a well-established group of Armenians and some Russian traders."[1]

As aggressive European powers expanded into Asia, they threatened the existing status quo. As early as 1641 the Japanese reacted to the threat by limiting European contact to a twice-yearly visit by the Dutch to a small island off Nagasaki. In 1760 the Qing closed most of China's maritime ports to outsiders and restricted foreign trade to Canton. The Tibetans too restricted European access, pressuring the Capuchins to close their mission in 1745, and then razing their church.

The cultural and political threat the mission had posed

This hand drum was formed from two human skulls. Its type is often used in monastic ceremonies. *(Land of the Lamas)*

to the eighteenth-century Tibetan religious establishment is obvious in the journal of Cassiano Beligatti de Macerata, a young Capuchin friar. He lambasted many of the seemingly bizarre Tibetan customs that still intrigue and repulse foreigners. He was horridly fascinated when Tibetans pulled the corpse of a Nepalese youth out of a river and "detached the head from the body in order to make from the skull a bowl to eat and drink out of, a custom followed by the Retroba religious community who are practicers of magic."[2] Objects made from human skulls are still on display in the Potala and other Tibetan shrines. There they still pique the interest and scorn of visitors, even those without the missionary's desire to eradicate the Tibetans' "barbaric" ways.

Moreover, as he became accustomed to Tibetan food, Beligatti, like contemporary visitors, began to take a perverse pride in his own constitution. Though he refused to eat raw yak flesh, Beligatti noted that he developed "the stomach of a Tibetan, that is to say, a fine hog. Accordingly it was by no means difficult for us to overcome our repugnance to eat the cooked flesh so rudely severed apart; also the *satu* made into a paste with water and rolled into a ball."[3]

In 1774 George Bogle, the first Englishman to enter Tibet, attempted to overcome this cultural gap by adopting Tibetan clothes and manners and trying to eat every food in good humor. But by the time this British East India Company representative arrived, Tibet was already less welcoming than it had been earlier. Bogle faced awesome political obstacles in his effort to establish a trading station and to open a back door into the lucrative Chinese market.[4]

But Bogle did manage to introduce a New World food that had a lasting impact in Tibet. As ordered by his superiors, he stopped frequently during his climb through Bhutan into Tibet to plant potatoes, establishing this crop as a staple in the diet of the region. Potatoes grew well in mountain soil. Tibetans took readily to this new form of starch and now serve it in a variety of Tibetan dishes, often curried.

Western impact on the culture and ecology of Tibet is also evident in two other New World foods now eaten there: chili peppers and peanuts. Unlike potatoes, though, neither is considered a standard item in Tibetan cuisine. The two appear in the spicy dishes of Sichuan restaurants that abound in Tibetan cities.

In contrast, sweet potatoes, also a New World crop, never sprouted in Tibet. The native Tibetan diet is almost unique worldwide in that it completely lacks sweets. Tibetan children are often given dry yak cheese as a kind of sweet substitute. Because it is aged for two or three years, it is so hard that it has to be sucked for several hours before it can be chewed.

By the 1990s a visitor staying at the Holiday Inn in Lhasa could enjoy sweet syrup poured over waffles. But travelers residing elsewhere could still sympathize with McGovern. After finally arriving in Lhasa after his long trek, he so craved sweets that he decided to buy any sugar he found, no matter how bad: "The sugar was filthy and sold in tiny paper parcels containing only a teaspoonful of the precious material, and these packets cost a rupee . . . apiece, but so great was my yearning for something sweet after months of abstinence that I squandered a small fortune on these sugar packets."[5] By contrast Bogle must have been so motivated to carry out his mission that he scarcely seemed to have noticed his lack of sweets.

Bogle and the Panchen Lama developed a close personal relationship; Bogle even married the Panchen's sister.[6] Unfortunately Bogle fell ill and died shortly after he returned to India in 1775. The British edited out of his journals his accounts of his Tibetan wife and children, who were sent to Scotland to be raised. In 1779, four years after Bogle left Tibet, the Panchen Lama died of smallpox while on a visit to Beijing. His death canceled any chance that Tibet might reverse course and welcome trade with the British. When a second British delegation visited Xigaze in 1783, the new Panchen Lama refused them.

Thereafter the Himalayas marked the boundary between the Asia Britain could conquer and the Asia whose ancient empire eluded it. Geography in this sense forged destiny for the Tibetans. George Bogle had noted that because of the mountains, any British troops that marched into Tibet would have to "consider all communications with the low country out of the question till they return."[7] Tibet's mountains foiled British plans for "immediate intercourse"[8] overland from India into the vast Qing empire. The image of Tibet as a mystical, impenetrable dreamland quickly grew.

In 1788 the British failed to respond when the new Panchen Lama sent them a desperate letter pleading for help to fend off an invasion by Gurkha troops from Nepal. The Panchen feared that if he turned to the Qing, he would compromise Tibet's independence.[9] Lord Cornwallis, the same general defeated by George Washington during the American Revolution, received the letter but refused to get involved. His clumsy reaction erroneously convinced both the Qing and the Tibetans that the British were aiding the Nepalese. In 1793 the Qing refused to grant better trading terms in its coastal ports to the British Macartney embassy to Beijing, partly because they resented Cornwallis.

The Qing worried that the Nepalese invasion could compromise Tibet, unsettle the Mongols, and thus disrupt the entire Qing empire. The dynasty mustered its declining resources and sent a new army to aid Tibet, the fourth military expedition to the area in seventy-five years.

One writer has called the campaign "the most difficult in history—far more of an achievement than Hannibal's crossing of the Alps—and one of the costliest up to that time."[10] Qing soldiers improvised lightweight cannon made of leather that could be carried through Himalayan passes. They forced back the Gurkhas and in 1792 reached the gates of Katmandu. The Qing compelled the Nepalese to return to the Tibetans everything they had stolen and to become a Qing tributary.

Subsequently the Qing took over Tibet's foreign relations and attempted to seal the country from contact with the West. They dispatched new *ambans* and delivered a large golden urn to be used in the selection of future Dalai Lamas by lot. For much of the next decade, the Qing exercised considerable authority in Tibet. Chinese culture became popular, including Chinese dress, housewares, and food. As historians have noted, "The great houses would employ Chinese cooks, much as French chefs have been employed in Britain,"[11] and the upper classes adopted the use of chopsticks.

Chinese chauvinists have occasionally pointed to this Tibetan taste for Chinese food and other goods as proof of China's annexation of Tibet. Yet no logical connection exists between the two. If there were, many parts of the United States, with their ubiquitous Chinese restaurants, would long ago have been annexed to Asia. Chinese cuisine enriched Tibetan culture just as egg rolls and pizza have added variety to the American diet. In the 1930s Sir Charles Bell described a feast at a Tibetan nobleman's house that resembles the Chinese-style banquet served today in fancy restaurants in Tibet:

> Sea slugs increase the strength of the body, seaweed removes hoarseness, fishes' abdomens are beneficial for bowel complaints, crystallized sugar and raisins relieve colds and coughs, while bamboo roots are good for the voice. As regards the fishes' abdomens, a gelatinous substance, it was explained to us, that not only did they relieve bowel complaints, but they were also useful when one swallowed a hair, as they took the hair down with them.[12]

Recently, as the Han population in Tibet has increased, Chinese restaurants have become plentiful in cities such as Lhasa and Xigaze. But only Hans and foreigners regularly frequent these restaurants. Tibetans eat only the Chinese foods such as *momo,* or dumplings, that have become a recognized part of the Tibetan diet. For their part, the Chinese who visit Tibet rarely sample Tibetan dishes. The fancy Chinese hotels in Lhasa have main Chinese dining rooms and separate, so-called Tibetan dining rooms where the Chinese managers frequently sneak fried rice or shrimp with peas onto the menu to satisfy foreigners.

*   *   *

Maintaining an army and government in Tibet over a long period of time proved too awesome a task for the Qing. By 1804, when the Eighth Dalai Lama died, the population of Lhasa had begun to accuse Tibetan officials of collaborating with the *ambans*.[13] The Manchu emperor yielded to these protests, reducing his garrison to 250 men and replacing imperial officials who had irked the Tibetans. In 1808 the Tibetans defied the Qing by refusing to use the golden urn to select a Dalai Lama. Thereafter, the few times they did use the urn, the child so chosen was "coincidentally" one whom the Tibetans had already selected.[14]

However they were chosen, few of these Dalai Lamas exercised much power. For almost all of the mid-eighteenth to the late nineteenth centuries, a religious regent ruled the country. After the Eighth Dalai Lama died, not one of his five successors lived to maturity, and few died a natural death.[15]

Nonetheless the family of each new Dalai Lama automatically became members of the Tibetan aristocracy. Many of these former peasant families prospered, enjoying luxurious ways of life and feasting on sumptuous delicacies.[16] By the twentieth century some of these families held vast estates with enormous numbers of serfs and slaves. Their mansions, some of which are still visible outside of Lhasa, housed groups of monks who prayed full-time for the families' fortunes. These wealthy Tibetans built special chapels in their mansions filled with guardian images to ward off ill fortune. When the head of a family died, his survivors would donate jewels and other valuables worth hundreds of thousands of dollars by today's standards to Lhasa's temples to assure him a good rebirth.[17]

During the nineteenth century, power passed from the Qing authorities and the Dalai Lama into the hands of these nobles. They came to constitute a de facto civil service, rising in the ranks according to ability. They replaced much of the older nobility and monastic authorities who had ruled local areas like independent kings. Under their leadership the Tibetan government expanded its authority both in central and in eastern Tibet. In 1829 the Tibetan government repossessed parts of Amdo from the Qing,[18] and later preempted the Qing in both Kham and Amdo.[19] In 1863, when a revolt broke out in eastern Tibet, the Tibetan government sent in troops, stationing a governor there permanently and reintegrating parts of Kham. Yet the governor of Sichuan continued to claim political control and to oversee the Chinese settlers in the region.

In the thus-confused legal situation that prevailed in Kham and Amdo, brigandage increased. Like the highwaymen of old England or the stagecoach robbers of the American West, these bandits preyed on travelers. They lay in wait in narrow valleys or at turns in the road, then swooped down on unprotected merchant caravans. A number of nomadic tribes and even monasteries in southeastern Tibet took to crime.

Many of these robbers were skilled horsemen and marksmen. They fired at their targets from under their horses' necks and then attacked with swords that dangled from their sides. The people from Golok and Nyarong were particularly notorious. The terms "Golok" and "Khampa" were considered synonymous with that of bandit, though these same people could be friendly and respectable when visiting Lhasa.[20] In the second half of the twentieth century, the Khampas led the struggle against the Chinese. Today the Goloks and Khampas are often held responsible for the ubiquitous thievery that Chinese visitors in particular complain about in Tibet.

In the middle of the nineteenth century, the one hundred Qing troops still in Lhasa neglected to fight even a few Khampa bandits. Most of the soldiers' fathers had been part of the original garrison, but their mothers were Tibetan. The men's wages often failed to materialize from the Qing and had to be supplied by the Tibetan government. In any case, the garrison had little to offer "in both quality and discipline."[21] In 1842, when a Sikh army pushed into central Tibet from Ladakh, the Qing offered no help. The Tibetan army repelled the invasion on its own and negotiated its own treaty with the Sikhs, regulating their border and their valuable wool trade.

Wool was the principal export from old Tibet, whose hills and valleys are still well-suited to sheep and goats. In the late nineteenth and early twentieth centuries, Tibet's wool became a major product in international trade. Much of it ended up in England or the Unites States.[22] The downy wool from Tibetan goats was and is prized as "cashmere," a name derived from neighboring Kashmir. This area was once controlled by Tibet and is now disputed by India and Pakistan.

Every year the Tibetans would drive huge numbers of mules and donkeys loaded with wool over the Himalayas into India and Nepal. At the turn of the century, Kawaguchi estimated that about "five thousand to six thousand mule-packs go to Darjeeling, about one thousand five hundred to Bhutan, about two thousand five hundred to Nepal and about three thousand to Ladak."[23] Pack sheep and goats sometimes shouldered twenty-five-pound loads along the treacherous alpine paths. At the end of their journey, they were usually slaughtered for meat.

After winding its way into south Asia, Tibetan wool was shipped throughout Asia and Europe. By the twentieth century, after a railroad was built from Calcutta to Siliguri, the Tibetan trade began to be drawn through Darjeeling, Kalimpong, and Gangtok. It often proved faster and cheaper to route goods intended for China to ports in India and then by sea to Canton, rather than by treacherous overland trails.

Today one of Tibet's most lucrative wool trades is its clandestine commerce with Nepal in *shatoosh*, supposedly

the warmest and lightest wool in the world. *Shatoosh* is obtained from the rare Tibetan antelope which is hunted and
slaughtered for its wool. This wool is woven into the finest
Kashmiri scarves, whose growing popularity has caused the
antelope to become endangered. Recently members of Tibet's
government-in-exile allegedly have used their political status
to smuggle the wool into Nepal and from there to India.

Nepalese involvement in this wool trade was already evident in 1854 when Nepal attacked Tibet in an attempt to secure favorable trading rights. The Tibetans yielded and
agreed to pay the Nepalese a large indemnity and to grant
them rights of extraterritoriality, giving Nepal an increased
share of its commerce in wool. Tibet and Nepal negotiated
the treaty as independent countries, but the Tibetans insisted
that the Qing be mentioned in the document. As one writer
explained, "the Tibetans themselves continued to profess
their obedience to Peking's authority for fear of the British
and the Nepalese."[24]

As a result, more Tibetan wool, salt, gold, and silver
flowed into Nepal. Tibetans also began to ship large quantities of musk, sheep, borax, and sulfur into south Asia and to
reexport more Chinese tea and silk as well.[25]

Only Tibet's rhubarb trade declined. By the eighteenth
century most Tibetan rhubarb (then a costly drug derived
from plants that grew as large as small trees and could be
spotted on hills from a mile away) was transported from
Tibet to Russia and then into western Europe. But beginning
in the 1770s the British East India Company developed a
mass market for a lower-quality drug that could be bought in
Canton and shipped by sea directly to Europe.[26] Much of this
was inferior rhubarb harvested from small plants[27] grown in
the central Chinese provinces of Sichuan and Shanxi.[28]

About the time they became more heavily involved in
the rhubarb trade, the British and many other Europeans
began to find ways to circumvent the prohibition on travel to

Tibet. Some hoped to find new goods for trade while others went on semiofficial government missions or simply wild adventures.[29] The experiences of many of these people helped create the aura of Tibet that Westerners recognize today and stoked later Chinese fears that the West desired Tibet as a stepping-stone into China.

As early as 1810 an English merchant named Gillman used a native agent in an unsuccessful attempt to import highly prized Tibetan cashmere.[30] In 1811 the eccentric half-mad Englishman Thomas Manning talked his way to Lhasa and actually met the Dalai Lama. His journal, discovered and published after his death, reads as if written by a modern tourist. He complained that while the Potala Palace "exceeded my expectations, the town far fell short of them. There is nothing striking, nothing pleasing in its appearance. The habitations are begrimed with smut and dirt. The avenues are full of dogs, some growling and gnawing bits of hide which lie about in profusion, and emit a charnel-house smell; others limping and looking livid; others ulcerated; others starving and dying, and pecked at by the ravens; some dead and preyed upon."[31]

A countryman of Manning's, William Moorcraft, entered Gartok in 1812 and returned to Tibet in 1819 to explore the possibility of importing the prized Tibetan horses across the Himalayas into India. The Tibetans turned down his request. In the ensuing years, British officials occasionally carried on border talks with the Tibetans. By the mid-nineteenth century, adventurous British travelers began to make a sport of venturing as far into the border regions as they could without being caught, a game in which Western backpackers still indulge. Even then some Europeans reached their supposedly forbidden destination. Two Lazarist fathers arrived in Lhasa from China in 1846. As Richardson has observed, "They regarded the Ambans as a mere ambassador sent to watch what the Tibetans did."[32]

In the half-century that followed this visit, a whole host of Westerners entered Tibet: adventurers, missionaries, traders, scientists, and simple eccentrics. Because Tibet had always been more open to Asians than to Westerners, the British employed 130 Indian and Sikkimese pundits to map the country. They pretended to be pilgrims and disguised their surveying equipment in their prayer wheels. Their exploits make exciting reading. The Royal Geographical Society awarded a gold medal to Nain Singh for his charting of central Tibet and the gold fields of western Tibet in the face of grave physical danger.[33] Another pundit, Kintup, or K.P., continued with his surveying of the Tsangpo River even after his disgruntled companion sold him into slavery. Kintup escaped and persisted in his original mission, returning to India four years later and receiving little reward or recognition for his work.[34]

Women were as brave and zealous as men in the exploration of Tibet. The Canadian doctor and missionary Susie Rijnhart watched her one-year-old son die during her journey and lost her husband to murderers. Yet once she remarried she returned to Tibet, only to die after giving birth to another son. The English missionary Annie Tayler trekked to within three days of Lhasa and then was betrayed by her abusive Chinese guide and had to turn back.

In the late 1800s a host of distinguished Russian explorers—Przhevalski, Roborovski, Koslov, and Orucheff—entered Tibet, collecting rhubarb roots and searching for a new route by which to import this commodity so important to Russian commerce. Nikolai Przhevalski, a scientist, considered by many to have been the greatest explorer of his age and for whom the Przhevalski horse was named, bullied his way with a group of Cossack marksmen almost to the gates of the capital. When the Tibetans arrayed their army against him, he was forced to retreat.

These kinds of exploits increased Qing and Tibetan fears

of imperialist incursions and created the background for contemporary Chinese suspicions. Anxieties about British motives were well founded, as the British spent much of the nineteenth century gradually encroaching on Tibetan territory. In 1835 British India acquired Darjeeling from the Raja of Sikkim. In 1846 the British took control of Kashmir; in 1861 they made Sikkim a protectorate; in 1865 Bhutan followed; and in 1886 they annexed Assam. These areas featured large Tibetan populations that had formerly paid allegiance to Tibetan authorities. By the late nineteenth century the British had taken control of almost all of Tibet's dependencies.

Though Tibetan influence had been limited in these mixed-population areas, the British completely changed the character of the region. In Darjeeling, for instance, British planters cleared the great forests that had once surrounded the city so that they could grow the famous tea named after the town. The small village known by the Tibetan name of Dorjeling ("the temple of the thunderbolt") grew into an important British hill station. After the British made Darjeeling, as they spelled it, the summer capital of the province of Bengal, European planters and Nepali-speaking Hindi workers and merchants poured into the area, just as the Chinese are now pouring into Tibetan towns on the other side of the Himalayas. By the time McGovern reached the city in the 1920s, the three Tibetan monasteries had already been overwhelmed by a British-organized Planters' Club, a number of European villas and hotels, and some Hindu temples and mosques. Today Buddhists comprise less than 15 percent of Darjeeling's population. Most of the Tibetans who live there are refugees gathered in a self-help center.

Kalimpong changed in similar ways after the British seized it from Bhutan. By the time of his arrival, McGovern found the Scotch Presbyterian mission dominant. He referred to the city as "the last outpost in British Indian Government" and noted that it was called "the Harbor of Tibet," a place where Tibetans came to "sell their goods, chiefly wool, and take back with them cheap knickknacks for sale in the markets of Shigatse and Lhasa. Kalimpong serves as the meeting-ground of Indian and Tibetan traders, just arriving to Lhasa, the Secret City; so that to see the caravan merchants coming in from the North was like having communication with another unseen, half-fanciful world."[35] Today this remnant of Tibetan character has disappeared, and Kalimpong stands simply as another Indian hill town.

In such outlying areas, the Tibetans could do little more than protest the British occupation. In central Tibet they tried to fend off the British by claiming that the Qing controlled their foreign relations. The ruse worked for a while. Then, in 1876, the British secured from the Qing government permission to venture across Tibet into China. This was part of a complicated exchange in which the Qing allowed the British to take over Burma and the British acknowledged the Qing's right to Tibet.

Under the terms of this Cheefoo Convention, the British gained permission to set up a trade center at Yatung, just inside Tibet's southern border. But the Tibetans refused to allow this, contending that the Qing "had no authority" to make these kinds of arrangements.[36] In 1887 the Tibetans challenged the British by setting up a checkpoint near the Sikkim frontier. When the British sent a force to this border the following year, a Khampa army of ten thousand soldiers ambushed and surrounded them. The British viceroy, who had to take time off from a hunt nearby to visit the frontier, found himself in serious danger. The British managed to flee by bribing some of the Khampa generals with promises of estates in Darjeeling and Kalimpong and "maharaja" titles. Glen Mullin, a chronicler of these events, notes that the term "Gyakar Khampa," or "Indian Khampa," remains a derogatory term in Tibet.[37]

Meanwhile the Qing, ever glad to bargain away territory it did not actually control, continued to grant the British rights in Tibet throughout the 1890s. The Tibetans continued to resist, claiming incongruously that the Qing ruler would not condone their direct contact with the British. The Tibetans prevailed with this lame excuse because the British were still heeding Bogle's warning about how difficult it would be to hold territory high in the Himalayas.

The British also allowed the Himalayan states of Nepal, Bhutan, and Sikkim to remain independent, though the British took over a considerable amount of their territories. Sikkim voted to merge with India in 1975 and is today an Indian state. Bhutan and Nepal remain autonomous countries, although India controls Bhutan's foreign relations.

Tibetans downplay the importance of geographical and other factors in preserving the independence of their country; instead they give credit to the Thirteenth Dalai Lama, or "Bodhisattva Warrior," as some have called him. He was the first Dalai Lama to negotiate directly with Western powers.

Chosen in 1877, he became the first Dalai Lama in more than a century to take power in his own right in 1899, when a seemingly miraculous escape from an evil hex greatly increased his reputation and authority.[38]

Allegedly the former regent had sewn a black mantra (a figure of a man with powerful curses on it) inside a pair of boots he gave to Lama Sogya, one of the Dalai Lama's tutors.[39] Tibetans believe that if Sogya had ever pulled on the boots for any length of time, his spiritual power would have worked to "synergistically increase the power of the black magic and end the Dalai Lama's life."[40] Although Tibetans consider the Dalai Lama a living god, even today they believe this curse could have killed him. Fortunately the official oracle discovered and removed the black mantra. The Thir-

While the current Dalai Lama is honored as a Nobel Peace Prize winner, the Thirteenth Dalai Lama is often referred to as the Bodhisattva warrior. The first Dalai Lama in almost a hundred years to survive into maturity, he is still honored as the man who created the modern Tibetan state. He learned to wax his mustache while in exile in India. *(Northwestern University Archives)*

teenth Dalai Lama did not use hexes to dispose of the orga-
nizer of the plot. He ordered the former regent to be "im-
mersed in a huge copper water vat until he drowned."[41] And
so the Thirteenth survived to lead his country's struggle
against first the British and then the Chinese.

The story is echoed in the popular tales of Tibetan magic
and mystery spread by Western writers such as Alexandra
David-Neel.[42] She claims to have seen levitating monks and
sorcerers so powerful they could freeze a man in his tracks
with a glance or split a head open with a word. Critics of
these tales rightly point out that they have confused scholars
of Tibetan history who strive to separate fact from fiction.
But as the account of the black mantra shows, many Tibetans believe these stories even more ardently than foreigners do, and have helped to spread them as much as foreigners
have.

By the end of the nineteenth century, Tibet had become a
focus of imperialist rivalries. The Dalai Lama had begun to
edge his country closer to an alliance with the Russians,
prodded by the curious Aguan Dorjiev, an ethnic Mongol of
Russian origin.

Dorjiev's life is a mystery; most sources even fail to list
his first name. One account claims he was in fact a highly
trained member of the Intelligence Service of the Russian
Foreign Office,[43] though this is doubtful. We do know that in
about 1880 he entered the Drepung monastery in Lhasa. He
became so accomplished as a scholar that the Tibetans chose
him to be one of the Dalai Lama's personal tutors.

In the late 1890s Dorjiev suggested to the Dalai Lama
that the tsar might become a sympathetic guardian who could
protect Tibet from the British. Dorjiev argued that Russia was
Shambala—the legendary messianic kingdom.[44] Realpolitik
mixed with mysticism. In 1898 the Dalai Lama sent Dorjiev
back to Russia, ostensibly to recruit donors for his monastic
college but also to do some diplomatic scouting.[45]

Dorjiev returned to Tibet offering an alliance with Russia.[46] After a second visit Dorjiev brought back word "that the Czar (Nicholas II) himself might become a Buddhist."[47] By 1900 the Russian press detected Dorjiev's missions, describing him as a special envoy from the tsar. At the same time Ekai Kawaguchi, the Japanese monk enrolled at the Sera monastery outside Lhasa, declared that the Russians had delivered firearms and other weapons to the Tibetans.[48]

The story scared the British even more than current rumors of foreign machinations in Tibet worry the Chinese. The British viceroy in India, Lord Curzon, fanatically feared a Russian plot to undermine the British position in Asia.[49] In 1903 he dispatched two hundred men under the command of Colonel Francis Younghusband to the Tibetan border to confer with the Tibetans and the Chinese. For five months the British waited for the Tibetans to agree to discussions. With winter approaching and the stalemating continuing, Curzon gave Younghusband permission to assemble a much larger force and enter Tibet.

In 1904 the advancing British army attempted to disarm Tibetan soldiers positioned behind a stone wall built to block the advance. A melée erupted and the outnumbered British fired automatic weapons on the Tibetans. In a haunting scene, the Tibetans walked slowly away in a trancelike retreat, with British guns continuing to fire. The British mowed down more than three hundred Tibetans (some claim more than eight hundred), suffering hardly a casualty themselves. Reports of the incident contrasted peace-loving, passive Tibetans with the bloodthirsty British. Disregarding their bad press and the growing outrage of the British public, British troops pushed all the way to Lhasa.

The Dalai Lama and Dorjiev fled to Ulan Bator (then called Urgu), the capital of Outer Mongolia. The Dalai Lama, of course, was held in almost as great repute by the Mongols as by the Tibetans. Even in the 1990s the Dalai

Lama excited great interest when he returned to Mongolia. As his visit wore on, however, he and the Grand Lama of Mongolia quarreled over their relative positions and even the heights of their thrones.

In Lhasa, Colonel Younghusband could not find any ranking Tibetans with whom to negotiate. The *ambans* claimed they had no authority to do so. Just before his forces had to retreat from the prospect of the Tibetan winter, Younghusband managed to pressure a powerful monk from the Ganden monastery to agree on a treaty. This "regent" persuaded the Tibetan national assembly to recognize British control of Sikkim and to establish consulate and trading centers in Gyangtze and Gartok. The British also would take control of the Chumbi Valley until the Tibetans paid an indemnity of half a million pounds or opened the trade marts (later it was stated this would be for a maximum of three years).[50] The Tibetans agreed to forgo relations with any other foreign state, making Tibet a semicolony of British India.

The Chumbi Valley is a narrow wedge of Tibetan territory on the south side of the Himalayas between Bhutan and Sikkim. Today its main city, Yatung, is considered by the Chinese to be their last outpost on their border with Sikkim and Bhutan. When border tensions between China and India have run high, natives have slipped in and out of Tibet along the forest paths that run near the city. Rain falls in abundance here, one of the few parts of Tibet where the main crop has always been wheat rather than barley. Mountain strawberries, azaleas, irises, and rhododendrons abound in the valley forests. The great *yetti* or abominable snowman supposedly lurks here.

Ethnologically, the people of the Chumbi Valley are distinct. The women are considered among the most beautiful in the Himalayas, and visitors from Bhutan and Sikkim still come in search of brides. The people speak a dialect and maintain customs that are unique. McGovern noted, "Unlike the true Tibetans, with whom filthiness is a virtue esteemed by the gods, the Chumbi people are occasionally known to wash themselves."[51]

This habit is particularly noteworthy because the Tibetan city of Pali that towers above the Chumbi Valley has for centuries been described by visitors as the filthiest in the world. McGovern claimed that so much refuse had been "thrown into the streets" that "these streets are now nearly on a level with the roofs of the houses, which look as if they were built underground. Pali is, in fact, buried in its own filth. Picturesque it certainly is, however, for on every roof there was a prayer-flag or two, and on many of them a heap of barley-straw and yak-dung."[52] Today it is not as picturesque, as the numbers of houses are almost evenly divided between old Tibetan structures and new cement-block Chinese buildings.

The Chumbi Valley did not remain under the British for long. Russians, Americans, Germans, French, and Italians all complained that the Younghusband expedition violated the recently issued Open Door Notes in which the United States had convinced the various governments involved in China to pledge noninterference in that country and to ensure equal rights in the area for merchants of any land.[53] Tibet was covered by the Open Door Notes only if it was considered part of China. Lord Curzon argued that the British "regard the so-called suzerainty of China over Tibet as a constitutional fiction—a political affectation which has only been maintained because of its convenience to both parties."[54] But, as Alastair Lamb observes, "in English political circles Tibet became a dirty word, and the Liberal Government of Campbell-Bannerman which came to power at the end of 1905 resolved to show that Britain had no aggressive ambitions towards Tibet whatsoever."[55]

In a 1906 convention with the Qing, the British gave up

almost everything Younghusband had gained except the new trade missions. In hindsight this may not have been such a good deal for the Tibetans. Today many Tibetan scholars argue that the British had no right to disregard the treaty they had signed with Tibet in order to cut a new deal with the Qing. At the time, however, the Dalai Lama did not want the original treaty with the British. He had fled Tibet and sought Russian aid. He never officially acknowledged the Tibetan-British treaty, making its validity dubious.[56] Not until 1911, after the Chinese invaded Lhasa, did the Dalai Lama protest the Anglo-Chinese Agreement on Tibet.[57]

At the time, Tibetans felt they had little to fear from the Qing. The dynasty had not exercised effective power in Tibet for almost a hundred years.[58] Unfortunately, shortly after the new treaty was signed, the Qing decided it needed to compete aggressively against Russian and English expansion into central Asia. The Qing built transportation and phone links to integrate Tibet into China. By 1907 a new Chinese *amban* had built a Chinese school in Lhasa and established a military academy to train Tibetan officers to enter a Chinese-style officer corps.[59] In an atlas published in Shanghai in 1910, the Qing for the first time showed Tibet as a part of China.

Beginning in 1905 the Qing also increased its presence in eastern Tibet. The six-thousand-man army of Zhao Erfeng brought the inhabitants of the semi-autonomous areas of Kham and the city of Batang under direct Qing rule. Butcher Zhao, as he was called, abolished Tibetan laws and all duties to Tibetan chiefs and religious officials. He even tried to settle Chinese peasants in the area. Though this last policy failed, the Chinese government repeated it on a much larger scale after 1950.[60]

During his trip across Tibet in the 1890s, Bower described Batang as the first city in "which any signs of Chinese authority are seen."[61] The Tibetan Buddhist monastery had dominated the town, which also had been a major center for Christian missions in Tibet around the turn of the century. Zhao "burned the great monastery at Batang to the ground and made his soldiers use the scriptures to resole their shoes. Many Tibetans were executed by decapitation or by another typically Chinese method, mass burial while still alive."[62]

No traces remain of the massacres of Zhao that many consider a precursor to the Communist cruelties of the 1950s and 1960s. Today Batang is an attractive town surrounded by lush vegetation. It retains a rich Tibetan character and, as it stands near the Sichuan border, it has become a favorite haunt for backpackers trying to hitch rides through Tibet. Markham, the first Tibetan town over the line, is a place where many people attempting to enter Tibet on the sly are turned back. In the market of this and other Tibetan cities, Khampas can buy hair extenders to create the appearance of wearing traditionally long hair even after they have cut their own hair to conform to the changing culture of the region.

The Great Thirteenth tried to halt Zhao's invasion of his country. In 1908, after Britain and Russia acknowledged Qing suzerainty over Tibet,[63] the Dalai Lama decided to visit China to make peace with the Qing. Instead he was humiliated by having to kowtow to the emperor on his birthday.[64] The Qing made it clear to foreign embassies that the Dalai Lama no longer ruled as the preeminent temporal power in Tibet. Then, quite auspiciously, both the Guangxu emperor and the empress dowager died, and the Dalai Lama officiated at their funerals.

Still the invasion continued. In 1910, shortly after the Dalai Lama returned to the Tibetan capital, Zhao Erfeng invaded Lhasa. Once again the Dalai Lama fled his country, and startled British border officials suddenly found him at their doorstep, seeking asylum. This was a precursor to his successor's flight to India almost fifty years later.

The Great Thirteenth did not remain long in exile. In 1911 a rebellion overthrew the Qing dynasty and established a Chinese republic. The Chinese-Manchu army in Tibet dissolved, and in 1913 the Dalai Lama reentered his capital. At about the same time the Khampas in eastern Tibet recovered much of their territory. New shipments of rifles from Russia increased the firepower of the Tibetan forces and made future Chinese governments even more paranoid about foreign meddling in Tibet.[65]

In 1912 the new President of China, Yuan Shikai, issued a proclamation claiming Tibet to be an integral part of China. Though the Dalai Lama replied that he had resumed the rule of his country, as he clearly had, Tibet's supposed subordination to China was fast becoming an important matter to Chinese nationalists.

The subject had not even been considered until 1902, when the Chinese reformer Kang Youwei accused the Qing of having concluded a secret treaty with Russia to cede Tibet. His misinformation helped panic Curzon into organizing the Younghusband expedition.[66] Anti-Qing activists also picked up the charge and began to accuse the Qing government of undermining Chinese sovereignty by ceding traditional territory. Kang's disciple, Liang Qichao, gave this powerful, highly charged indictment intellectual validity by advancing the notion of a greater Chinese nation that would continue to occupy Tibet. Liang developed this position in 1904 after a visit to the United States. In opposition to the anti-Manchuism of the American-educated nationalist leader Sun Yatsen, Liang posited a Chinese multinationalist state that would inherit all the land and peoples of the old Qing empire.[67]

At the time Liang formulated his position, few other nationalist writers even mentioned Tibet. The young Hunanese revolutionary Yang Shouren talked about ultimately establishing an Asian central government that would consolidate

Tibetans, Mongols, Muslims, and other races in the Qing empire and "repel the white menace."[68] But most other political thinkers wanted nothing to do with the Tibetans. Before 1911 the well-known Chinese nationalist writer Zhang Binglin argued that Tibet and Mongolia were not part of China, though strangely enough he maintained that Japan and Korea were. Indeed, most maps of the Qing empire showed Korea, Manchuria, Taiwan, and China proper, but not Tibet.

All this changed after the Chinese republic was established in 1911. At first many Chinese felt they had taken part in an exclusively Chinese movement. In the heady days of the revolution, many Chinese turned on Tibetans, Manchus, and other major ethnic groups whom they felt the Qing had favored. Before they abdicated, the Manchus demanded official protection. To safeguard them, the new Chinese government of Yuan Shikai issued the so-called Manchu-Mongol-Uigur-Tibetan Articles of Favorable Treatment. This declaration guaranteed the four non-Han peoples equality with the Han, a decision incorporated into the design of the new flag of the Chinese republic.

In deeming the Tibetans and their territory an official part of China, the government was making itself vulnerable to the demands of nationalists who were insisting that no official Chinese territory be ceded. The idea that the Chinese nation consisted of five races—Chinese, Manchu, Mongol, Muslim, and Tibetan—eventually became an official part of the nationalist Sun Yatsen's political program. But as Dru Gladney has pointed out, "While Sun recognized five peoples of China, his ultimate goal was still assimilationist, to unify and fuse all the peoples into one Chinese race."[69] Sun Yatsen himself put it quite bluntly: "The name 'Republic of Five Nationalities' exists only because there exists a certain racial distinction which distorts the meaning of a single republic. We must facilitate the dying out of all names of individual peoples inhabiting China, i.e., Manchus, Tibetans, etc. . . . We must satisfy the demands of all races and unite them in a single cultural and political whole."[70] Although under the influence of the Communists, Sun modified his position on this issue in the 1920s, the thrust of it never changed.[71] The problem is, as one recent writer has perceptively put it, that "From their ethnocentric view . . . the Han do not believe that the culture and territorial claims of minority groups are equal to that of the superior Han civilization."[72]

Sun, who was himself Cantonese, sought to unify the various ethnolinguistic groups of China into a single Han people. Juxtaposing the Han against non-Han groups gave the Han a clearer identity, which could help prevent the vast differences among the various Han groups from becoming an issue.[73] Neither Sun Yatsen nor his successors could recognize the independence of Tibet or the other nations for fear that if they did, it might unravel the concept of a Chinese state dominated by the supposedly superior Han. If the Han were not considered superior to other peoples, everyone might just as well wish to remain Cantonese, Hunanese, Sichuanese, or whatever.

In twentieth-century China this has been not merely a theoretical issue. Even before the breakup of the Qing, a number of revolutionaries had demanded provincial autonomy. Shortly after the establishment of the Chinese republic, China divided into separate warlord states. Chinese unity was (and some observers would argue still is) so tenuous that the government feared that granting autonomy to Tibet or any other part of China might set off a chain reaction that would imperil the republic.

The fact that foreign imperialist governments bolstered the various warlords has also worried the present Chinese government. As Tibet has become a cause outside of China,

The Drepung monastery was once the home of the Dalai Lama and the world's largest monastery. Located on a hill about seven kilometers from Lhasa, it was a city unto itself, complete with its own army of fighting monks. *(Northwestern University Archives)*

this has increased Chinese fears that imperialist "splitists" are once again trying to divide and weaken China so they can take advantage of it.

Ironically the Chinese have used the fragile unity of the various Tibetan groups to enhance their own power in Tibet. When returning to his country in 1913, the Dalai Lama referred to Tibet as a "small, religious, and independent nation" which had driven out the Chinese and preserved the country's Buddhist faith and destiny.[74] But when he attempted to regulate some of the monasteries, restrict coercive officials, and prevent inhumane punishments such as the "amputation of citizens' limbs,"[75] the Panchen Lama, the monks of the Drepung monastery, and other prominent members of the religious aristocracy refused to cooperate, egged on by the Chinese.

In 1913 the Dalai Lama had fewer than three thousand ill-trained troops under his command to combat Chinese incursions and quash rebellions within his own community. Thus he leaped at the opportunity to send his representative to a conference with the Chinese and the British to resolve peacefully issues about his country's borders and political structure.

The setting for the conference, the English hill station at Simla, was unintentionally symbolic of the fluctuating fate of the region. Today Simla is the capital of the Indian state of Himachal Pradesh, a mountainous area on the edge of the Tibetan plain where many Tibetan-related people once lived. The British took the territory from the Gurkhas of Nepal in 1814, and in the 1820s began to build what soon became the most popular British hill station in India, favored as a retreat from summer heat. The huge old palace of the British viceroy still looms at the edge of town. Not far from Simla stands Dharamsala, the location of the Tibetan government-in-exile and the home of the Dalai Lama.

The conference participants agreed to divide Tibet into two zones. Central Tibet would be called Outer Tibet; the disputed territory in Kham and Amdo would be called Inner Tibet. The conferees drew the border line separating the two areas between the Yangzi and Mekong rivers. Outer Tibet would be quasi-independent. The Tibetans needed only to consult with the Chinese before making major decisions and to agree to call the region an autonomous area of China. In official parlance, the Chinese would be granted suzerainty, not sovereignty, over the territory. The only right the Chinese would be granted in Outer Tibet would be that of stationing an *amban* and three hundred troops in Lhasa. The Chinese, however, would govern Inner Tibet and could send troops and officials there. The Tibetan government in Inner Tibet could continue to appoint its own monastic officials.

This division was proposed by the British "to keep Lhasa-controlled Tibet separate from Mongolia by as much Chinese territory as possible."[76] By so doing the British hoped to prevent the Russians from exploiting the developing military alliance between Tibet and Mongolia.[77] The Tibetans agreed to what they were told would be a temporary division, because the British assured them protection against the Chinese. But the Chinese government refused to accept the treaty its own negotiators had initiated. The Chinese rightly surmised that the treaty would have made Tibet into a de facto British protectorate.[78]

Even without having a signed treaty, the British persuaded the Tibetans to agree to a new border. This so-called McMahon Line changed the Tibetan border with Bhutan and India from the base of the Himalayas to their summits, and thus ceded considerable land to the British. The Indians still respect this border while the Chinese still dispute it (though in practice they accept it) as unfair to the Tibetans.

Shortly thereafter, the British furnished the Tibetans with five thousand rifles, provided military training for Tibetan soldiers, and agreed to educate four young Tibetans in Britain. In 1917 the Tibetans thus managed to defeat the Chinese army in Kham and to extend the border between the two countries to the Upper Yangzi River. In a few months Tibetan troops had regained much of their territory and could have taken much more if the British had not insisted that they agree to a truce.[79]

By the time World War I ended, the Dalai Lama had authorized an aggressive program to enlarge and modernize the Tibetan armed forces. The British trained Tibetan soldiers in Gyangtze, assisted in the development of a modern police force, and helped with the construction of a telegraph line from Gyangtze to Lhasa. They even opened an English school in Gyangtze for Tibetan children.

McGovern arrived in Tibet soon after the new army had been assembled. He amusedly described the soldiers as being trained "along strict European lines," standing in their "British uniforms" with their "modern rifles" beside offi-

cials and high priests dressed in their medieval costumes. . . .
To make matters worse, at the most solemn and sacred mo-
ment in the whole procession the regimental band struck up
'Should a Body Kiss a Body Comin' through the Rye?' "[80]

Alongside this modern army stood Tibet's older army
provided by the country's great families and large monasteries. McGovern notes, "A quainter procession could scarcely
be imagined. There were three main groups, one armed with
bows and arrows, one with spears, and one with guns—but
such guns. They were all muzzle-loaders, of old seventeenth-
or at latest eighteenth-century design—top-heavy, lopsided
but wonderfully inlaid and decorated. Any one of them
would have found a place of honor in a historical mu-
seum."[81]

By the time McGovern arrived, the contrast between the
two armies had begun to excite opposition. Most of the
money needed to fund the new army's expansion came from
a land tax. Virtually all land in Tibet was owned by either
aristocrats or monasteries and was worked by serfs. The
more the need to support the military grew, the more taxes
were increased on these estates. In effect the old aristocracy
was paying for the army that would in turn diminish the nobility's authority. Moreover, military leaders often came from
families of low social position and were, as Bell has suggested, "regarded with jealousy by the nobility and gentry."[82]
These new leaders did not always approve of the nobility's
traditional privileges which decreed that "The Tibetan landlord can have his tenant beaten as severely as he wills, short
of killing him. He may put his neck in the heavy cangue
[wooden yoke], his feet in iron fetters. . . . In mutilating, the
hand may be severed at the wrist, or the leg at the knee. Or,
in rare cases, the lower half of the nose may be cut off. Or
both eyes may be put out. . . ."[83]

Like Tibet's aristocracy, its religious establishment opposed the army's growing influence. Before the twentieth

century, almost all government revenues funded the monasteries, not the military. Monks became so resentful of the army that they "broke the windows in the Commander-in-Chief's house. . . . A little later on his wife's jewelry was stolen to the value of about three thousand pounds."[84] The foreign manners and dress of the new troops exacerbated the situation.

Animosity grew strongest in eastern Tibet. By the 1920s the Lhasa government had stationed ten thousand troops in this area, virtually the entire Tibetan armed forces. And the levies Lhasa imposed were the most severe here. When I spoke with the present Dalai Lama, he quoted a saying popular among his fellow Amdowas in his youth: "Do not trust central Tibetans or Chinese."[85] Local authorities in eastern Tibet resisted any interference in their affairs and protested the new levies even more than the monasteries did.

The Dalai Lama increased Tibet's new army slowly, by five hundred or six hundred per year, but his gradual approach did not fool anyone. Monks repeatedly massed in Lhasa to demonstrate against the army and the alien ways it seemed to promote. In 1921 the Dalai Lama ordered the army to surround the Loseling Buddhist college, which had been a hotbed of action against his new policies. To the surprise and chagrin of the conservatives, the troops arrested about sixty monks, paraded them around the city, flogged them, and shackled them with cangues around their necks. As a result, the monasteries temporarily submitted, but their discontent continued. The Dalai Lama responded by replacing the monks of Loseling with some from central Tibet. Loseling's original monks were largely of eastern Tibetan origin, and the Dalai Lama feared they would likely "combine with China against Tibet."[86] Their replacement, however, simply heightened Tibet's internal frustrations.

In the 1920s the Panchen Lama, like most other Tibetan leaders with large estates, resisted paying taxes to the army.

The Panchen Lama and the Dalai Lama had long been at odds. At the time of the Younghusband expedition the Panchen Lama sidled up to the British as the Dalai Lama fled their approach. In 1922 the Panchen appealed to the British for help in resisting the Dalai Lama. When the British refused to intervene, the Panchen Lama fled to China the following year, and remained there for fourteen years. His flight gave added solace to the Chinese and made the nationalist cause in Tibet even more difficult.

After the Panchen fled, members of the Dalai Lama's reform movement began to fight among themselves. If the Dalai Lama had moved forcefully against the monasteries and confiscated their estates, he might have defended and expanded his reforms, and created the basis of a modern society in Tibet. Unfortunately he did not, because he dared not give more power to the army that even he, like the rest of the religious community, feared. In the mid-1920s rumors were rife in Lhasa that the military would soon depose him, ending all his secular powers. As Melvyn Goldstein has observed, the Dalai Lama "chose in the end to weaken the military rather than risk their deposing him."[87]

By 1925 the reforms had ground to a halt. In a few short months the Dalai Lama transferred and demoted commanders and cut off the military's source of funds. He removed the British-trained officers who had helped defeat the Chinese in 1918. During the next few years the army and police force deteriorated, the English-language school closed, and even the government mail service ceased.

By 1930 the central Tibetan government no longer had the power to keep peace in eastern Tibet. In 1931 two monasteries in Kham—Beri and Dargyas—fell into conflict. Some of the Khampas sought the support of the local Chinese warlord, Liu Wenhui. After he intervened on the side of the Beri monastery, the local Tibetan regiment came to the aid of the Dargyas monastery. By 1932 the Chinese had pushed back the Tibetans west of the Yangzi River.

At about the same time, another monastic dispute in the Xining area caused Ma Bufang, the local Muslim warlord, to intervene on behalf of one monastery while again Tibetan troops backed the other. The fighting this time raged until 1933, when the Thirteenth Dalai Lama died and the Tibetan army lost most of the territory it had gained.

Thus the Tibetans long took advantage of international power rivalries to keep the British, Russians, and Chinese at bay. By so doing, Tibet preserved its traditional institutions to a degree almost unprecedented in the world. But by the 1930s these foreign rivalries helped convince the Chinese that they needed an interest in Tibet to preserve their own security and territorial integrity. As the Tibetan government weakened and the Chinese government strengthened, Tibet assumed an increasingly vulnerable position.

FIVE

❦

The "Liberation" of Tibet

In recent years Chinese settlers have been flooding the cities of central Tibet. They demolish old houses of wood and stone with curving roofs and fluttering prayer flags and erect ugly flat-topped concrete structures with ersatz decor. As the population, architecture, and even lifestyles of Lhasa, Xigaze, and other Tibetan cities become sinicized and homogenized, Tibetans decry the annihilation of their race and culture.

Concerns that Tibet faces the loss of its cultural and ethnic uniqueness are not new. Throughout the reign of the Thirteenth Dalai Lama, conservatives worried that Tibet might lose all that made it special. But Tibetans feared his reform movement more than the huge influx of Chinese settlers.

By the time the "Bodhisattva Warrior" died of a short illness in 1933 after more than thirty years of rule, not a single plane had ever landed in Tibet, and only six automobiles had entered the country. Three cars had twice wound their way from Yatung to Gyangtze in a quickly abandoned attempt to institute an improved transport system. The other three had been brought in pieces to Lhasa from India and then reassembled. The military leader Kunphela liked to use one of the twin Austins, while the Dalai Lama intermittently tooled around town in the 1931 Dodge. Lhasa did feature a telegraph line and a small hydroelectric plant that supplied meager power to a few places in the city. But few of the other changes that had overtaken the world had come to Tibet during the fifty-eight years of the Thirteenth's life.

The traditional aristocracy and the theocracy had resisted reform in Tibet. It was, of course, hardly the only country whose elite feared losing their power to change. The same specter haunted China, Thailand, India, and many other nations. But because Tibet had moved slowly in adopting the features associated with modern life, the idea that the country remained a remote and pristine mountain kingdom filled with occult lamas and barbaric practices remained particularly fixed in the minds of both foreigners and Tibetans.

The imagery and tone the French traveler and Tibetologist Alexandra David-Neel used to begin her highly regarded book, *Magic and Mystery in Tibet,* lingers today. With great reverence, she begins with a long-awaited meeting with the Dalai Lama while he was in exile in India after the turn of the century:

> "Learn the Tibetan language," he told me.
>
> If one could believe his subjects who call him the "Omniscient," the sovereign of Tibet, when giving me this advice, foresaw its consequences, and consciously directed me, not only towards Lhasa, his forbidden capital, but towards the mystic masters and unknown magicians, yet more closely hidden in his wonderland.[1]

At that time Tibetans talked about the "special" nature of their society, unpolluted by the secular materialistic concerns of the outside world. Both outsiders and Tibetans saw their society as an ethnically pure, unchanging one. Coincidentally in 1933, the year the Dalai Lama died, James Hilton published the work that most epitomized this image, the novel *Lost Horizon,* which described Shangri-la, a valley hidden in the Tibetan Himalayas where no one aged and nothing changed.

In the real Tibet, however, people did die. In his last will and testament, the Great Thirteenth pleaded with his countrymen to institute change or risk losing all that was special about their country. Writing at a time when not even the most prescient scholar predicted that Mao Zedong and his followers might triumph in China, the Dalai Lama ominously prophesied that the Communist menace would soon sweep into Tibet from neighboring lands. He begged his people to prepare for this threat. Otherwise "even the names of the Dalai and Panchen Lamas will be erased, as will be those of the other lamas, lineage holders and holy beings. The monasteries will be looted and destroyed, and the monks and nuns killed or chased away."[2]

Tragically there was no one in Tibet with sufficient power, vision, and character to take up the Dalai Lama's challenge. Two leaders most capable of spearheading the reform movement were Kunphela and Tsepon Lungshar. But Kunphela was a dubious character who had worked his way up from attendant to the Dalai Lama to military leader. He drove around town in one of the Austin A-40s that had been presented to the Dalai Lama. The soldiers of his crack Drong Drak Makhar regiment cut their hair short and wore fancy Indian uniforms, reinforcing in the minds of many Tibetans the foreign and "unpure" ways of the reformers.[3] Tsepon Lungshar, on the other hand, was a forceful and mercurial aristocrat who had spent time in England. After the Dalai Lama's death, Lungshar joined the old elite[4] to undermine Kunphela's troops and to send him into exile.

After they had used him to dispose of Kunphela, the abbots of the main monasteries in Lhasa muscled Lungshar aside and quickly resumed the old practice of granting tax concessions, interest-free loans, and other privileges to noble families and important monasteries. When Lungshar tried to regain power, he was charged with plotting to overthrow the government and replace it with bolshevism.[5] In 1934 the government sentenced him to be blinded by having his eyeballs pulled out. "The method involved the placement of a smooth, round yak's knucklebone on each of the temples of the prisoner. These were then tied by leather thongs around the head and tightened by turning the thongs with a stick on top of the head until the eyeballs popped out. . . . The mutilation was terribly bungled. Only one eyeball popped out, and eventually the *ragyaba* had to cut out the other eyeball with a knife. Boiling oil was then poured into the sockets to cauterize the wound."[6]

Practices such as these reinforced the barbaric image of Tibet and weakened the possibility that the nation could win internal and external support for retaining its distinct culture and independence. The new Lhasa officials further rolled back reforms by disbanding large portions of the army and restricting the purchase of arms and ammunition from the government of India.[7] The Tibetan leadership opposed funding the new soldiers and feared that they could not be trusted.

The British-trained army became like the carefully crafted butter sculptures that now appear in Lhasa during the great Lantern Festival on the fifteenth day of the first month of the year. At this festival, statues of butter fashioned in the finest filigree stand on display and melt, vividly illustrating the Buddhist doctrine of impermanence.

In the late 1930s Tibet was left with an old-fashioned military that was "ill-fed, and paid practically nothing. . . ." Live ammunition was kept "sealed in strong rooms and none . . . issued without the personal attendance of the

Prime Minister, the Cabinet, and the two Commanders-in-Chief." When provided, "it frequently burst the barrel of the rifle and seriously injured the soldier." Practice drills were so rare that each would become a spectacle that the entire population of Lhasa, including several thousand monks, turned out to watch. At one such event, Chapman described how "The more enterprising women had opened small stalls where they sat beneath umbrellas selling apricots, greasy-looking cakes, tea and cigarettes."[8]

With their military reduced to theater, the Tibetans were obliged to negotiate with the Chinese. But the talks in 1934 were a charade. As at Simla, the Tibetan government did not mind yielding formal sovereignty in return for territorial concessions. But the Chinese could not grant the latter, for the Guomindang did not control any territory bordering Tibet. Ironically for a government trying desperately to maintain its traditional order, these discussions resulted only in the Tibetans allowing the Chinese to install in Lhasa a modern technological marvel: a wireless machine.

The Chinese later used the presence of the official (actually more of a technician) they posted to operate the radio to prove they had maintained a long-term presence in Tibet. A recent writer has criticized the Tibetans for their diplomatic ineptness in giving the Chinese this opening.[9] It would be more just to note that the fact the Chinese resorted to this kind of sophism indicates the absurdity of the logic that justifies their occupation of Tibet and further illustrates their frequent tendency to substitute appearances for reality in Tibetan-Chinese relations.

The Tibetans certainly were naive to believe that old-fashioned posturing could continue to preserve their society. Yet in their defense, their efforts almost worked. The negotiations so alarmed the British that in 1935 they sent a delegation to Tibet to counter what they believed was the growing Chinese influence. When the leader of the delegation, F. W.

Williamson, grew ill during his visit, the Tibetan National Assembly refused to grant the British permission to land a plane to evacuate him. Tibetan authorities feared it would annoy the monks and create a precedent that would make it difficult to deny the Chinese landing privileges. The British air force also decided its plane could not land and take off again at Tibet's altitude, and Williamson died. In spite of this tragedy, however, the British too left a wireless machine and officer in Lhasa.

The Panchen Lama added another twist to this complicated political situation by announcing he would return to Tibet. He had gained the support of important Chinese leaders, notably the famous right-wing intellectual Dai Jitao. Dai had developed an interest in Buddhism and in expanding the borders of the Chinese state to include Tibet. He and his associates helped the Panchen Lama assemble a Chinese military escort to help him reassert his authority in Tashilhunpo.

A great natural corridor in Tibet extends from the banks of the Tsangpo River—not far from the Panchen Lama's Tashilhunpo monastery in Xigaze—north through the Nyenchen Tanglha range into the Changtang plateau. This corridor opens into some of the most religiously significant valleys in Tibet. When the passes are open, pilgrims, traders, and hermits trek along this path. In the Tsangpo River valley itself, especially near the town of Lhaze (not to be confused with Lhasa), about 150 kilometers from Xigaze, stand the three major shrines once favored by the Panchen Lama. Thus in 1936 Lhasa authorities feared that the Panchen with Chinese backing might use his hold over Xigaze and his close relationship with the residents of Lhaze and the valleys to the west of the Yarlong Zangpo River to rally the Tibetans of this region to his side if he invaded.

But the Chinese government was in no position to

launch a new military invasion of Tibet. When the Panchen realized he would be on his own, he traveled no farther than Kham. As a Chinese report sarcastically noted, he seems to have been delayed "by snow in spring and winter and by rain in summer and autumn."[10]

The Panchen Lama's abortive threat to the Tibetan government ended in 1937 when he died. Nonetheless, in a curious twist, the Panchen Lama played a major role in the selection of a new Dalai Lama. On his trip he had paused at the Kunbun monastery in Amdo where he had interviewed potential candidates. When the search team from Lhasa came to Amdo to look for candidates, they respectfully spoke only with those boys the Panchen Lama had picked as possibilities.

A number of signs convinced Tibetan officials that they would find the new Dalai Lama in the place where the Panchen had looked. The body of the Thirteenth Dalai Lama, which had been seated facing south in a salt-lined coffin, suddenly slumped over so his head faced northeast. Auspicious clouds began to ring the mountains on the northeastern side of the city. When officials observed these portents and dispatched a search party to the small village of Taktse, the two-and-a-half-year-old boy they had come to investigate spontaneously recognized the leader of the expedition—traveling incognito as a merchant—as a monk from the Sera monastery. Moreover the boy identified various artifacts of the Thirteenth Dalai Lama's, calling out about each: "It's mine. It's mine."[11] The fact that the Great Thirteenth had once visited Taktse served as another sign. And finally, the boy chosen happened to have two brothers who were lamas, one of whom was a high-ranking lama from the nearby Kunbun monastery. Thus the sacred figure who was to preside over Tibet during its time of most radical change appears to have been picked in the most traditional manner.

By choosing the candidate from Amdo, the selection

team inadvertently gave an otherwise peripheral area an important role in national politics, which later greatly complicated Tibetan-Chinese relations. At the time the boy was found, even the nearby Kunbun monastery was so out of touch with Lhasa that caravans between the two areas ran only twice a year.[12]

This situation has changed since the Chinese built the Qinghai-Tibet highway, the highest road in the world. Opened to traffic in 1954, the highway runs 1,930 kilometers between Golmud, a city in Qinghai, and Lhasa. It transports 85 percent of the goods carried into and out of the region, bringing products ranging from marmalade to color televisions into Lhasa. To the uninitiated, it seems incredible that this highway could drastically alter the relationship between Amdo and central Tibet. In spite of recent attempts to repair it, two-thirds of the route remains frozen most of the year, and seasonal thaws cause parts of it to sink. The Chinese truckers who ply this route are paid about two hundred yuan or thirty-five dollars a month. They drive heavily overloaded Dongfang trucks so primitive that they each come equipped with a large iron crank to turn over the engine, as the electric starter often fails. In the morning cold, drivers must often heat their engines with blowtorches before they can crank them. Subzero winds blow into the trucks' poorly heated cabins. Once they get going, the trucks grind up the high passes of the Tanggala Mountains and then burn their brakes descending into the grasslands of the plateau, often with sparks flying. Yet these vehicles, primitive as they may be, have integrated Amdo into central Tibet in a way that was impossible to imagine when the search party ventured forth to find the new Dalai Lama sixty years ago.

When the new Dalai Lama was chosen, it proved difficult to bring the boy to Lhasa. Both the Chinese Muslim warlord who dominated the area and the Tibetan monks at the local Kunbun monastery demanded payoffs. After more than a year of negotiations, officials from Lhasa had to dole out 400,000 silver coins to the warlord Ma Bufeng and give the monastery "a set of the late Dalai Lama's clothes, one of his thrones and decorations, a 108-volume Kangyur written in gold, and a full set of the Tengyur."[13]

The 400,000 silver coins the Tibetan government paid Ma indicated the huge amount of bullion once stored in the central treasury. Today in Lhasa the central market near the Barkhor is crowded with vendors selling Indian, Chinese, Tibetan, and even French Indo-Chinese silver dollars. Many of these are forgeries crafted to fool tourists, but their ingenious variety attests to the continued sophistication of Tibetan metalworking.

Surprisingly gold has never greatly fascinated Tibetans, although they fashion it into the extensive amount of jewelry they wear. Perhaps this is due to the fact that gold has seemed so plentiful in their country. During his stay in Tibet during the late 1940s, Heinrich Harrier found gold so abundant that he could spot bits of it when swimming in the rivers near Lhasa. The Tibetans, he reported, collected it only where it could be easily obtained, scooping it out "in the Changtang with gazelle horns."[14] Recently the Chinese have begun to exploit Tibet's mineral wealth much more systematically. Some critics claim that exploiting the country's resources of gold and other precious metals has been one of the main goals of the Chinese occupation of the country. By the mid-1990s some were claiming that a gold stampede was taking place in Tibet. In some regions, Muslim Chinese were said to be pouring into the hinterland, panning for gold.

Once the prerequisite payoffs were made by the Tibetan government, the Dalai Lama was finally released. In late 1939 the boy who was to represent the temporal and religious essence of the Tibetan state rode into Lhasa. He seemed remarkably oblivious to what was in store for him.

Writing with considerable hindsight in 1991, the Dalai Lama recalled that he spent "a great deal of his time squabbling and arguing" with his older brother during the journey, to the point where they almost tipped over the conveyance. The drivers repeatedly had to stop and summon his mother to set things right.[15]

Meanwhile, in 1936, just as the Tibetans engaged in their traditional process of selecting the new Dalai Lama, a harbinger of radical change arrived in their midst. In that year Chinese Communists occupied much of Kham, fleeing their own country in their epic journey later known as the Long March. Tibetans responded by pounding the Communist troops.[16] These seasoned Chinese veterans were so terrorized that they "danced and sang and cried" when they escaped Tibet. When they again saw "Chinese peasants," they "touched their houses and the earth" and "embraced them."[17] Later some of these same soldiers took their revenge on Tibet, making the Tibetans regret they had not better prepared for the Communists' return. Unfortunately the ease with which the Tibetans dispatched the Communists reinforced the Tibetans' belief that they could continue to muddle along without altering their traditional ways.

In the long run, however, the invasion had a major effect on the region. As they pursued the fleeing Communists, Chinese nationalist leader Jiang Kaishek's forces for the first time entered Sichuan directly and forced the local government to fall in line with the central Chinese authority. That proved to be just in time. In 1937 when the Tibetans finally decided on their candidate for Dalai Lama, Japanese soldiers crossed the Marco Polo Bridge separating Manchuria from north China and began the Pacific side of World War II. Forced to flee west, the battered Chinese government relocated its headquarters to Chungking in Sichuan province.

Today Sichuan is the staging point for entrance into

Tibet. In the Sichuan capital of Chengdu, tourists scramble for tickets to take the bumpy flight in an aging Boeing 707 over the Himalayas into Lhasa. The truly adventurous try to hitch rides on trucks and buses for the difficult and often dangerous journey through what was once Kham.

Kham has changed drastically since the 1930s when Tibetan conservatives were still concerned with preserving their nation's cultural and ethnic "purity." In 1955 the Chinese Communists merged a huge part of Kham into Sichuan, doubling the size of the Chinese province. Kham's government has been completely altered and its former character is rapidly disappearing.

Fortunately the beauty of the region remains. In what is today part of northern Sichuan, near the Gansu border, lies the nature preserve Jiuzhaigou, literally "Nine Stockade Gully." Former Premier Zhao Ziyang once described the scenery as the most gorgeous in the world. Here pandas wander through bamboo forests and mountains soar above valleys and lakes. But the Chinese government plans to make the territory into a major tourist attraction, necessitating radical change in the infrastructure of the region. When complete, this part of Kham will probably lose much of its Tibetan character as well.

Farther to the south, the Tibetan towns of Kangding, Dege, Chamdo, Batang, and Markam are now mixed-population areas at the center of Sichuan's thriving logging industry. Kangding is the opening to this area. Once known as Dajianlu or Dartsedo, it was the name of a territory established during the Qing dynasty. Today the Han clearly predominate and the place has lost much of its old border-town ambiance. A road has been built by the Communists through the territory, connecting Sichuan to central Tibet. Although it is a remarkable feat of engineering, it is nonetheless plagued by landslides and washouts that kill a few foreign travelers and many more natives every year. The Chinese try

Yaks, the "ships of the plateau," are central to the Tibetan economy. Their bodies are used for transport, their carcasses for meat, their hair for wool, and their dung for fuel. There are three varieties: wild, domesticated, and dzos, a cross between yaks and cattle. *(Northwestern University Archives)*

to restrict foreign passage on the route to protect tourists' safety and to control access into Tibet.

During World War II the Chinese headquartered in Sichuan had also needed to transport supplies through this area. The increasingly isolated Chinese government there had proposed to build the present road through Kham and across central Tibet, but the Tibetans objected. Logistical problems made it difficult, and alternate sources of supply eventually convinced the Chinese to abandon the proposal.

American pilots took up much of the slack, flying Douglas and Curtis Commando transports on the risky trans-Himalayan fly-over between China and India. The hazards of soaring over "the hump" in propeller-driven planes were somberly recalled in 1994 when the Chinese uncovered the bodies of American pilots whose plane had crashed into the Himalayas fifty years earlier.

Most of the $800 million in supplies that Washington gave China during World War II was transported by air. The

Tibetans allowed nonmilitary goods to be carted across their country along existing paths into China. Once again their refusal to change appeared to pay off. Many Tibetans made fortunes packing goods across the country for the Chinese. All it took was a mule or yak to flourish. This new revenue set off an inflationary spiral in Tibet (similar to that in China and many other countries in the region) at the end of the war that caused protests against the government.[18] Yet through the 1940s the Tibetans continued to conduct business more or less as usual, making little effort to strengthen their position.

The Tibetans managed to retain their identity and independence for so long and with such little effort largely due to three factors. First, the British saw Tibet as a desirable buffer between China and their colony in India. Second, China was too divided to consider invading Tibet, and in any case did not think an invasion was necessary. Third, Tibet was so different from its neighbors and would have been so costly to occupy that it was unlikely that anyone would bother to do so, at least as long as the Tibetans remained wedded to their traditional ways.

After World War II, two zealous new superstates suddenly surrounded Tibet. This new reality quickly and dramatically shook the country out of its torpor.

In 1947 the British retreated from the subcontinent. The newly independent Indian government of Prime Minister Jawaharlal Nehru came to power claiming to be an anticolonial regime. The Tibetans lost no time in asking Nehru to return to them the vast territories seized by the British in the Himalayan highlands stretching from Assam to Ladakh, especially Sikkim and Darjeeling. Instead of recognizing this opportunity to strengthen Tibet as a buffer zone, the Indian government ignored its request. The Indians instead proceeded to take over the British extraterritorial rights to maintain trade agents and military escorts in Tibet; to run mail and telegraph services there; and to try their citizens in Tibet under their own laws rather than Tibetan law. In 1949 the Indian government dispatched troops to Sikkim and formally claimed this one-time British protectorate with its large Tibetan population as an Indian dependency.

Historically Bhutan and Sikkim have been largely ignored by the outside world. But in 1994 their central role in the Tibetan community became clear during a bizarre dispute over the selection of the latest incarnation of the Karmapa, the head of the Karma Kagyu lineage of Tibetan Buddhism. He is known as the "Black Hat Lama" because of the antique ceremonial crown he wears. The Karmapa's line of incarnations predated that of both the Dalai Lama and the Panchen Lama. After the Chinese occupied Tibet in 1949, the Karmapa fled to Bhutan and then to Sikkim, where many of his followers lived. He eventually built a new monastery in Sikkim. Unlike the Indian town of Dharamsala, to which the Dalai Lama fled in 1959, Bhutan and Sikkim were areas with already large Tibetan populations. The monastery soon began to play an important role in the politics and culture of the Tibetan communities on the Indian side of the Himalayas.

The tension between the Tibetan government-in-exile and the monastery in Sikkim became apparent after 1981, when the Karmapa died in a U.S. hospital. A decade passed with no sign of his reincarnation. Then one of the four regents at the Rumtek monastery in Sikkim discovered a slip of paper hidden inside an amulet he was repairing. On the paper the Karmapa had written that his reincarnation would appear in a district of eastern Tibet near where the school had originated. Until this time, the favorite candidate for Karmapa had been a member of the royal house of Bhutan. Before the search could be conducted, the regent died in a mysterious crash of his recently repaired BMW. Nonetheless,

two of the three remaining regents found a boy, Ugen Thin-
ley, near the spot where the note had claimed he would be.
The Dalai Lama himself certified the selection, and the child
was enthroned in Tibet in 1992. The Chinese also approved
the reincarnation for the first time since 1959.

But a third regent with close ties to the king of Bhutan
and the Indian government had refused to go on the search
party. He brought forward a new candidate. Supporters of
the two contenders fought with one another on the streets of
Sikkim, rocking the Tibetan community throughout the
world and roiling the Dalai Lama. Questions arose about the
role being played by the Bhutanese government and the regent linked with it in the disposition of the great wealth of
the monastery in Sikkim. Many quoted a prophecy made by
a Karmapa five hundred years ago. It warned of the future
domination of Tibet by powerful neighbors, and of a threat
to the succession of Karmapas stemming from an insider
who would wreak havoc "by the power of his twisted aspira-
tions."[19]

The Bhutan government has played a pivotal role in this
dispute. Recently it has in some ways become a greater center for the preservation of unadulterated Tibetan culture and
religion than even the government-in-exile in Dharamsala.
The Bhutan monarchy has required its citizens to wear native dress and has insisted that all buildings conform to traditional architecture. The government has expelled up to 15
percent of the population in three years in order to be rid of
those of Nepali and Hindi origin.[20]

The Indian government has not objected to Bhutanese
actions, as it has been anxious to prove its religious tolerance. Former Tibetan lands were part of a border region disputed by neighboring Pakistan and contiguous to other
territories occupied by a Muslim population not eager to be
under the authority of the Hindu-dominated Delhi government.

For India, the most sensitive part of this border region was Kashmir, where today a war between India and Pakistan may erupt at any time. In the early 1990s the historic importance of this territory to all the countries of the region again became evident with the discovery by Chinese scholars of a huge complex of ruins and caves filled with giant, centuries-old religious murals. Archaeological digs at the Piyang and Donga sites show that this was part of the northern route that brought Buddhism to much of east Asia. The cave dwellings that have been uncovered contain murals depicting Buddhist legends, historical events, and the lives of royalty. Buddhist scriptures there are painted in Tibetan characters in gold on a blue base. The artifacts found date from the mid-eleventh to the thirteenth centuries. Scholars believe that the ruins were the site of a royal complex and likely are older than ruins near Lhasa. Archaeological evidence indicates that the region was once an important trading center along the Silk Road and had long been a focal point for the various cultures of the area.

In the mid-twentieth century, as the Indians increasingly claimed border areas, the Chinese worried that their national pride as well as their military and economic security might be endangered if they did not gain control over this strategic region with its long history of influence on trade and culture throughout east and Southeast Asia. This was particularly true following World War II, when China was in the midst of a civil war. The two contending armies both used nationalist sentiment to rally the masses to their sides. Under these circumstances, Russian and Indian incursions into these regions inflamed Chinese passions to keep Mongolia, Tibet, and Turkestan under their authority. Neither the Communists nor the Chinese nationalists, the Guomindang, dared give up their claims to Tibet. No one seemed to appreciate Tibet's traditional role as a buffer between China and India.

In 1943 the Guomindang leader, Jiang Kaishek, under

pressure from nationalist groups, declared that the Tibetans
were Chinese. The Tibetans and other minorities, he said, all
had common ancestors. Any differences were due "to religion and geographical environment. In short, the differentia-
tion among China's five peoples is due to regional and
religious factors, and not to race or blood."[21] If this statement did not make clear the Guomindang position on Tibet,
the 1946 Guomindang National Congress certainly did. The
Tibetans sent a delegation headed by the Dalai Lama's
brother to China, hoping to present a letter to the assembly
declaring Tibet's quasi-independence. None of the Tibetan
statements appeared in Chinese newspapers. Instead the Chinese listed the Tibetans as members of the convention, implying therefore that they accepted Chinese rule. Adding
insult to injury, after 1950 photos of the Tibetans at this convention were used to show that the Tibetans had earlier acknowledged being a part of China.

Sadly the Tibetans had no allies to whom they could
turn for help. They had been so concerned about preserving
their own identity that their government had not even established formal trade ties with countries outside the region. All
their trade with the West went through India, and the Indians paid them only in rupees. As the Tibetan finance minister
told the American journalist Lowell Thomas in 1949, "We
must find a way to trade directly with the dollar world."[22]

In 1948 the Tibetans sent their first trade delegation to
the United States and Britain to purchase gold bullion to
back up their currency and to secure a new outlet for their
wool. None of Tibet's neighbors made it easy for them. The
Tibetan delegates traveled through India where they were
pressured to repudiate Tibet's claims to the area taken by
the British.[23] Then the embassies of the major powers in
India, which had never seen Tibetan passports, refused to
recognize them. The Tibetans finally secured a British visa
in China and a U.S. visa in Hong Kong.[24] But when the Chi-

nese became enraged about this, the United States promised
the Chinese that it would not accept Tibetan passports in
the future.[25] In addition, the United States refused to allow
the Tibetan delegation to meet the president without the
Chinese ambassador present. Because the Tibetans would
not accept this caveat, they settled for a meeting with U.S.
Secretary of State George Marshall. He arranged for them to
buy gold worth about $250,000. This was an ironic indig-
nity for a country so concerned about preserving its traditional ways that it had failed to exploit its own vast gold
resources.

The Tibetan delegation's visa for England had expired
during its stay in the United States. The British therefore
needed to renew the visa in order to admit the delegation. To
avoid alienating the Chinese, the British cunningly altered
the date on the old visa to make it current. The British could
thus tell the Chinese that they had not granted the Tibetans a
new visa. The Tibetans arrived in Britain and even managed
an audience with the prime minister.[26]

Publicity over this diplomatic hairsplitting attracted the
attention of anti-Communists in the United States. In early
1949, as it appeared clear that China was about to fall to the
Communists, some officials in the State Department began
to consider making Tibet "one of the few remaining non-
Communist bastions in Continental Asia."[27] The American
broadcaster Lowell Thomas visited Tibet with his son in the
summer of 1949, publicizing the Tibetan cause and advocat-
ing shipping "arms and advice" to Tibet. Thomas argued
"that there is sufficient manpower in Tibet for defense pur-
poses, if it is properly equipped and trained."[28] Early in 1950
the right-wing commentator Philip Jessup also broadcast an
appeal to support anticommunism in Tibet.

But the talk was not followed by action. The rhetoric
simply provoked Chinese fears that the United States might
use Tibet as a base to stage an attack on China in the same

way that in the 1930s the Japanese had used Manchuria. The Chinese were determined not to let this occur.

By this time the Communist attitude toward Tibet had gone through even more radical transformations than the attitude of the Guomindang. In 1922, even as Guomindang leader Sun Yatsen was formulating his hard line on the minorities question, the Second Party Congress of the Chinese Communist party acknowledged that Tibet as well as Mongolia and Turkestan were all independent states that might choose to become part of a Chinese Federated Republic. Throughout the 1920s and into the 1930s the party continued to suggest that Tibetans should have full autonomy and equality. In the late 1930s, however, the Communists retreated from this position. In a 1936 interview Mao Zedong, who had begun to reflect increasingly zealous nationalist sentiment, asserted that the "Tibetan peoples, likewise, will form autonomous republics attached to the China federation."[29] By 1938 he had dropped any mention of autonomy and was claiming that a unified Chinese state would grant the Tibetans and other minorities full equality with the Han while respecting and preserving the minorities' cultures and languages.[30]

In early 1950 the Chinese Communists massed a huge army along the Tibetan border. The Tibetans could send only a few thousand poorly trained forces to fight a highly trained and seasoned Chinese force of about twenty thousand, which in turn was backed by the entire People's Army of five million soldiers—more than the combined population of all of Tibet. Desperately the Tibetans tried to implement a new reform movement and import weapons and other foreign equipment, but it was too little too late. The Tibetan army was so inured in traditional ways that soldiers brought their wives and children to the front with them.

Even today Tibet continues to be the poorest, least developed area of China. Tibetans have used this fact as a double-edged sword. On one hand, Tibetans can point to their poverty to show the ill treatment they have received at the hands of the Chinese. On the other hand, Tibetans can decry efforts to change and develop their country as an attempt to destroy its unique qualities. This has proven particularly true because most efforts at change have involved the immigration of more Chinese into Tibet. Chinese workers generally have higher technological skills than their Tibetan counterparts. Tibetans worry that eventually all they might have left are majestic mountains.

Terrain was one advantage the Tibetans held against a Communist advance. Moreover, unlike all the other areas that the Communists conquered, "there was not a single Communist party member in Tibet proper. There were no guerrilla bases to link up with and few who could advise the party on how best to proceed."[31] After the Korean War began in 1950, the Chinese might have been reluctant to battle if the Tibetans had roused enough resistance to rally the United States behind them. Instead the Chinese staged a lightning raid and captured the Tibetan radio station on the farthest northeastern section of the border. Then they launched a propaganda campaign, announcing they would lower the onerous taxes that the Lhasa regime had levied on Tibetans and promising religious freedom. This campaign weakened the resolve of much of the population, including many members of the monastic community.

More disheartening to the Tibetans was that the man in Amdo who claimed to be the new Panchen Lama had cabled the news that he would back the new Chinese Communist government. He sent a telegram to Chairman Mao praising him for "having completed the salvation of the country and the people" and suggesting that "the realization of the democratic happiness of the people and revival of the country are only questions of time and it will not be long before Tibet is liberated."[32] Even in the face of a national threat, Tibetans could not put aside traditional divisions and rivalries.

In October 1950, on the eve of the Chinese entrance into the Korean War, the Communist army advanced into Kham. Large numbers of Khampa irregulars accompanied the Chinese troops. They met little resistance. As the Chinese military communiqué succinctly put it: "The battle began on October 7 and was concluded on October 15 after a total of twenty engagements."[33] The main Tibetan force in Kham surrendered without even a skirmish. The invasion ended in less than two weeks.[34] The Chinese reported no casualties while they claimed that only 180 Tibetans were killed or wounded.[35] Thus the way had been cleared for an advance to Lhasa.

Many have blamed the quick defeat in Kham on the Tibetan commander, Ngabo Ngawang Jigme. He thought the Tibetans had no hope of resisting the Chinese army, so he dismantled most of the fortifications his predecessor had erected.[36] When the attack finally came, "Ngabo lost his nerve. He radioed Lhasa for permission to surrender. When it was denied, he packed his belongings, took off the long gold-and-turquoise pendant earring hanging from his left ear, changed his yellow silk robes for the plain gray serge of a junior official and decamped in the middle of the night. With the discovery that the governor had fled, Chamdo erupted in panic."[37] While Ngabo's actions may have hastened the inevitable, without outside help—and none materialized at this point—there was no chance the Tibetan army could have won.[38] A more vigorous defense would simply have prolonged the fighting and resulted in unnecessary destruction.

Following the occupation of Kham, the path was opened for a quick Chinese advance into central Tibet. A second Chinese army massed in Amdo. Another, much smaller Chinese force made a daring and difficult crossing of the Kunlun Mountains from Khotan (Hotan) in Xinjiang and entered western Tibet. The Chinese confronted the central Tibetan government on both its western and eastern flanks.[39]

The small Central American country of El Salvador made a last-ditch effort to place the Tibet issue on the United Nations agenda, but no other nation cared to deal with the volatile situation. Both Britain and India actively opposed the request, as did the Soviet Union. The United States decided that because India, the state most concerned, didn't support Tibetan independence, neither could Washington.

The Chinese suggested that the sides discuss a peaceful surrender. The fifteen-year-old Dalai Lama officially took power late in 1950, and early in 1951 fled with his government to Yatung, the Chumbi Valley city perched on the Tibetan-Indian border. Here he was poised to cross into India and immediate exile if the Chinese swooped into central Tibet and tried to capture him. From his refuge, the Fourteenth Dalai Lama sent a high-level delegation to China led by Ngabo Ngawang Jigme, the governor of Chamdo who had abandoned his troops when the Chinese invaded.

Shortly after the Tibetans arrived in Beijing in 1951 to a warm welcome, the Chinese presented them with the so-called Seventeen-Point Agreement. Although the document unambiguously declared that Tibet had "a long history within the boundaries of China,"[40] it also declared that "The Central authorities will not alter the existing political system in Tibet."[41] It further pledged that the Dalai Lama could remain in office and that Tibetan religious customs and institutions would be preserved. The agreement promised that social and economic reforms would not be forced on the Tibetans. Ominously, however, the document called for the integration of the Tibetan army into the Chinese forces and the establishment of a military and administrative committee in Lhasa to implement the agreement. Because the Tibetan delegates claimed to fear that many of its subtleties would not be understood by other Tibetan officials, the delegation signed the agreement without consulting their own government.

In the hills near Yatung the Dalai Lama received word

that his government had accepted the document for "the peaceful liberation of Tibet" while listening one evening to the Tibetan-language broadcasts of Radio Peking. "I could not believe my ears,"[42] he recalls, and was even more surprised when he heard the clause proclaiming that "The Tibetan people shall return to the big family of the Motherland—the People's Republic of China."

Within a matter of days, representatives from the United States contacted the Dalai Lama and urged him to go into exile and spurn the Chinese agreement.[43] His brother wrote that he had met with the American consul in Calcutta and that the Americans had stated that if he "were to go into exile, some arrangement for assistance could be negotiated between our two Governments."[44] Later the Dalai Lama noted that at that time he doubted the United States would sacrifice "unlimited casualties" for the sake of the Tibetans.[45] Clearly his assessment was realistic.

Members of the Tibetan religious establishment pressured the Dalai Lama to remain in Tibet. Fearful of exile, they thought he could help them keep the agreement with the Chinese. As a result, the Dalai Lama returned to Lhasa. On September 28, 1951, the Tibetan National Assembly formally convened and ratified the new agreement. A month later the Dalai Lama sent an official confirmation to Mao Zedong accepting "the peaceful liberation of Tibet" and recognizing China as the "motherland."[46]

Many accounts have since claimed that the Chinese coerced the Tibetan delegation in Beijing into signing the Seventeen-Point Agreement and that it is therefore illegitimate. The Dalai Lama himself notes that "Ngabo had not been empowered to sign anything on my behalf, only to negotiate. I had kept the seals of state with me at Dromo to ensure that he could not. So he must have been coerced."[47]

It seems clear that the Chinese pressured the Tibetan negotiators by threatening an imminent invasion unless their terms were accepted. But no evidence has yet been produced that the Chinese personally threatened the delegates. In any case, no matter how the delegation signed the compact, the government in Tibet also accepted it. The Dalai Lama and his officials may not have been happy with the accord, but after learning its details they did not flee into exile or rise up in violent opposition to the Chinese occupation. Nor did they repudiate the agreement and demand that a new one be negotiated. As obnoxious as many parts of it were, the Tibetans also recognized that the agreement offered many concessions to them.

The Chinese have not been forthcoming about exactly how good a deal they offered the Tibetans. To this day the Chinese argue that the acceptance of this agreement marked the official Tibetan acknowledgment that Tibet is and always has been a part of China. But the very existence of the Seventeen-Point Agreement clearly shows that this is not the case and indicates that in the 1950s the Chinese viewed the region as distinct from the rest of China.

For one thing, China did not sign such agreements with other areas it "liberated." Only in Tibet did China acknowledge that it was dealing with a political, cultural, social, and ethical system so different from its own that China needed to guarantee Tibet's political and religious autonomy. The existence of the agreement indicates the Chinese recognized Tibet as a separate and independent ethnic area that deserved different treatment from the rest of the country. Tibet was not to be an integral part of China but an area with special status.

Not long after the agreement was signed, Mao Zedong noted that in Tibet "our army finds itself in a totally different minority nationality area." He was acutely aware that it was military force and not support of any kind from the Tibetan people that had enabled the Chinese to enter Tibet, and admitted that while the Tibetans "are inferior to us in military strength, they have an advantage over us in social influence."[48]

The differences between the two groups are so immense that it is hard to believe anyone could seriously argue that they are the same people. The spoken languages of Tibet and China are mutually unintelligible. The Chinese write in ideograms while the Tibetans use a phonetic system adopted from India. The overt sexuality of many Tantric, or mystical Indian Buddhist, practices associated with Tibetan Buddhism are so anathema to the Chinese that modern authorities in Beijing have covered with cloth the statues of copulating figures in the Tibetan Buddhist temple the Manchus built in the city.

Nonetheless, during the first ten years of Communist rule the Chinese kept to their agreement and did not treat Tibet like other parts of China. During this period Tibetans continued to have many rights and privileges normally accorded an independent state. For instance, the Chinese did not prevent the Nepalese from enjoying extraterritorial status in Tibet in the early 1950s. As late as 1952 the Dalai Lama sent his customary tributary mission to Nepal and suggested hopefully that "there will be no hindrance to continuing the age-old relations between my government and yours. I pray God that our relations may become stronger than ever."[49]

In 1953 the Chinese revoked Nepalese privileges in Tibet, closing Nepalese courts and taxing Nepalese traders. Yet throughout the 1950s the Chinese continued to acknowledge the special relationship between Nepal and Tibet. In 1956 the Chinese gave the Nepalese permission to establish trade agencies in four Tibetan cities, including Lhasa and Xigaze. Nepalese merchants received the right to trade in a number of Tibetan cities. The Chinese also "permitted traditional practices like cross-frontier trade and conceded grazing rights, travel rights, and the rights of pilgrims."[50]

Even today Nepalese merchants own some of the most sophisticated shops on the Barkhor, the holy pilgrimage street circling the Jokhang Cathedral in Lhasa. These shops sell everything from phony antiques to ugly plastic baubles. While leading a group of students to Tibet in the late 1980s I was amused to see that our Sichuan guide was thrilled to be able to buy cheap imported plastic bracelets from the Nepalese merchants. She claimed the prices were far cheaper than those in the ample markets of Chengdu.

In the 1950s the Chinese did not directly control internal policy in Tibet. They only influenced the Dalai Lama; they could not command him. Although the Chinese occasionally pressured the Dalai Lama on policy matters, social and religious institutions in Tibet remained largely untouched. The Dalai Lama himself has written that after the "early spring, 1952, there followed a period of uneasy truce with the Chinese authorities."[51]

The Chinese military presence during this period also remained low-key. In 1951 three thousand members of the Chinese Eighteenth Route Army entered Lhasa and twenty thousand more troops arrived in central Tibet. But this was only a small fraction of the number of troops the Chinese sent to the region a few decades later, and the soldiers' presence in these first years caused few major problems. The sudden population influx, however, created a temporary food shortage. The Chinese exacerbated the situation by distributing silver dollars to the monasteries and to the old elite to win them over to their side. The resulting inflationary spiral led to both popular and governmental protests, but they did not last long.

The Chinese constructed an airfield about ninety miles north of Lhasa and also began building the two roads already discussed, one from Sichuan via Kham and the other from Xining in Amdo or Qinghai. These new transportation facilities allowed the Chinese to bring in supplies (and more troops) from outside Tibet. "In two days a single truck" was now able to "carry goods which formerly required 60 head of livestock more than 12 days to move."[52]

Central Tibet, in effect, managed to preserve much of its old ethnic purity while outlying ethnic areas did not fare as well. In Amdo, for instance, the region where both the Dalai Lama and the Panchen Lama were born, change was much more drastic. Amdo was annexed to China in the early 1950s and rapidly gained the reputation it has today as China's "Far West."

The Chinese turned this desolate region they called Qinghai province into their gulag, housing political prisoners and storing atomic wastes there. The Chinese government encouraged their own people to settle in this inhospitable region, and a growing population of Han farmers, oil explorers, and workers soon began to overwhelm the Tibetan natives. The change was slow at first but occurred more rapidly than in central Tibet.

By the 1990s the Han population in the province greatly outnumbered the Tibetans. Han settlement has continued to accelerate, especially because hundreds of thousands of Chinese miners have been streaming into the area every spring and fall to pan the rivers and dig the sandy deserts of the plateau for gold. By 1991 there were said to be more than ten active gold mines in the province, producing more than two hundred kilograms of gold annually. The presence of these mines has aroused the resentment of Tibetan nomads who fear that the water they depend upon to sustain their herds is becoming polluted as a result of the digging.

Since 1980 Chinese authorities have attempted to settle the Tibetan nomads by building concrete barracks for them. Approximately twenty reserves have been organized, including the 237,000-square-kilometer Changtang Reserve. Chinese tourist agencies, such as the Hunting Association, organize safaris for foreigners to hunt threatened species in these areas. The agencies charge outrageous prices ranging from fifty dollars for a rare Koslow pika (a kind of wild hare) to fifty thousand dollars for an endangered wild yak.

In the 1950s, as they were beginning this transformation of Outer Tibet, the Chinese refrained from interfering in central Tibet. The Communists permitted the central Tibetans to engage in a wide range of activities that they prohibited in China proper and even in Kham and Amdo. The Chinese did not expropriate businesses or cooperatize land in Tibet. The Tibetans, like other minority groups in China, were not bound by the new Chinese marriage law, which set a minimum age for marriage, limited the amount that could be spent on wedding ceremonies, outlawed polygamy, and established a procedure for divorce. Many Tibetan traders grew rich selling to the Chinese foreign goods that were no longer available in China itself. As one scholar has pointed out, "As late as 1958, luxury items that had all but disappeared from Chinese markets were available in Tibet. Swiss watches and expensive cameras and fountain pens were reportedly available in Lhasa at prices considerably below those in Hong Kong."[53]

The Dalai Lama was inspired by the social and political reform sweeping China. He wanted to imitate Chinese efforts and divide the old Tibetan monastic lands among the peasants. But Chinese administrators supported Tibet's old landlord class in opposing the plan. The Dalai Lama canceled some of the corvée taxes and agricultural debts the peasants had traditionally assumed, but did not attempt land reform.

In early 1954 the Dalai Lama, to the chagrin of some of his followers, accepted an invitation to visit China. He stayed for almost a year, learning Chinese and touring the country. Forty years later he still fondly remembered how interested he was in the changes he saw during his visit. The

Chinese leaders, especially Chairman Mao Zedong (though not Zhou Enlai), particularly impressed him. The Dalai Lama actually wrote a number of poems and letters praising Mao's rule. When the First Assembly of the Communist party took place, the Communists elected the Dalai Lama vice-president of the Steering Committee of the People's Republic of China, an impressive though largely honorific title that demonstrated the close relationship between the two sides.[54]

By this time, however, problems had started to brew in Tibet. After 1955 the Communists abolished the Guomindang-created province of Sikang and made the land east of the Jinsha River part of Sichuan province, doubling the size of the province and placing virtually all of Kham under direct Chinese control. Increasingly they treated most of what had been Kham and Amdo as an integral part of China. In effect they applied different standards for the two-thirds of the Tibetan population in eastern Tibet than for the remaining one-third outside it.

For instance, the Chinese almost immediately made plans to harvest the great Tibetan forests in Kham between Litang and the Yangzi. At the beginning of the 1990s the southeastern parts of what was once Tibet still held some of the largest wooded tracts in China. The clear-cutting of these forests has already decimated half of them. The only saving grace is that the Tibetan loggers are still using handsaws and winches rather than chainsaws and heavy cranes, and are not plowing up the land with earthmovers like their counterparts in Malaysia and Indonesia.

In the 1950s when this blight was just beginning, the elite in Kham resented the Chinese contractors who employed Tibetan laborers in timber camps. The hiring of these workers and the introduction of new work patterns curbed the elite's authority. When the Chinese paid Tibetans to build roads, serfs no longer depended on their masters. When children were paid to go to school, they no longer were subject to traditional Buddhist ideals. When the Chinese persuaded Tibetan nomads to settle down, they destroyed a traditional Tibetan way of life. The introduction of cars and trains made horse-breeding obsolete. The U.S. boycott of Tibetan wool as part of a general embargo on all goods made in Communist China hurt Tibetan sheepherders. As the Communists began to interfere with their activities, confiscate their weapons, and prevent religious observances, the Khampas edged closer to rebellion.

In this climate of resentment, Chinese failures were blown out of proportion. For instance, in 1954 the Chinese began to distribute marginal land to beggars and itinerant workers in Kham. Much of the land was too poor to farm, and the people who occupied it lacked the skills they needed to take advantage of what usable land there was. This was the kind of well-meaning mistake that bureaucrats blunder into all over the world. But in Kham it inflamed the Tibetan elite, who believed (correctly) that the Chinese were eroding their traditional prerogatives. Because the Chinese had initially showered them with silver dollars and other favors in return for their support, the elite resented all the more the growing loss of their position.

Fears mounted as the Chinese reorganized the old administrative districts in Kham, dividing the area into *xiang*, a Chinese political unit roughly the equivalent of a county. The Chinese handpicked the officials to run the *xiang*, usually from the peasantry. At the same time they introduced new forms of taxation on land, livestock, and houses, and on monastic valuables.

Communist land policy grew increasingly radical in late 1956 and 1957. Although the land was not turned into agricultural cooperatives as systematically in Kham as in China proper, the Khampas resented the cooperatives more. When the Tibetans defied them, Chinese administrators reacted harshly, carrying out public beatings and executions. The Chinese probably did not treat the Tibetan resisters any worse than they did people in many other parts of China, but because the Chinese were seen as an alien force, their methods met with greater criticism. Moreover in Kham a dissatisfied traditional elite could resist the Chinese government and then take refuge in the neighboring area that was still governed by the semi-autonomous central Tibetans.

The increasing hostility of the Chinese Communists toward religion made matters worse, alienating more of the traditional Tibetan authorities who had welcomed the Chinese in 1950. "Monks and nuns were subject to severe harassment and publicly humiliated. For example, they were forced to join in extermination programs of insects, rats, birds, and all types of vermin, even though the Chinese authorities knew that taking any form of life is contrary to Buddhist teaching. If they refused, they were beaten."[55] Growing Chinese immigration into Kham upset the Tibetans further.

In 1956 the Chinese People's Liberation Army besieged and destroyed a monastery at Litang in Kham. A woman warrior named Dorjee Yudon urged her people "to rise against the Chinese. Dressed in a man's robe and with a pistol strapped to her side, she rode before her warriors to do battle with the enemy."[56]

The United States helped to instigate this revolt. A number of sources have now documented this aid—ex-agents,[57] journalists,[58] and, most recently and authoritatively, the historian Tom Grunfeld.[59] The Tibetans also have begun to talk about it. The Dalai Lama acknowledges the contacts his brothers and others had with U.S. agents and mentions that later in 1959, CIA-trained rebels helped spirit him out of the country.[60] As the Dalai Lama's statement implies, the CIA not only supplied weapons and equipment to the rebels, it also trained commando squads and smuggled them out of and back into the country. Some of this training was quite imaginative. The CIA conducted special classes for the rebel leaders in the mountains of Colorado, where the high altitude conditions were similar to Tibet and parachuted the commandos back into Tibet.

Regrettably, however, the CIA did not provide high-caliber aid. The Dalai Lama himself has claimed that the CIA harmed the rebels more than it helped them. Rather than supply first-rate equipment, the Americans, he has reported, "dropped only a few badly made bazookas and some ancient British rifles which had once been in general service throughout India and Pakistan and thus could not be traced to their source in the event of capture. But the mishandling they received whilst being air-dropped rendered them almost useless."[61] The rebels remained poorly armed and poorly organized. As late as 1958 at least twenty-three different rebel groups existed. Some were true freedom fighters while others were bandits disguised as rebels.

The Chinese could have dealt easily with the rebellion had it remained confined to Kham or even Kham and Amdo. But in central Tibet the quasi-independent government could act independently of the Chinese authorities and give succor to the rebels. This became the Achilles heel of the Chinese. When refugees from Kham and Amdo fled into central Tibet, many officials actively aided and protected them. Posters and leaflets denouncing the Chinese appeared all over Lhasa. Anti-Chinese meetings took place. Khampa and Amdowa merchants raised funds to aid the rebels. Many government leaders, including the Dalai Lama and his family, had come from Kham and Amdo, and they sympathized with the stories of dissidents from these areas.

Complicating the situation further, the Chinese had begun tinkering with the structure of Tibetan government, offering the Tibetans both more and less independence and heightening Tibetan frustrations. Toward the end of 1955

the Chinese and Tibetans formed the Preparatory Committee
for the Autonomous Region of Tibet (PCART), a concept
that originated in talks between the Dalai Lama and Mao.
Mao agreed it was too early to implement the Seventeen-
Point Agreement in Tibet and suggested that a new organization be established to lead the Tibetans down the road to
autonomous rule. The Dalai Lama eagerly concurred.

What made the prospect of the PCART particularly attractive to the Tibetans was that only five of its fifty-one delegates were to be Chinese. But when the PCART was
established, only fifteen delegates were selected by the Tibetan local government, ten were from the Panchen Lama's
committee, ten from the People's Liberation Committee of
the Chamdo Area (in Kham), and eleven from other sectors.
In practice this meant that even the Tibetan delegates were
appointed by the Chinese and were fiercely loyal to Beijing.
Moreover the Chinese State Council was given what
amounted to veto power over any actions of the PCART.
Many Tibetans considered the organization a sham, and
their sense that they had been tricked by the Chinese only increased unrest in central Tibet.

In 1956 the Dalai Lama attended a conference in India
celebrating the 2,500th anniversary of the birth of Buddha.
Chinese Foreign Minister Zhou Enlai happened to be passing
through New Delhi at the same time as the Dalai Lama, and
with the aid of Indian Prime Minister Nehru, the Dalai Lama
put his case to the Chinese official. Zhou Enlai agreed to
postpone reforms in Tibet, and Mao publicly announced in
1957 that "it has now been decided not to proceed with democratic reforms in Tibet . . ."[62] Mao put land reform in
Tibet on a back burner and halted the construction of roads,
dams, schools, and even a hydroelectric plant. The Chinese
recalled many of its cadre working in Tibet.

The Dalai Lama appears to have been satisfied by these
Chinese efforts. Shortly after Chinese leaders gave him these

reassurances, the Dalai Lama returned to Tibet. His brother, with the encouragement of the CIA, had tried to prevent him from leaving India. Still, rebellion in Tibet continued to escalate. The newly armed Tibetan rebels viewed Chinese moderation as a sign of weakness. In the summer of 1957 open warfare erupted in much of Kham and Amdo. The Chinese responded by bombing towns and villages and torturing and imprisoning increasing numbers of Tibetans.

In 1958 the radicalism of the Great Leap Forward reverberated throughout China. Only central Tibet was not subject to this campaign. Elsewhere the Communists attempted to organize China's vast rural population into large-scale communes in which all property was owned in common. Huge work teams tilled the soil. In Kham and the rest of what was considered China proper, traditional patterns were totally disrupted and class struggle ensued.

In minority areas throughout China, local officials pushed the use of Han customs and the Han language, a particularly sensitive issue in Kham and Amdo. The situation was made worse because the Great Leap created starvation throughout China and caused many Chinese to flee into Kham and Amdo.

By 1958, as the Great Leap intensified and the CIA sent increasing numbers of arms into Kham, the rebels attacked the main Chinese units in Kham, routing them and disrupting the land route into Lhasa. The Chinese ordered new troops to the area, and soon their forces swelled to at least 150,000 soldiers. As Chinese troops advanced into Kham, increasing numbers of the then outgunned rebels sought refuge in Lhasa.

Tension and paranoia mounted on both sides as the refugees created growing numbers of disturbances in central Tibet. In April 1958 the Chinese government sent a special police force to Lhasa to deal with the crisis. But just one month later they could not prevent the rebels from eradicating a one-thousand-man Chinese military post only twenty-five miles from Lhasa.[63]

Chinese officials urged the Dalai Lama to deploy his army against the rebels, but he refused. In January 1959 the Dalai Lama declined to attend a meeting with Mao in Beijing. The Chinese now worried that he might join the rebels. The Tibetans feared that Chinese commanders in Lhasa would seize the Dalai Lama and issue orders in his name.

Two months later the Chinese commander invited the Dalai Lama to come to Chinese military headquarters in Lhasa to see the performance of a visiting dance troupe. When the Chinese suggested the Dalai Lama attend the performance without his usual retinue of armed guards, the Tibetans grew suspicious of Chinese intentions.

Tom Grunfeld has recently argued that the resulting melée may have been set up by Tibetan leaders (though not the Dalai Lama) eager to provoke a confrontation.[64] The Dalai Lama has stated forthrightly that he set the date for the visit and that even after a number of Tibetan authorities had begun to argue that the invitation was a ruse that would enable the Chinese to seize the Dalai Lama, he still agreed to attend.[65]

Whatever the cause, word spread among the people that the Chinese might try to capture the Dalai Lama. Tibetans began to mass outside the gates of the Norbulingka, the summer palace where he stayed. Fearful of provoking the mob, the Dalai Lama canceled his visit by writing a letter to the Chinese. He stated his desire to attend the performance and regretted his inability to do so, "owing to obstruction by the people, both religious and secular, who were instigated by a few evil elements and who did not know the facts. This has put me to indescribable shame." He further insisted that, "Reactionary, evil elements are carrying out activities endangering me under the pretext of protecting my safety."[66]

In spite of the Dalai Lama's continued respect for the

The Norbulingka or Summer Palace was begun in 1755. The New Palace was completed in 1956 by the present Dalai Lama. The Chinese shelled it in 1959.

Chinese and his annoyance with the swelling Tibetan rebellion, the crowd grew larger and more militant as time passed. According to some accounts, by March 12 as many as thirty thousand people mobbed the outside of the palace.[67] A group of junior officials, some of the Dalai Lama's personal bodyguards, and the remaining popular leaders exacerbated the situation. They held a meeting in which they denounced the Seventeen-Point Agreement and declared that Tibet no longer recognized Chinese authority.

The Dalai Lama tried to calm the crowd but his actions had little effect. The Tibetans became convinced that the Communists intended to launch an attack after several shells fell near the palace. The Dalai Lama took these to be warning shots fired by the Chinese. Grunfeld suggests that these shells instead may have been fired by Tibetan rebels eager to provoke the situation.[68] He notes that the scenario that led to the flight of the Dalai Lama was one earlier outlined in an Indian paper said to be close to several leaders in the rebel camp. The Chinese deny firing the shots and ask "if the People's Liberation Army really wanted to attack, why was it that it only fired two or three mortar shells and did not venture to fire one more shell after they had fallen into a nearby pond."[69] Despite its good logic, this argument fails to address the question of whether the shots were a warning or the action of a few rash soldiers.

Hotheads on both sides hoped for a confrontation. The Great Leap had undermined the control of the Chinese central government and caused its officers and officials to take unwarranted, unwise, and often provocative actions all over China. The same unrest had provoked the rebels into continuing their attacks on a weakening Chinese government.

Fearful of capture, the Dalai Lama and a small retinue donned disguises and slipped into the crowd. He made his way out of the city and then fled by horseback toward the Indian border, accompanied by several Tibetan-trained CIA operatives. In spite of Nehru's hesitations, the Indians allowed him into the country. He was soon joined in exile by thousands of followers.

With the Dalai Lama gone and the population in an uproar, Chinese troops entered Tibet in large numbers. Unfortunately the Tibetans did not adequately plan their revolt. Only a minority of the population took part, and the Tibetan army did not fare well. The uprising was confined mainly to Lhasa. Two weeks after it had begun the Chinese announced it had mostly ended. But the Chinese considered the events an abrogation of the Seventeen-Point Agreement. On March 28 the Chinese ordered "that from that day the Tibetan Local Government which had instigated the rebellion was to be dissolved and the Preparatory Committee for the Tibet Autonomous Region should exercise the functions and powers of the Tibetan Local Government."[70] The Chinese seized direct authority and proceeded to disassemble the old Tibetan political structures and sack many of the monasteries and religious institutions. Tibet was no longer considered a special case by the Chinese.

An era had ended. For the first time since the thirteenth century, the Tibetans did not control their own country, either directly or indirectly. Their attempt to preserve their traditional political system and culture had failed. Ironically, even as the Dalai Lama's personal power lapsed, his world prestige grew and so did world recognition for the unique political and cultural institutions the Tibetans had created. The world press hailed the Dalai Lama's escape as a mystical and magical flight through the Himalayas, depicting the Tibetan struggle as one of pure good versus absolute evil. As he fled into exile, the media moguls and movie stars who still flock to him today raced to India to be by his side.[71] Ironically it was only by fleeing the country at a time when the old order was being completely routed that he and his followers finally woke up the world to the potential tragedy of Tibet losing its cultural and ethnic uniqueness.

SIX

❧

The Deluge

Foreign visitors traveling to Tibet in the 1980s and 1990s generally stay at the sterile-looking and politically controversial Lhasa Holiday Inn. In the summer the hotel resembles its counterparts in the United States, though the Hard Yak Cafe features yak burgers rather than hamburgers. In the winter, however, the Lhasa Holiday Inn becomes a completely different place with what must be the coldest rooms and lobby of any major hotel in the world. Even during the day when the sun makes the outside temperature relatively warm, the lobby temperature still hovers below freezing. Rushing to and from the dining room is a bone-chilling experience. As I ran to dinner one evening, swearing and shivering in my long underwear and heavy sweater, a friend jokingly asked me if my mother had not instructed me always to wear a jacket in the lobby of a hotel.

There is no heat to speak of in the bedrooms either. During the day the south-facing rooms are heated by the sun's rays. But at night small electric space heaters, when turned on full, either fail to work or blow the room's fuses. During the cold months, rarely more than three or four hardy souls stay in the huge hotel that bustles with activity in the spring and summer.

Under the best of circumstances, Tibet is an inhospitable though fascinating place. After 1959 the country became like the Lhasa Holiday Inn in winter—a cold shell. The region retained its old name and much of its outward appearance, but the Chinese quickly chilled its political climate and tried to transform its culture.

On March 25, 1959, five days after the flight of the Dalai Lama, the Chinese dissolved the Tibetan government. A month later the Panchen Lama, the second-most important leader in Tibet, sent a telegram to the Chinese central government expressing his continuing support for its regime. A few days after the telegram arrived, the Chinese brought the Panchen Lama to Lhasa and made him chairman of the Preparatory Committee for the Tibet Autonomous Region. He called on Tibetans to support the Chinese government. The Chinese also installed two prominent aristocrats—Pebala Choliehnamje and Ngabo Ngawang Jigme—as vice-chairman and secretary general of the new government. Ngabo was the collaborator who had first surrendered Kham and then led the team to negotiate the Seventeen-Point Agreement.

The new Tibetan government added six branches to its administration. The first and most ominous of these was the Public Security Department, the Chinese equivalent of the KGB. The new administration also established a Public Health Department, a Department of Industrial and Commercial Administration, a Communications Department, a Department of Agriculture and Animal Husbandry, and a Counselors Office.[1] At the same time, the Communists reorganized the country into seventy-two rural counties and seven special administrative districts. In every village they began to create an organization to keep track of all facets of people's lives.

A few weeks after the reorganization of the Tibetan government, the Second National People's Congress meeting in Beijing declared: "The existing social system in Tibet is an extremely backward system of serfdom. The degree of cruelty which characterized the exploitation, oppression and persecution of the laboring people by the serf-owners can hardly be paralleled in any other part of the world."[2] The congress made it clear that the Chinese would use their ability and power to free the Tibetan people from slavery. The Chinese announced that they would soon begin what were called "democratic reforms" to build a "new Tibet."[3]

Although they claim them as compatriots, the Chinese actually think of Tibetans as slovenly and backward. The Chinese dislike Tibetan cuisine, customs, and religion. They determined in 1959 to transform Tibet into a place in which they could feel more comfortable. In all fairness we should note that racism toward their fellow Asians is by no means confined to the Chinese. Even the Tibetans have been guilty of it. And the Japanese are notorious for the derogatory way they describe the Koreans and other Asians. The Japanese explorer Kawaguchi, who lived as a Tibetan for several years, openly derided many Tibetan characteristics, noting that the Tibetan "never washes his body; many have never been washed since their birth. . . . They are quite as black on their necks and backs as the African Negroes. Why then are their hands so white? It is because they make dough with their own hands with flour in a bowl, and the dirt of their hands is mixed with the dough. So the Tibetan dishes are made of dirt and flour, and the Tibetans eat with their teeth black with sores. It is a sickening sight!"[4]

Chinese racism differed from that displayed by Kawaguchi and other Asians because the Chinese displayed it toward a people they claimed were their fellow Chinese. Yet the Chinese continued to treat Tibet differently from the rest of China. In late 1959 for instance, the government announced there would be a "speedy realization" of the social-

It is a curious Tibetan custom to greet a person by sticking out the tongue. This is usually done as a sign of respect to someone of apparently higher social station and is sometimes even repeated at the end of each spoken sentence. *(Land of the Lamas)*

ist transformation that would bring the radical movement then spreading throughout China into Tibet.[5]

But after the moderates prevailed in Beijing in early 1960, they abandoned the extreme policies of the Great Leap, dismantled the communes, and announced that the "democratic reforms" in Tibet would be carried out in two stages. First they would eliminate slavery, end corvée labor, and reduce rent and interest in a campaign to be called the "three antis and two reductions" (antirebellion, anti-Ula [the Tibetan corvée], and antislavery). After completing this, they would progress to the second stage—the redistribution of land. While land redistribution had been carried out in China in the early 1950s, it differed greatly from the collectivization implemented in the rest of China in increasingly radical steps in the mid- to late 1950s.

To carry out the first stage, the Chinese abolished "the old regime in the villages" and established peasants' associations "to exercise the functions and powers of the lowest level of government in the rural areas."[6] The government also confiscated herds belonging to rebels and launched a campaign in the monasteries "to oppose rebellion, privileges and exploitation" while still protecting "freedom of religious belief and lamaseries and cultural relics. . . ."[7]

The "democratic reforms" actually began before the Chinese government officially announced the new policy. Within a matter of months, the Communist party had moved on to land distribution. The Chinese did not send their most sophisticated or sensitive officials to Tibet, and few of them found it easy to distinguish between the "good" Tibetans who supported the Chinese and the "bad" ones who had supported the rebellion. Many "good" Tibetans did not receive compensation as they had been promised for the goods taken from them. The few Tibetans who were paid for their confiscated property still suffered from a loss of prestige and position.

In 1961 a moderate new government realized that the situation in Tibet was running out of control. It consolidated its position in Beijing and further reversed the ravages of the Great Leap. The party announced that the socialist transformation—that is, collectivization—would not be carried out in Tibet for five years, though it had taken place seven or eight years earlier in the rest of China. The Communists also declared they would give the rebels' goods and livestock to the deserving "in their own tribes" and that the children of rebels were to receive their fair share.[8]

To the Tibetan peasants the Communists gave the land

they had confiscated as well as interest-free loans of seeds and grain. The Chinese ended serfdom in Tibet and bestowed on each peasant an average of about six acres, far more than most had ever owned. By 1960 the government triumphantly declared:

> During Tibet's democratic reform, the people's government confiscated the land of the rebellious serf-owners and their agents and bought up the surplus land of those serf-owners and agents who did not take part in the rebellion. This land totals over 2.8 million Ke [one Ke is about one-fifteenth of a hectare] and has been distributed to 800,000 former serfs and slaves in the agricultural areas, who formerly did not own any land. . . . Under the leadership of the Communist Party, over 100,000 households of emancipated peasants organized themselves into more than 15,000 agricultural mutual-aid teams last winter and this spring. . . . By extending the sown acreage by 340,000 Ke this year, building many irrigation canals, accumulating large amounts of fertilizer and improving farming methods, they achieved a good harvest this autumn.[9]

The Communists claimed that grain production in 1960 increased 15 percent over 1959, which had been a bumper year. Moreover, officials in certain counties claimed a 100 percent increase.[10] By 1961 the Chinese government could boast that Tibet had had a bumper crop for three consecutive years, an impressive achievement. During the same period the rest of China experienced a decline in agricultural production. The Han agricultural specialists dispatched to Tibet introduced new and improved techniques and provided better fertilizer, irrigation, and seeds. Peasants who owned property for the first time probably found themselves working harder.

Unfortunately few Tibetans derived long-term benefits

from this growth. Chinese settlers streamed into Tibet as cadres and agricultural experts. They increased the population and depleted what otherwise would have been an expanding agricultural store.

Other changes produced similarly mixed results. The Chinese strove to develop Tibet's industrial potential as they had transformed the country's agricultural base. By the spring of 1960 the first modern hydroelectric power station was built with a generating capacity of 7,500 kilowatts. The Communist party also proudly declared that "an iron and steel foundry is under construction; the blast furnace was completed in three months and the first vat of molten iron was produced on October 1, 1960. Now Tibet has such new industries as an iron and steel industry, hydro-electric power, motor car repair, the manufacture of farm implements, serums and animal medicines."[11] Unfortunately in industry as in agriculture, the new Han settlers rather than the Tibetans were able to take advantage of much of this new development.

Nor should anyone assume that in this rush for progress Tibet became heavily industrialized. Even in the mid-1990s, when the country was in the midst of an unprecedented building spree, only a few factories and little industry could be found in the country. Outside the cities the roads are poorly built, often washed-out, and characterized by numerous hairpin turns. In the cities the streets are not much better. Sheep are still used to keep down the grass even at the posh (by Tibetan standards) Lhasa Holiday Inn. Where there is electricity, power outages are frequent. Travelers cannot find more than a handful of real taxis in all of Lhasa; instead of cabs, there are three-wheeled rickshaws. Most are open to the air, and some are adorned with fancy red-and-white canopies and feather dusters. Private vans also ply the main roads in Lhasa, picking up passengers for one yuan each. At the Gyangtze carpet factory, the most famous in Tibet, much of the work is done outdoors. Women spin the wool squatting in the yard with dogs and babies roaming in and out interrupting them. In the 1960s Communist development destroyed much of the old Tibetan infrastructure but did little to industrialize or even electrify most of Tibet.

In the xenophobic atmosphere that prevailed in Tibet after 1960, many Han cadre thoughtlessly and sometimes cruelly vented their prejudice against the Tibetans. Many of these cadre resented being sent to Tibet and used the opportunity to enrich themselves at the locals' expense.

Making matters worse, some Communist leaders believed Marx's dictum declaring religion to be the "opiate of the masses." They had little tolerance for Tibetan customs that seemed so radically at odds with their own. The contrast between the opulence of Tibet's temples and monasteries, to which ordinary citizens contributed everything including their own children, and the seeming poverty of everyday life appeared to confirm this Communist aphorism. The close relationship between political power and religion also gave the Communists an added incentive for attacking these religious structures. Unfortunately many Chinese seemed to relish the opportunity.

The new government arrested monks, nuns, and other traditional leaders with whom they had previously cooperated. They emptied the monasteries of all but a few elderly monks and then dismantled many of the historic structures. They also jailed much of the old aristocracy. Ironically the Chinese punished those who had chosen to stay rather than flee with the Dalai Lama. Many of those who had remained had been loyal to the Chinese government.

The assault on religion and tradition in Tibet was a harbinger of the Great Proletarian Cultural Revolution that was to sweep all of China five years later. The attack foreshadowed what the Cultural Revolution was to become—an effort to equate and reduce to one common denominator all disparate cultures and groups in greater China.

By late 1960 the Communists had organized a little over half of Tibet's countryside into 8,400 mutual-aid teams. These cooperative units pooled labor like the Chinese organizations had in China before collectivization. In late 1962 the party declared that "over 90 percent of the region's peasant households joined the mutual-aid teams for agricultural production."[12] At the same time the Communists formed work brigades in Tibet like those created in China in the early 1950s. They commandeered able-bodied adults to build the roadways and other facilities necessary for continued industrialization. Although this may have been essential for development, it of course riled many Tibetans.

The government also began to force nomads to build pens to confine their stock and to store grain, supposedly in the interest of increasing production. It was a wasteful policy not well adapted to the fragile ecosystem of the Tibetan plateau, where nomads drove animals from pasture to pasture to avoid overgrazing. In China many peasants killed their animals rather than turn them over to the public domain. In Tibet farmers and herders did the same. Fewer animals meant more surplus grain, which helped increase Tibetan food stocks but did not translate into more protein or even more bulk in the Tibetan diet.

In their reorganization of the Tibetan countryside, the Chinese Communist party centralized food storage and distribution. The Chinese took advantage of this to siphon off grain from the countryside to feed its troops in Tibet. Food shortages developed. During the lean years in China from 1960 to 1963, many in Tibet suffered even though their harvests increased.

Today Chinese troops are everywhere in Tibet. On the two-hour drive from the Lhasa airport to the capital, visitors glimpse soaring peaks and valleys, horses, dogs, sheep, and little houses with prayer flags fluttering from their roofs. They also see one walled army encampment after another. Although the army tries to keep a low-key presence when civil unrest is moderate, soldiers remain constantly on guard in the major cities, and roadblocks suddenly appear even in remote areas to check the credentials of travelers. The presence of troops strains the frail Tibetan infrastructure and causes resentment among Tibetans.

As unrest continued to grow in the 1960s, the Chinese clamped down harder and party control became pervasive. The party distributed rations and allocated work. The party also controlled the movement of the people, confining them to their villages in a form of socialist enfiefment previously applied to the rest of China and particularly loathsome to the usually free-roaming Tibetans. The Communists held public trials of so-called reactionaries and encouraged children to denounce parents and friends to inform against friends.

Tibetan cadres were as arbitrary and authoritarian as their Chinese counterparts. The Chinese employed growing numbers of young Tibetans who had studied in China to carry out their new policy. According to published documents, "Before the anti-Communist revolution broke out, the Chinese Communists had trained only 6,000-odd Tibetan cadres. By August 1965, the number of Tibetan cadres in the whole Region had risen to more than 16,000, with 1,500-odd working as leading cadres at and above district level in the various Party and government organs in Tibet. In addition to this, there were 20,000-odd basic-level work cadres who were originally serfs or slaves."[13] The Communists used these local officials to try to popularize their program. But because of the high level of suspicion between the Han and Tibetan populations, few if any of these cadres moved up to high office.

Tension in Tibet also affected neighboring India. Soon after "liberation," the Indians bent over backward to cooperate with the Chinese. In 1952 the Indian government agreed to conduct relations with Lhasa through Beijing and two years later formally recognized Tibet as part of China. The Indians agreed to relinquish the extraterritorial privileges originally granted to the British. As part of the deal, the Indians withdrew their escorts and special representatives stationed in Tibet.

In the mid-1950s, however, when the Khampas threatened to cut off the roads into Tibet from Sichuan and Qinghai, the Chinese constructed a new road along an old caravan trail from the northwestern province of Xinjiang into western Tibet. The road they built passed more than a hundred miles inside the Indian-claimed Aksai Chin plateau.

The Aksai Chin had once belonged to Tibet, and therefore after 1950 it was arguably part of China.[14] But the Indians considered it to be in Ladakh, a section of Kashmir that is now disputed between India and Pakistan. As one scholar has written, "Any Indian surrender of Kashmiri territory to any foreign power would of course be a most unfortunate precedent highly detrimental to the arguments which India was then raising in support of her claims and would provide potential ammunition for her Pakistani opponents."[15]

If the Chinese had quietly attempted to negotiate this issue with the Indians, they might have been able to avoid making the control of the territory a matter of Indian national pride and identity. The Aksai Chin was a worthless, unsettled piece of land that was unoccupied and unguarded.[16] But instead the Indians were shocked to discover that a road had been built on their territory. They found out a year after its completion in 1957, when the Chinese published a map that showed the highway. Having just witnessed how the Chinese had treated the Tibetans, many Indians became convinced of the aggressive and hostile nature of the new Chinese regime, and the Indian government began to protest what they considered a Chinese intrusion.

In 1959 the Chinese moved their troops to the border after the Dalai Lama fled to India. Livid that the Dalai Lama denounced their government from the safety of Indian soil, the Chinese feared that the Indians might take advantage of the unrest to launch a Younghusband-style invasion to liberate Lhasa and reunite the Tibetan groups in India with those in Tibet. The Chinese felt especially alarmed that many of those fleeing Tibet were picking up arms in India and returning to carry on a guerrilla struggle against the Chinese.

With no buffer zone between them, the two forces began to brush up against one another. In 1959 Indian and Chinese troops clashed, killing an Indian soldier. The Russians later argued that the Chinese planned the skirmish to disrupt Khrushchev's visit to the United States. Whatever the case, it aggravated the tension between China and Russia and led to their growing ideological split as well as increased Russian support for India. This heated up the friction between China and India. Periodic clashes followed by attempts to moderate the disputes continued for much of the next year.

In the fall of 1962 the Indians moved more troops into the area, and Chinese troops launched a major offensive against them. Battles raged throughout the winter as the Chinese won victory after victory. Early in 1963 the Chinese ceased firing and pulled back most of their forces. Thereafter the two sides retreated to their old lines, the Chinese remaining in control of the Aksai Chin. By this time China and Pakistan had allied, and the latter had conceded Chinese control over territory it had claimed near the disputed road. Because Pakistanis no longer disputed Chinese control over the Aksai Chin, India had no reason to do so.[17]

Although this remains a heavily patrolled border, today as relations ease between India and China, Hindi pilgrims again make the strenuous journey to west Tibet to pay

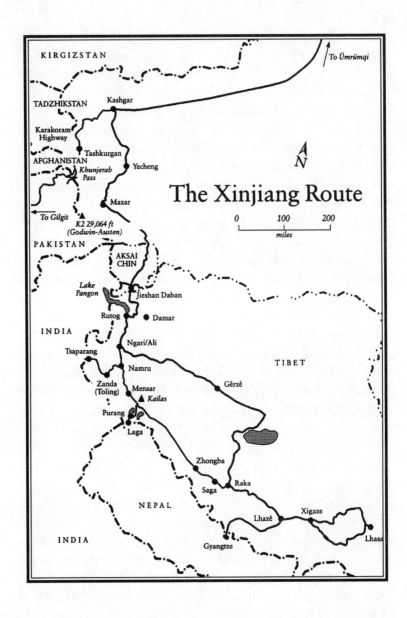

KIRGIZSTAN

To Ürümqi

TADZHIKSTAN

Kashgar

Karakoram
Highway

Tashkurgan

AFGHANISTAN

Yecheng

Khunjerab
Pass

Mazar

The Xinjiang Route

To Gilgit

K2 29,064 ft
(Godwin-Austen)

0   100   200
                miles

PAKISTAN

AKSAI
CHIN

Lake
Pangon

Jieshan Daban

Rutog

Damar

Ngari/Ali

INDIA

Tsaparang

TIBET

Namru

Zanda
(Toling)

Mensar

Gêrzê

Kailas

Purang

Laga

Zhongba

Saga

Raka

NEPAL

Xigaze

Lhazê

Lhasa

INDIA

Gyangtze

homage to Mount Kailas and to bathe in the holy waters of Lake Manasarovar. Even without these holy sites, the trip would promise close encounters with wildlife as well as spectacular vistas.

As India gradually toned down its conflict with China, the United States continued to stir up the situation. In 1959 the CIA began to train Tibetan guerrilla fighters at a high-altitude camp in Colorado and then sneak them back into Tibet to destabilize Chinese control over the area. Initially Pakistan served as the conduit for these CIA-trained fighters. But the CIA also prevailed on the Nepalese to provide sanctuary for the Tibetans.

In 1960 the government of Nepal allowed the Tibetan resistance to set up a base in Mustang, an isolated Nepalese province with a largely Tibetan population set high in the Himalayas along the two countries' borders. From here the freedom fighters raided Chinese units in Tibet, disrupting transportation on the new Xinjiang-Tibet road. This base operated until 1974 when the growing accord between the United States and China, threats against Nepal on the part of the Chinese government, and internal dissension among Tibet's rebel bands forced the base to close.

India continued to assist the Tibetans even while it edged away from direct conflict with China. After the 1962 war, the Indians, according to John Avedon, created a secret "entirely Tibetan force charged with the mission of guarding the world's highest border.[18] By recruiting these Tibetans into the Indian army, the Indians availed themselves of Tibetan alpine skills and avoided provoking the Chinese by aiding independent Tibetan efforts against China.

In the face of this pressure, the Chinese consolidated their grip on Tibet. In 1963 the Communists completed the regional elections necessary for the establishment of the Tibet Autonomous Region. Provincial elections followed. On September 1, 1965, the delegates formally convened. Eight days later they proclaimed the Autonomous Region of the People's Republic of China. This effectively abolished the system of civil and religious rule that had characterized Tibet for more than a thousand years.

The Communists sought to purge the influence of the leaders who had upheld the ancient Tibetan system. In 1964 they formally dismissed the Dalai Lama, dropping the pretense that he had been abducted and taken abroad. They also removed the Panchen Lama from office, though most had previously seen him as a loyal supporter of Beijing. In 1964 the Panchen had given a public speech in which the Chinese had expected him to condemn the Dalai Lama, but he had failed to do so. At this time, the eve of the Cultural Revolution, anyone who stood apart from China's so-called proletarian movement came under attack, especially feudal relics. Many of the Panchen's supporters had been arrested in 1960; now it was his turn.[19] The Chinese subjected him to a seventeen-day trial in which they publicly humiliated him, accusing him of everything from treason to sexual indiscretions. The court sent him to prison, where he remained until the mid-1970s.

Recently the Chinese have honored the loyalty of the Tenth Panchen by constructing a *stupa* (shrine) and a hall in his memory in the Tashilhunpo lamasery in Xigaze. Although he was flawed, the Panchen nonetheless had gained considerable affection among the Tibetan people. In 1993, the year after its completion, more than a hundred thousand Tibetan disciples as well as domestic and foreign tourists visited the memorial that boasts first-class architecture and frescoes. In 1994 plans were under way to add a transmigration altar more than six feet tall.

The political transition that removed the Dalai Lama from office and imprisoned the Panchen Lama occurred shortly before the start of the Cultural Revolution. By the summer of 1966 Red Guard groups at the behest of Mao Zedong and Lin Biao had launched their campaign "to sweep away the freaks and monsters" of political power and tradition. They struck minority areas particularly hard. Hatred of superstition easily melded with traditional Chinese prejudices against non-Han minorities. In any case, foreign religious traditions were overwhelmed by a movement striving to carry out a radical vision of sameness.

By July Red Guard groups began to trickle into Tibet. At least one writer has suggested that many, if not most, of them may have been returning Tibetan students, as it was difficult at that time for Han groups to enter Tibet.[20] Under pressure from the Red Guard, Tibetan peasants and workers were forced to study Mao Zedong's teachings. In the cities the newly arrived self-appointed guardians of the revolution began to criticize everyone in authority, from Chinese Communist officials to Tibetan monks.

The situation grew worse after August 1966 when Mao began urging the Red Guards to take their revolution into the countryside. Their numbers grew. They rampaged through the streets of Lhasa, pillaging palaces and temples. They even sacked the Jokhang, the ancient and holy cathedral of Tibetan Buddhism, and transformed it into a guesthouse for visitors.

All over China, Red Guards desecrated and destroyed beautiful sacred buildings and artwork. Well before the Cultural Revolution, Tibet had become a target for Communist wrath. The strong relationship in the region between Buddhism and governmental and societal authority convinced many young zealots that this area bore particularly corrupt and exploitative feudal traditions. The country possessed a great number of impressive temples on which to wreak havoc. By the end of the revolution, only a few of the more than two thousand monasteries and temples that had once dotted Tibet remained. Many had been destroyed brick by brick.

Although Tibetan sources sometimes imply that the Cultural Revolution was a Chinese plot specifically directed against Tibetans, in fact throughout China historic relics and temples were destroyed and innocent people were tortured. Some Chinese leaders actually tried to steer the Cultural Revolution away from Tibet. In the summer Chinese Prime Minister Zhou Enlai issued a special decree ordering the Red Guards out of the country. He repeated his commands in October, forbidding Han groups to enter Tibet. But the Red Guards ignored his commands, like many other orders given by Chinese leaders in those heady days. By late fall all the Red Guard groups in the country were Han. Even when officials gave the Red Guards a farewell banquet, they refused to leave.

When the Red Guard groups began to fight among one another, most ordinary Tibetans were at best bystanders and at worst innocent victims of the fractional violence. But some relished the chaos and its results. Many secretly sympathized when the Red Guards targeted General Zhang Guohua and his party secretary, Wang Jimei. These two had helped organize the regime that replaced the Dalai Lama. Early in 1967 when the Red Guards forced Zhang to flee to Sichuan, central authority collapsed. Some Tibetan rebel groups then used the chaos to attack both inside and outside the border, sometimes blaming the violence they caused on feuding Red Guard groups. At the same time many Tibetan workers walked off their jobs and refused to listen to their Chinese employers.

One former Red Guard has suggested that as a result of the Cultural Revolution, "For the first time the broad ranks of workers were able to give their superiors a piece of their mind without fear of being beaten down as anti-party, anti-socialist elements." It was a time when "factories disbursed long-overdue overtime pay, raised the limits of compensation on certain items of medical insurance, and expanded the coverage."[21]

In China this popular movement probably reached its height in early 1967 with the creation of the short-lived Shanghai commune. It crested later in Tibet. In June 1969,

mass disobedience occurred when the entire population openly defied the ban on religion by celebrating Saka Dawa—the anniversary of Buddha's birth, enlightenment and death. The following month office workers in the capital walked off their jobs, ostensibly to celebrate World Solidarity Day. Erecting tents in Lhasa's old *lingkas* or picnic grounds by the Kyichu River, they opened their Little Red Books on the ground, as though studying, and proceeded to play dice and mah-jong for an entire week. Outside Lhasa, in Lhoka, resistance took a less playful turn. There, 3,000 young Tibetans attacked the PLA, killing 200. Two months later, 200 more troops were killed in Tsethang; similar uprisings were reported to have occurred in five areas of western Tibet as early as 1967. By the summer of 1970—long after Red Guard fighting had subsided, communes had been imposed and war preparation begun—a major revolt broke out across southwestern Tibet, in which more than 1,000 Chinese soldiers died. . . .[22]

Before this rebellion ended, it had spread to more than eighteen counties and entailed a greater loss of life than that incurred in the 1959 rebellion.[23]

Meanwhile, the Cultural Revolution sped up the forced communization of the Tibetan countryside. The Chinese had formed their original communes in the Lhasa and Xigaze areas in the early 1960s, a year or two after they quelled the rebellion. But the Communists did not begin to apply them to the rest of the country until after 1965 with the formation of the Tibetan Autonomous Region. By the summer of 1970 they had created more than a thousand communes covering a little over a third of the country. Following the Cultural Revolution the Chinese worked to extend this radical administration. By the end of 1975 they had pushed more than 90 percent of the Tibetan peasantry into communization.

Although these were far smaller administrative units than those formed in China during the height of the Great Leap, the freewheeling Tibetans did not take well to them. The communal authorities forced the people to give up much of their private property, sometimes even small objects such as hammers, knives, and ropes. The Chinese promised to compensate them for their property, but rarely paid them or paid them inadequately.

With their incentive to work removed, the people's productivity plunged. The timing of this drop was terrible, as growing numbers of Chinese flooded Tibet. The Chinese sent former Red Guards to the countryside supposedly as part of a campaign to encourage urban and rural dwellers to trade skills, but often simply as a way to rid the cities of troublemakers. The disruptions devastated the region. By early 1968 famine again began to roll through the rural areas. From 1968 to 1975 the population grew as work output declined. Food shortages steadily worsened, and Chinese rule in Tibet became increasingly discredited.

In 1971, in the wake of the failed coup against Mao by his former subordinate Lin Biao, Lin's supporters in Tibet were removed from office and new military and civilian officials were appointed. By this time it had become clear to many Chinese authorities that without relaxation of their harsh policies, they would be unable to govern Tibet. Officials in Beijing began to praise the special characteristics of the various ethnic groups, including the Tibetans.[24] The Chinese again allowed people to wear native dress and eased restrictions forbidding travel and religious practices. They even began covert talks with the Dalai Lama.

Tibet's situation improved even more after 1977. Zhou

Enlai and then Mao Zedong died, and the Gang of Four, the Maoist henchmen blamed for the devastations of the Cultural Revolution, were arrested. Deng Xiaoping, who had briefly returned to office in 1973 before being purged again in 1976, regained political power. A Cultural Revolution group in Canton once claimed that in the early and mid-1950s, Deng had been the principal architect of the conciliatory policy toward the Dalai Lama.[25] Yet most critics certainly would not consider Deng to be a friend of the Tibetan people. Moreover the Chinese eased their policy in Tibet even before Deng returned to office. But it is true that in the late 1970s, after he began to gain real authority in China, Deng, a native of Sichuan, the Chinese province closest to Tibet, did recognize the counterproductivity of the harsh Chinese policy in the region.

By the time the Chinese began to change their policies toward the Tibetans, they had already created massive destruction throughout Tibet. The architecture, religion, economy, and politics of this formerly independent nation had been so battered and the people so embittered that it was difficult for them to feel anything but defensive and hostile toward the Chinese. The revolution had brought them almost nothing in terms of genuine aid or benefits. Reconstruction left little more than the ugly concrete block structures that now congest Tibetan cities and appear incongruously in the countryside.

In their own defense the Chinese point out that this had been a tough time for everyone in China. First the Great Leap Forward had caused economic chaos and starvation throughout China. And then the Cultural Revolution had attempted to obliterate all local and regional distinctions and to amalgamate everyone and everything into the Great Proletarian Culture. The Tibetans, however, claim the Chinese had committed cultural genocide against them. The Great Leap and Cultural Revolution were Chinese campaigns, and,

SEVEN

❦

The Uncomfortable
Decade

I visited Lhasa in January 1991, leading a class of students from the East Asian Department at Colby College in Maine who were studying Tibet. The plane had barely come to a stop on the runway when our Chinese guide gathered the students together to give them two warnings. Visitors to Lhasa, she declared, should spend their first day resting as they would need a chance to adjust to the altitude and climate. Next, she continued, we should not venture on our own into the huge open-air market that runs along the Barkhor, the pilgrimage route encircling the Jokhang temple in the center of Lhasa. The Tibetans, she told us, were uncontrollable and dangerous. The Barkhor could be risky.

The guide's warnings served instead to motivate the students. Despite feeling tired from the trip, and sick from the altitude, about an hour after we arrived every one of them had crept out of the hotel to tour the Barkhor. They delighted in the noise, the sights, and the crowds. Our guide had never been to Lhasa before. At first she sulked about having been disobeyed. But she was not much older than the students, and when she saw the interesting bargains they were finding and the fun they were having, she soon joined in. She was both fascinated and repelled by what she saw, and always guarded. She never walked alone, instead positioning herself in the center of a bevy of students. When a monk stopped them and asked what nationality they were, she answered quickly, "We're all Americans."

Our guide demonstrated the unease most Chinese feel in Tibet. Although they argue, as our guide did, that Tibet is an inalienable part of China, the fact is they feel foreign amid Tibetans. It felt safer to our guide to relate to the Tibetans as an American than as a supposed Chinese compatriot.

Many Chinese confronted this dilemma after the early 1970s. When the Chinese reversed the oppressive policies of the Cultural Revolution, Tibetans began to vent their animosity toward them more openly. Chinese liberalization increased in 1978, when the government again permitted Tibetans to contact relatives outside the country.

In 1959 many of these relatives had fled to India or nearby Nepal, where about twenty thousand Tibetans officially settled. Protected by a special tax status granted by the king of Nepal, they flourished. Some traded in jewelry and *thankas,* the Tibetan Buddhist religious scrolls. As late as 1995 Tibetan crafts were often cheaper and better made in Nepal than in Tibet itself. The Tibetans also created Nepal's rug industry, and by the 1990s it earned the tiny kingdom more than $200 million annually. European countries threatened to boycott this Tibetan-owned industry, however, if it did not stop using child labor. In addition, Tibetans owned a number of low-budget hotels, easily recognized because of pictures of the Dalai Lama in their offices.

These Tibetan refugees enhanced Nepal's glamour and allure. In the 1960s and 1970s they were partially responsible for establishing Katmandu as an essential stop on what became known as the Raj Trail, making the city a mecca for Western travelers seeking cheap drugs and spirituality. A sec-

The Barkhor, near the Jokhang temple in Lhasa, is filled with peddlers, beggars, and crafts people trying to snag some of the pilgrims' money.

tion of Katmandu where many Tibetan merchants set up establishments became known as Freak Street because it catered to foreign "freaks." As the city has become more upscale, growing numbers of reputable stores have opened there, providing travelers with food ranging from yogurt and enchiladas to German brown bread.

By the early 1980s the sophisticated Tibetans from Nepal were carrying goods and messages back and forth into Tibet, stoking their relatives' interest in the outside world and supplying them with anti-Chinese propaganda. The prosperity of these emigrants revealed what those left behind had missed while suffering under Chinese rule.

By the 1990s Dharamsala had diverted some of the allure once held by Katmandu, as India is home to more Tibetan refugees than Nepal. Many of them have congregated

Although much of the Tibetan rug industry has now moved to Nepal, the best rugs are still made in Gyangtze. Women sit on the ground, often surrounded by their friends and children, and spin the wool out by hand.

in the old British hill station above Dharamsala that is called McCloud Ganj, where the Dalai Lama has established the Tibetan government-in-exile. Monks, backpackers, Tibetan restaurateurs, drug dealers, and Tibetan dogs crowd the still beautiful setting. Accommodations are bare-bones but cheap. Students on vacation often find themselves staying in rooms next door to the likes of Richard Gere or other movie stars paying homage to the Dalai Lama. At night, glossy-eyed druggies join sincere backpackers at lectures denouncing the Chinese. By the mid-1990s some Tibetan intellectuals had formed a group known as the Amye Machen Institute, dedicated to an intelligent discussion of Tibetan and Chinese issues. Unfortunately liberal Tibetans who suggest that some aspects of Tibet's situation may be improving or that serious problems existed in the country before the Chinese occupied it can find themselves quickly drummed out of town. Many of the most conservative and reactionary Tibetans in Dharamsala are still propped up by Westerners who look to them as spiritual guides and mentors.

In 1992 I saw articles pasted on the doors of government buildings in Dharamsala announcing the imminent collapse of the Chinese economy just as it had begun to boom. The Tibetan government-in-exile distributed an article that claimed the former secretary general of the Chinese Communist party, Hu Yaobang, generally acknowledged as somewhat sympathetic to Tibetan issues, was dismissed in 1983.[1] In fact Hu remained head of the party until 1987 and continued as a member of the politburo until his death in 1989. Even the Dalai Lama mistakenly claimed that after Hu declared he would withdraw 85 percent of all Chinese personnel from Tibet in 1981, "he [Hu] then remained in office for only a few months. Then he himself was dismissed."[2]

In recent years many Tibetan Communist leaders have begun to send at least one of their children to be educated in Dharamsala. In this way the leaders can keep a foot in each camp—that of the Tibetan government-in-exile and that of the new Tibetan government in Lhasa. Many ordinary Tibetans also ship their children to Dharamsala for a year or two to learn English. When these students return to Tibet, their new English skills qualify them for highly paid jobs such as those of government guides or hotel or restaurant workers. They also carry messages and anti-Chinese propaganda back to their homeland, flaming resentment and sparking rebellion.

This kind of foreign contact became possible after the late 1970s when Beijing reopened communication with Dharamsala and initiated a long-distance dialogue with the Dalai Lama. In 1978 Gyalo Thondup, the Dalai Lama's older brother, accepted an invitation to come to the Chinese capital for discussions on his brother's behalf. The Chinese also allowed fifty Tibetan teachers living in India to teach in Tibet.[3]

More important, at this time the Chinese government permitted Tibetans within Tibet more freedom and initiative. For instance, the American-educated academic Tashi Tsering became a professor at Tibet University and compiled the first Chinese-English-Tibetan dictionary. Tashi had fled Tibet in the late 1950s, making his way to the United States where he graduated from Williams College and did graduate work at the University of Washington. In the early 1960s he returned to Tibet to work with the Chinese in helping his people. This was shortly before the start of the Cultural Revolution, and anyone with an American education was suspect. Tashi was imprisoned and tortured for almost a decade. He was not released until the 1970s, when the Chinese government reversed the policies of the Cultural Revolution and began to look again to those with foreign training and education to improve life in Tibet.

Tashi's continued willingness to work with the Chinese government was unusual. For many other Tibetans, the Chinese relaxation in restrictions allowed the Tibetans to make public and obvious the hatred the two peoples often feel toward each other. In 1980 the Chinese government allowed the Dalai Lama's older brother to visit Tibet to see how much the welfare of Tibetans had improved. Tibetan crowds mobbed the delegation, demonstrating their disenchantment with Chinese policies while sharing their respect for the Dalai Lama.

Colorful women peddlers can be found in the Barkhor and outside many of the major tourist attractions in Lhasa, offering everything from bracelets to knives to prayer wheels. Their brightly colored vests, hats, and waist bands illustrate the importance of dress in Tibetan life and the extent to which it provides a spectacle for foreign visitors.

The visit forced the Chinese to confront the extent of Tibetan dissatisfaction with their policies. The government held a special meeting in Beijing to discuss how to "improve the relationship" between Chinese and Tibetans.[4] In 1980 Hu Yaobang, Deng Xiaoping's protégé and the future secretary general of the Chinese Communist party, led a high-level delegation on a historic visit to Tibet to see firsthand the state of the region. The Chinese had been boasting for years that they had liberated the Tibetans from serfdom and were subsidizing their efforts to improve their lives. But what the Chinese saw appalled them. And they were quick to dodge responsibility, blaming Tibetan poverty and oppression on the leftist policies of the Cultural Revolution. The outspoken Hu sarcastically asked if all of China's aid to the region had simply been thrown into the Yarlong Tsangpo River.

The delegates promised political autonomy or "having the right to decide for oneself" for Tibet. They also pledged that, regarding "economic issues, Tibet should be treated as a special case and with flexibility according to Tibet's own conditions." They even suggested that "All ideas that ignore and weaken Tibetan culture are wrong."[5]

This was quite an admission for the Chinese who continue to state publicly their prejudices against Tibetans. In a 1991 article in the *Beijing Review* publicizing economic reforms in the region, correspondent Li Rongxia wrote:

> On my return from Tibet, one of my friends asked me, "What did you eat in Tibet, butter and roasted barley?"
>
> As a matter of fact, restaurants in Tibet provide the same kind of food as in the inland. Tibetan food is served on special occasions as a sign of respect for visitors.[6]

As this comment illustrates, even the Chinese seemingly sympathetic to Tibet often equate development with the sinicization of the region. The idea of eating in a Tibetan restaurant disgusts them. Like some Americans who want to see a world filled with McDonald's, the Chinese wish for a Tibet crowded with Chinese restaurants. They envision a Tibet where Tibetan food is served only to tourists in dining rooms like that of the Holiday Inn in Lhasa.

In spite of this attitude, in the early 1980s the Chinese made a major effort to grant new freedoms and opportunities to ordinary Tibetans. The government eliminated taxes in rural areas, waived school tuition payments, and abolished the newly established commune system. Officials even withdrew many Chinese cadres and replaced them with Tibetan ones, though the Chinese never came close to recalling 85 percent of Chinese personnel as promised by Hu Yaobang. The Communists also eventually admitted that forcing Tibetans to raise wheat instead of barley had been a mistake. The Han had considered barley an inferior grain and had failed to recognize that it was better suited than wheat to Tibetan growing conditions.

In 1981 another Tibetan government-in-exile delegation arrived in Beijing for negotiations and proposed that the entire Tibetan plateau be reunited in one administrative unit. Hu Yaobang seemed interested and responded that "this is a new idea which needs to be considered."[7] If it had been enacted—despite the enormous administrative roadblocks in its way—this proposal could have brought about the resurrection of a government that presided over an area almost equal to that of the traditional Tibetan state.

Although the authorities quickly put this possibility on the back burner, about forty-five monasteries with fourteen hundred monks reopened. By 1981 as many as ninety thousand people a month were again visiting the Jokhang temple in Lhasa.[8] Donations flowed into monasteries. Tibetans complained that Chinese officials stole most of the charity money they donated, but the restoration and rebuilding of the temples continued. Parents began sending their children to monastic schools. Religious institutions regained an important focus in people's lives and became a center for anti-government activity. A decade later the Dalai Lama told me that he thought that too many temples and monasteries were being built in Tibet, and that more resources should be spent on building schools instead. "It's wasteful to have so many people becoming monks and nuns," he noted, openly showing his desire to increase the decimated Tibetan population. "They should at least wait until they are older and have had a couple of kids."[9]

After land was returned to peasants in the wake of Hu Yaobang's visit to Tibet, living standards increased dramatically. According to government reports, the annual income rose from 127 yuan to 220 yuan between 1979 and 1982, an almost 200 percent increase.[10] Of course, as at least one scholar has pointed out, the rise in the standard of living was due mainly to the elimination of the taxes; actual output in 1984 compared to 1980 declined considerably.

> Some agrarian methods introduced earlier, such as irrigation works and machinery, decreased after the implementation of the reforms. In 1986, as compared to 1979, there was a seventy-four percent reduction in sales of fertilizer, with an equal percentage reduction in sales of farm machinery. Beyond an initial jump, the rise in the standard of living was very limited and, by 1987, the average rural annual income was only 361 yuan, which after adjustment for inflation (in Tibet one of the highest rates compared to China), actually represents a negative increase between 1985 and 1987. The return to traditional agrarian methods, while generally better for the population in comparison to the period under the communes, has in fact returned the rural areas to an almost subsistence level of living, not the goal of a progressive economic policy.[11]

As conditions improved, the Chinese were caught in a dilemma. They needed Tibetan leaders to help them transform Tibet, but the only Tibetan leaders loyal to the Chinese were conservative, poorly educated hard-liners. Many were Tibetan in name only. An example was Tian Bao, an ethnic Tibetan named in the late 1970s as chairman of the People's Government of the Tibetan Autonomous Region, placing him second in command of the territory. Born Sangye Yexe in a Tibetan area now part of Sichuan, he joined the Red Army with his brother in 1935 and took part in the Long March.

In 1992 the Dalai Lama told me that Tian Bao had accompanied him to a banquet during his visit to Beijing in the mid-1950s. Tian Bao became a bit tipsy, and when the Dalai Lama later showed him movies of Lhasa, Tian Bao placed his hands on the Dalai Lama's chair and made a religious sign. The Dalai Lama thought this showed that even a dyed-in-the-wool Communist such as Tian Bao retained some feelings of loyalty to his original Buddhist beliefs.[12] Clearly this was the message the Chinese hoped to convey when they appointed Tian Bao to office in Tibet. But as the Dalai Lama was quick to admit, Tian Bao was not the type to support the reform movement. He felt closer to the conservative Chinese military leaders stationed in this sensitive border region than to the progressive officials from Beijing.

The Panchen Lama was one of the few Tibetan leaders who could successfully act as a conduit to convey both the demands of the Tibetan people and the ideas of the Chinese government. After the Panchen had resurfaced in 1978, the Chinese dissident Wei Jingsheng reported that the harsh conditions of Chinese prison life had caused the Panchen Lama to attempt suicide.[13] Nevertheless the Panchen declared his loyalty to the new regime, and in 1980 the Chinese government named him vice-chairman of the National People's Congress. In this position he demanded the increased use of

the Tibetan language and of native Tibetan dress, but he refused to take a more forceful leadership role.

The Chinese expected the Tibetans to be grateful for Chinese
"help," but instead the Tibetans were resentful and their
growing demands increasingly drained Chinese resources. By
the mid-1980s the Chinese were growing concerned about
the vast sums of money they had spent in Tibet. A 1983 report claimed that the Chinese had expended 6.39 billion
yuan (close to $4 billion at that time) on Tibet, or about
1,400 yuan for every person in the country.[14] Even if this figure did not take into account the resources the Chinese were
taking from Tibet, by the mid-1980s the Chinese had become
aware that the occupation of Tibet was draining resources
that they desperately needed elsewhere. Rather than withdraw, however, the Chinese decided to pour in good money
after bad to increase production. In early 1984 the Chinese
government decided to undertake forty-three major new
projects in Tibet, most of which were designed to promote
tourism.

Because it lacked adequate numbers of qualified Tibetan
construction and tourism workers, the Chinese government
decided to allow Chinese immigrants into Tibet on a supposedly interim basis to help with these projects. The Law on
Regional Autonomy for Minority Nationalities of the People's Republic of China, adopted in 1984 at the second ses-
sion of the Sixth National People's Congress, expressed the
prevailing attitude.[15] Tibetans and other minority nationalities were "backward" and in order to develop needed the
help of "advanced nationalities" such as the Han.[16]

Nonetheless the Communists continued to try to ap-
pease the Tibetans. In 1985 the Chinese appointed Wu
Jinghua head of the Chinese Communist party and the real
powerbroker in Tibet. Wu belonged to the Yi ethnic group

that is closely related to that of the Tibetans. The Yis had experienced many of the same problems with Chinese cadres as had the Tibetans. Wu was a much more progressive official than Tian Bao or any of the other power holders previously in Tibet.

As soon as he assumed his role, Wu appeared in native Tibetan dress (earning the sobriquet the "lama secretary" from the hard-line Chinese cadres under him). During the next few months he appeared at religious ceremonies and even made donations to monks. He relabeled the streets of Lhasa using their old Tibetan names. He began far-reaching reforms to return local administration to the Tibetans, especially in rural areas, distributing large amounts of grain and other aid to alleviate hunger there. Wu tried to force all cadres, officials, and People's Liberation Army officers under fifty years of age to learn Tibetan, a language he himself did not speak.

Meanwhile, Tashi Tsering, the Tibetan academic who had returned from the United States, retired from the university and moved to the Barkhor, the giant bazaar in the middle of Lhasa. As a sign of the changing times, he became involved in a whole range of new enterprises, including setting up a private school to teach Tibetans English and working as an agent for a U.S. importer of Tibetan rugs and handicrafts.

With the exception of a few people like Tashi, the more power the Chinese put into Tibetan hands the more the frustrations of the Tibetans surfaced. Improving conditions in Tibet did not necessarily make Tibetans feel kindly toward the Chinese or the Chinese to feel comfortable around Tibetans. Chinese police and military officers resented being assigned to their lonely post far from home and were quick to quell any sign of a protest, often brutally and with little provocation. Tibetans reciprocated with anger and violence.

It became harder for progressive officials such as the

new Tibetan party leader Wu Jinghua to combat the conservative opposition that was spreading throughout China. By late 1986 conservatives feared that the economic and political reforms initiated by Hu Yaobang were weakening the party's—and their own—position and authority. Conservatives began to press for his overthrow, and their cause gained momentum in December and January when student demonstrations rocked China. The party removed Hu from his key leadership role, giving credence to rumors in Lhasa that Hu had been ousted at least in part because of his policies in Tibet.[17]

In September 1987 the Dalai Lama delivered a speech to the Human Rights Subcommittee of the United States Congress which was denounced by the Chinese media. Two Western observers close to the Tibetan Independence Movement and in Lhasa at the time, claim that "a rainbow over the Potala on September 25 and three earthquakes on September 26" led monks from the Sera monastery to consult an oracle who told them they "must demonstrate."[18] On September 27, 1987, a group of monks took to the streets of Lhasa in protest.

The Chinese authorities beat the demonstrators, incensing the population of Lhasa. In October another group of monks protested, and again the Chinese flailed and detained them. Thousands of Tibetans marched to denounce the police actions and demand that the monks be released. When protesters stormed a local police station to free the prisoners, the police opened fire and killed several marchers, creating a cause célèbre for the movement. Though it appeared that the incident would further ignite the explosive situation, both sides backed off temporarily.

But as long as Tibetans and Chinese lived side-by-side in the same country, it would prove extremely difficult to make peace. Recently the outspoken Chinese dissident, Wei Jingsheng, offered a personal analogy to illustrate the misunderstanding and antipathy between the two groups. When he fell in love with and tried to marry a Tibetan girl in his youth, Wei recounted, the idea horrified his parents and friends. And when his family finally consented, then *her* parents would not even consider the possibility of a Chinese son-in-law.

On June 15, 1988, with the situation between Chinese and Tibetans still tense, the Dalai Lama gave the speech to the European Parliament assembled in Strasbourg, France, that was to help him win the Nobel Peace Prize. The Dalai Lama told the delegates that he was willing to accept less than full independence for Tibet. Under his plan China would continue to control Tibet's foreign relations and to station troops in the area, and Tibet would still remain subject to de facto Chinese sovereignty. In what the press referred to as a "Hong Kong–style" solution, his plan also called for the creation of a democratic government in Tibet complete with its own bicameral legislature and independent legal system. The government would exercise control over the region's domestic affairs. The Dalai Lama stated his hope that Tibet could ultimately become a zone of peace.[19]

His was a noble effort. By stating publicly that he was willing to accept at least nominal Chinese sovereignty over his country, the Dalai Lama was making a genuine concession to Beijing. If accepted, his plan would have returned Tibet to a democratic version of its pre-1911 situation rather than to the complete independence the country enjoyed between 1912 and 1950. Nepal had declared itself a "zone of peace" in 1975. The Dalai Lama's proposal would have extended this sphere across the Himalayas.

Unfortunately his effort was too little, too late. By 1988 the Chinese faced other political crises and dismissed his proposal. So did Tibetan radicals excited by the new militarism they saw sweeping Tibet.[20] The pressure from Tibetan exile groups became so intense that the Dalai Lama backed away from his proposal for a while and partially repudiated it. In the following months the Chinese objected to the contention in the Dalai Lama's speech that Tibet had historically been an independent state that China had taken by force in 1950. And the Dalai Lama created obstacles for negotiations with the Chinese by insisting that a foreign lawyer remain associated with the proposed negotiating team.

Meanwhile, in China people grew uneasy about rampant inflation and a runaway economy and disgruntled with the political leaders unable to control the situation. A generation that thought itself unique clamored for a break with the old order.

Tibet led the way. On December 10, 1988, about thirty Tibetans, disappointed that an anticipated visit by the Dalai Lama had failed to come about, marched into the center of Lhasa to confront the authorities. Government spokesmen claimed that the police fired warning shots into the air to frighten the crowd, and a melée erupted. Foreigners who witnessed the incident reported that the Chinese police fired directly into a crowd of peaceful protesters. One person died and thirteen were injured, including a woman from the Netherlands. In an apparent attempt to justify the injury of a foreigner in this incident, the Chinese labeled her an agent of the Dalai Lama.[21]

The Chinese government also ousted Wu Jinghua and replaced him with Hu Jintao, a Chinese official with a take-charge attitude and a reputation as a reformer. Yet with conflicting orders from the central government, Hu Jintao proved just as indecisive as his predecessors.

This violent crackdown prompted even the Panchen Lama to speak up. Visiting Tibet in January 1989 he reportedly declared, "Chinese rule in Tibet has brought more destruction than benefit to the Tibetan people."[22] Shortly afterward the Panchen suffered a massive heart attack and died at the age of fifty-one while visiting Xigaze. Tibetans claimed that the Chinese poisoned him. This was an ironic charge concerning a man many Tibetans had previously labeled a Communist pawn and had belittled for marrying a Chinese woman and for succumbing to many secular pursuits. No evidence of the crime was offered, but suspicions grew in the volatile atmosphere.

The Panchen's death increased tensions in Lhasa. In February demonstrators flew their banned national flag over the city for the first time in thirty years. In the confused political atmosphere, the Chinese police peacefully stood by and watched, allowing the banner to remain in place for several hours. At about the same time, worried authorities banned the annual *Monlam* festival celebrations in Lhasa, fearful of another protest. Demonstrations continued into 1989 and grew more serious in late February and early March. As March 10 approached—the thirteenth anniversary of the failed Tibetan uprising and the subsequent flight of the Dalai Lama—monks and their supporters began to take to the streets.

On March 5 about forty people began a peaceful demonstration in front of the Jokhang temple in Lhasa. According to foreign observers, Chinese police watching from the roof pelted the demonstrators with empty beer bottles. A few angry protesters threw stones back at them. The police drew their guns and fired into the crowd, killing three people. About an hour later, a mob of angry students from Tibet University rushed into the city and drove the police out of the Tibetan quarter.

Over the next few days the demonstrations escalated. At least three times soldiers poured into the city, shooting wildly into the crowds. But when Tibetans pelted them with stones from the rooftops of neighboring buildings, the army retreated, giving the people a sense of victory and further inflaming their militancy. The crowds zeroed in on stores run by Chinese, pillaging them and forcing their owners to flee.

For a while it seemed that the demonstrators had "liberated" whole areas of the city. But the Tibetans were deluding themselves. With policy confused the Chinese troops did not know how tough they could be, but there was never any question about who really held the balance of power.

One exiled Chinese dissident has claimed that the Chinese response was even more cynical than it appeared. The former journalist Tang Daxian, who now lives in Paris, told the American reporter for the London-based *Observer,* Jonathan Mirsky, that agent provocateurs working under orders from Beijing actually began the demonstrations. Tang claims that on March 5 these agents, disguised as monks and ordinary civilians, burned down a prayer flag pole in Lhasa and led a raid on a government granary. This helped precipitate the conflict and gave authorities the chance to crack down.[23]

On March 7 Chinese Premier Li Peng imposed martial law in Lhasa. The next day more than two thousand soldiers entered the city and began arresting rioters. The Chinese dragged thousands of Tibetans from their homes and placed them under detention. Foreigners reported hundreds of casualties.

The Chinese government blamed the disturbances on a small number of conspirators whom they labeled "splitists." These splitists, the Chinese claimed, were egged on by foreign interests. Chinese Premier Li Peng spoke of "outrageous foreign interference" in the region. One of my students, Alex Day, who had been visiting Tibet that March, was trapped in a small hotel known as the Yak in the old Tibetan part of town while the fighting raged outside his door. After the army quelled the unrest, it ordered foreigners out of the area, charging tourists exorbitant fees for the transportation they forced them to take to return home. When Alex Day protested that the government was making a profit on his expulsion, the Chinese hauled him into a local police station and accused him of being one of the foreign splitists. When he showed them his student identification card to persuade them not to charge him the high tourist rate for travel, the Chinese police told him that student cards were valid only in China, not in Tibet!

Few Chinese proponents of democratic rights spoke out against the suppression of the Tibetans. Two notable exceptions were the 1987 dissident leader Fang Lizhi and the writer and philosopher Wang Ruowang. Most other leading intellectuals either supported the government's actions or refused to comment. On college campuses in Beijing, many of the students later to be active in the democratic movement argued that the Tibetans had provoked the government. The only solution, one claimed, was "to wipe out the Tibetan language and culture." Native Tibetans, another suggested, "are spiritualistic. It is our duty to develop them into materialists." Even Taiwanese spokesmen supported the Chinese government's quelling of the riots.

A few months later Chinese students realized their mistake. Chinese democratic demonstrations erupted after Hu Yaobang's death in April 1989. In June government tanks and guns crushed the demonstrators in Tiananmen Square. Chinese intellectuals realized that they had allowed the army to crush the Tibetans the way it was now crushing them. Many Chinese began to reevaluate the demands of the Tibetans. After 1989 it became common for Chinese dissidents in the West to share a platform with Tibetan leaders, and the two groups met and talked on a number of occasions. Differences remained, but a much greater understanding of each other's problems developed.

In the 1990s young, urban Chinese intellectuals are searching for a spirituality they feel they have lost and are expressing a new appreciation for Tibetan culture and ideas. Tibetan

Buddhism and many Tibetan writers are beginning to attract a cult following. Chinese artists paint and sculpt the "ethereal" Tibetans. At some avant-garde shows in Beijing in the late 1980s and early 1990s, the majority of pieces apparently displayed Tibetan themes. These works reflect a growing Chinese view of the Tibetans as their alter ego. Tibetans are still seen as spiritual and direct when the Chinese increasingly regard themselves as materialistic, logical, and opaque. Like the Chinese guide who accompanied my students to Lhasa, young Chinese marvel at the intensity of Tibetan devotion and the mystical nature of their society. The Chinese see themselves as a sophisticated people, yet they long to be primitive peasants enamored with religious values, as they picture the Tibetans in their patronizing stereotype of them.

In the wake of the Dalai Lama's 1989 receipt of the Nobel Peace Prize, Western interest in Tibet has also grown. Members of the award committee all but admitted that the Dalai Lama's prize was a slap at China for its massacre of democratic activists in Beijing.[24] The honor nonetheless made the world aware of Tibet. By the early 1990s an often zealous Tibetan support network existed in most major Western cities and even in many places in what was once the Soviet bloc.

In 1991 George Bush became the first American president to meet formally with the Dalai Lama; a few years later Bill Clinton became the second. In the spring of 1991 the United States launched a Tibetan-language service of the Voice of America. It also made Tibet an issue in U.S.-Chinese trade negotiations.

Scientists are giving more credence to fears that the Chinese environmental devastation of Tibet is creating climatic change around the world. As noted earlier, every major river in east Asia, Southeast Asia, and south Asia originates in Tibet. These rivers ultimately filter into the lands and seas of the world's most populous and fertile region. By the 1990s some scientists argued that "the frequent and devastating landslides and floods in Nepal, North-eastern India, Bangladesh, Burma and China" are due "to the massive deforestation in Tibet."[25] A more modest study pointed out that more than 65 percent of China's medicinal herbs grow only in Tibet and mostly in forested areas,[26] and that the Chinese slashing of these forests places these resources at risk.

In the late 1980s the Dalai Lama outlined a five-point peace program that emphasized clearing nuclear missiles and nuclear wastes from the region (the Chinese have stationed some in Qinghai) and turning it into a "zone of ahmisa (peace and nonviolence)."[27] By 1990 the Dalai Lama proposed turning Tibet into "the planet's largest natural preserve."[28] He has accused the Chinese of wantonly cutting the once vast Tibetan forests, stripmining the soil, overgrazing the plains, and using agricultural pesticides and chemical fertilizers that have destroyed the delicate ecology of his country.

At the 1992 Earth Summit in Rio de Janeiro, the Dalai Lama pointed out that as early as the seventeenth century Tibetans "began enacting decrees to protect the environment."[29] He envisioned a country whose people could return to the simple life of their ancestors. The Dalai Lama's ideas may have sounded naive, but other Tibetan leaders shared them. Before his death the Panchen Lama voiced similar concerns, condemning Chinese efforts to build a hydroelectric plant on Yamdrok Lake to supply electricity to Lhasa.

Yamdrok Lake is one of Tibet's most sacred bodies of water. The road to the lake from Lhasa climbs through gorgeous alpine scenery and through herds of yaks, donkeys, and sheep. Rock and snow avalanches usually block the road, which perpetually needs repair. Frequent hairpin turns on what is often just an icy, narrow dirt path often terrify travelers. Then suddenly from a summit comes a glimpse of the lake's tranquil, turquoise waters. On this peak Tibetan pilgrims have placed prayer flags and cairns, enhancing the exotic beauty of the scene.

When my students and I reached this site, I stood in the rarefied air gasping for breath while admiring the lake's pristine beauty. I was amazed that our driver and guide pulled out cigarettes and smoked them, oblivious to the effects of the altitude. Next to our bus several of my students were suffering from altitude sickness, while those who had struggled over to look at the lake with me were sweating from the effort.

Later we ate lunch on the cold, sunny shores of the lake while a nomad woman watched. My students gathered up our trash, but our guide threw the plastic containers and glass bottles out of the bus onto the ground, where the nomad woman gratefully collected them.

If the Chinese have their way, however, the fate of Yamdrok Lake, one of the largest freshwater bodies of water in the Himalayas, may be grim. The Chinese plan to blast through the mountains from the "life-power lake" down to the Yarlong River, to create a drain tunnel along the lake bottom that would generate hydroelectric power. This probably would destroy the watershed around the lake, muddy the lake's water, and possibly even deplete it altogether in fifty years. The Panchen Lama's opposition to the project forced the Chinese to suspend construction of the hydroelectric facility in 1986. But after the death of the Panchen Lama in 1989, the Chinese ignored an international campaign against it and resumed work on the plant.

In 1991 China responded to some of this worldwide criticism by announcing its plans to make the Qiangtang (Changtang) or "Northern Wilderness" into one of the world's largest wildlife reserves. The region encompasses approximately 800,000 square kilometers in northwestern Tibet. It is home to many endangered species, including snow leopards, golden-haired monkeys, blue sheep, and wild donkeys.[30]

The Chinese have also stopped trying to force the Tibetans to adopt inappropriately intensive methods of raising livestock, permitting the return to a more environmentally responsible and productive system of animal husbandry. A recent study by two prominent American anthropologists has noted that nomad groups have reverted to old patterns of herd management, moving yaks and sheep back and forth between high and low pastures depending on the condition of the soil and the time of the year.[31]

These remedial efforts do little to stop the Han laborers streaming into the country in increasing numbers, radically altering the population and delicate environmental balance of Tibet. As the cultural patterns of the rice- and wheat-eating Han become predominant in Tibet, the barley-growing Tibetan peasants and nomadic Tibetan herders will inevitably be forced aside.

In 1984 the first group of Chinese workers was scheduled to leave when the large-scale government construction projects ended. Instead, after 1985 the growing number of tourists created a need for more Chinese guides, drivers, and mechanics. Migrant workers followed to build Chinese restaurants catering to their countrymen's needs. Han beggars, peddlers, rickshaw drivers, carpenters, and other tradespeople soon flooded the streets of Tibetan towns. By 1989 reports estimated that seventy thousand to eighty thousand Han lived in Lhasa alone, turning the town into a Chinese city. This huge number of immigrants has placed great pressure on agriculture and transportation facilities, threatening the fragile ecostructure as well as Tibetan culture.

A 1989 article referred to Tibet as the new Chinese "Wild West frontier." Han entrepreneurs and adventurers "see the Tibetans as filthy, backward and superstitious—but loaded with money. They hawk their wares or scheme like mad to get what money they can get out of the Tibetans. They neither understand nor care for Tibetan culture or society."[32] Although they live in Tibet, the Chinese do not live with the Tibetans. A recent study has confirmed what observers have long maintained—that there is almost no social interaction between Chinese and Tibetans living in Lhasa.[33] The Han settlers threaten to overwhelm the country and to eliminate Tibetan society, as they have already done in large parts of Kham and Amdo.

In an attempt to show their concern for Tibetans, Chinese authorities have instituted an affirmative-action policy to promote Tibetans into desirable jobs. This often comes at the expense of more experienced and qualified Chinese who have been working for longer periods of time. The Tibetans now earn more for government or education work than their Chinese counterparts in China as well as in Tibet. At the Minorities School in Beijing, for instance, Tibetan teachers are paid considerably more than their Chinese colleagues. Yet affirmative action has not helped many Tibetans, because only a small number want these public-sector jobs, which pay less than jobs in the private sector. The affirmative action policy has not prevented the Han from owning and running most stores and businesses in Lhasa and other cities in Tibet. Thus the Tibetans are not only being overwhelmed by vast numbers of Han moving into their country, they are also being economically deprived by skilled, well-financed Han entrepreneurs and workers. And the few Tibetans in public-sector jobs suffer resentment from those Chinese who are demoted or denied a promotion.

To raise the educational level of Tibetans, the Chinese have tried to compel Tibetan university graduates to become teachers. These Tibetan graduates resent being sent to primitive rural towns to teach children while their Chinese colleagues monopolize lucrative jobs in Lhasa such as those of tourist guides. The few native Tibetans who do become guides are generally only middle-school graduates who have taken night courses or have visited Dharamsala to qualify.

Because these guides are trained less then their Chinese counterparts, they appear to compare unfavorably. This rein-
forces the negative stereotype the Chinese have of Tibetan
abilities.

In spite of such efforts, the educational level of Tibetans
remains abysmal. There are so few teachers of the Tibetan
language that in the mid-1990s only 6 percent of Tibetan
students could take Tibetan language classes. Tibetan students study their native literature during the period in which
students in standard Chinese schools learn English. This
leaves Tibetans at a disadvantage when they enter the university, as a knowledge of English is often required for many
classes. Tibetans also struggle in businesses such as tourism,
in which contact with English-speaking foreigners is frequent. Moreover, because Tibetans have trouble keeping up
with Chinese students in Chinese classes throughout the
country, Tibetans find it more difficult even to earn admission to college.

The Chinese have tried to compensate for some of these
problems by giving Tibetans special preference on national
exams. But Tibetans do not appreciate this advantage because the Chinese have also given similar treatment to the
Han who live in Lhasa. Indeed, Chinese working in Tibet receive hardship pay. And while the Chinese have developed a
program to send promising Tibetan youths to China to
study, these students come back with a good Chinese education but little knowledge of their own culture.

These contradictions and conflicts are only the beginning. The more contact the Chinese and the Tibetans have
with each other under Chinese rule opposed by the Tibetans,
the more the two groups learn to distrust and dislike each
other. As the Han population increases in central Tibet, Tibetans worry that their culture will become extinct even in
their own heartland. They need look no further than eastern
Tibet to see the horrors the future may hold. What was once

Amdo has already been turned into Qinghai province, an area with a ratio of approximately three Chinese to one Tibetan, or 2.5 million Chinese to 800,000 Tibetans.[34] Similar figures probably hold for the area of Kham that is now part of Sichuan.

In 1990 approximately 2 million Tibetans lived in the Tibetan Autonomous Region (the figures vary from 1.8 million to 2.19 million). Tibetan sources estimate that the Chinese population in the region already almost equaled the Tibetan. The Han have concentrated mainly in Lhasa, Xigaze, and the major cities, where they have constituted the majority of inhabitants.[35]

The Chinese government disputes these figures, claiming the Han population of the TAR to be only 81,000 or about 3.7 percent of the total population of 2.19 million people.[36] Chinese figures pointedly omit the estimated 150,000 to 250,000 soldiers in the area as well as their support and administrative staffs and families. Troop figures are also open to question; one recent source has dubiously claimed that only 40,000 Chinese soldiers are stationed in the region, not the higher number other observers have noted.[37] More important, Chinese statistics do not include the vast numbers of unregistered laborers who have flooded Tibetan cities in recent years.

In small numbers, immigrants might be welcomed. In historical times Chinese, Indian, Persian, and Mongol immigrants made major contributions to Tibetan society. In 1992 the Dalai Lama suggested to me that even recent Chinese immigrants could become Tibetan if they learned the language and assimilated the culture. He cited the example of a Chinese monk, now deceased, who entered a Tibetan monastery and ended up thinking and writing more like a Tibetan than most Tibetans.[38] With the Chinese flooding their country, however, few Tibetans can be as sanguine about this possibility as the Dalai Lama appeared to be.

Native Tibetans fear that the Chinese are systematically exterminating their population. Some have made wildly sensational charges, for example that the Chinese routinely kidnap Tibetans to drain their blood to supply hospitals in Beijing. Tibetans claim the Chinese have instituted a rigid birth-control policy that has forced women at term to have abortions. The Tibetan government-in-exile in Dharamsala states: "The ferocity with which Tibetan women and even the young girls are subjected to forced sterilization and compulsory abortions leaves us with no doubt as to the motives of the Chinese government: to slowly annihilate the Tibetan race."[39]

Some of these charges are open to question. In Qinghai and in Sichuan, as in the rest of China, the Chinese have instituted a birth-control policy that allows only one child per family. This has resulted in a restrictive birth-control policy in Kham and Amdo. But the Chinese have applied the policy much more leniently to the Tibetans and other so-called minority groups than they have to Han Chinese. Reports even from the government-in-exile in Dharamsala indicate that in the early 1990s Tibetans in eastern Tibet were not subject to punishment unless they had two children.[40]

In the TAR itself, both Judith Banister of the U.S. Census Bureau[41] and Susan Greenhaigh of the Population Council[42] found that birth restrictions on the population are limited. Two American anthropologists—in a study bitterly denounced by some pro-Tibetan groups—found virtually no birth-control restrictions on Tibetans outside of Lhasa. The scholars' research shows that contrary to what exile groups claim, the Tibetan population is growing at a very rapid rate.[43] In Lhasa they discovered that Tibetan cadres have been limited to two children per family while the Han have been restricted to one child per family. Furthermore the American researchers noted that the Chinese government could apply only economic penalties against Tibetan official

families who had more than one child. In 1990 the government announced that it would apply the same two-children-
per-family policy to ordinary Tibetans in Lhasa as well. But
as of the mid-1990s the Chinese had made no effort to institute this policy aside from providing easy access to birth control and abortions.

Ironically the fear and anger Tibetans voice in response
to perceived Chinese efforts to expunge their culture and
race are echoed by Indian resentment of Tibetan encroach-
ment on their country. This bitterness has developed in spite
of the fact that the Indians have no cause to fear they will be
overwhelmed by the Tibetans. In 1994, after a Tibetan
stabbed an Indian youth to death in a fight over a televised
cricket match, violence burst out against the Tibetan population in Dharamsala.

During the Indian youth's funeral, a right-wing Hindu
politician yanked the shroud off the corpse, reached into the
cadaver's open stomach, pulled out a length of intestine, and
held it high. "This is what the Tibetans have done!" he cried,
causing the mourners to rampage. Shouting "Death to the
Dalai Lama!" and "Long Live Deng Xiaoping!" the mob
stormed the compound of the Tibetan government-in-exile,
smashing windows, setting fires, and destroying furniture.
The mob then looted Tibetan shops and beat up refugees. In
the following days, pamphlets threatening to murder Tibetans appeared as did a petition calling for the Dalai Lama
and Tibetans to get out of India. For a while tension ran so
high that the Dalai Lama began to speak of moving his government-in-exile to another location.[44]

This kind of ethnic conflict has flared in other parts of
the region as well. In neighboring Bhutan the Tibetan-related
population is actively threatening Hindu immigrants. Bhutan
has enacted punitive and discriminatory laws to prevent Hindus from Nepal from entering Tibet and overwhelming its
native population. In 1990 eighty thousand terrified

Nepalese fled Bhutan, and the Bhutanese refused to take them back.

Yet while the Tibetans dislike the Chinese and want them to leave, many Tibetans act as if they need the intruders. As the Dalai Lama has pointed out, "Tibetans owning vegetable gardens lease them out to Chinese settlers. Also, despite the availability of Tibetan tailors and carpenters, people employ Chinese for reasons of convenience."[45]

These contradictions within the Tibetan community have made it easier for the Chinese to enact a radical immigration policy. In 1992 the Chinese promoted Hu Jintao, the man who became the chief official of Tibet in 1989, to the Standing Committee of the Politburo of the Chinese Communist party. Chen Kuiyuan replaced Hu Jintao in Tibet. Chen has opened Tibet's door to migrant laborers and entrepreneurs from the rest of China. And he has begun a bold new economic program.

In 1992 Chinese authorities announced a plan to open Tibet to outside investment. They completed a major expansion of the Lhasa airport and extended air links from Lhasa to Beijing, Katmandu, and Hong Kong. To promote foreign investment from the rich Tibetan expatriate community, the Chinese also planned to turn an area near the Tibetan-Nepal border into a free economic zone. In 1993 the government approved forty-one joint-partner enterprises with foreign countries, mostly with Nepal but also with nations such as Germany and Malaysia. A number of export enterprises grew, mostly specializing in traditional handicrafts such as rugs. By 1994 the Tibet Trust and Investment Company had become the first Tibetan company whose shares are traded on the Shanghai Stock Exchange.

Han entrepreneurs pioneered many of these investments, opening most of the restaurants and businesses that have blossomed throughout Tibet. Chinese businessmen and manufacturers have even copied traditional Tibetan handicrafts and begun to mass-produce them. Economic growth has augmented the physical development of Tibet and has improved the well-being of the Tibetan population. But older Tibetans have grown alarmed as they see Chinese stores replace traditional Tibetan buildings in Lhasa and Tibetan youths substitute blue jeans and video games for traditional dress and Buddhist prayer services.

Some young urban Tibetans have begun to talk openly about creating a compromise situation to bridge the differences that divide the Tibetans and Chinese. These intellectuals believe that Tibet is so economically interwoven with China that a split would be disastrous. Many have spent so much time learning about China and studying Chinese that they have developed a vested interest in retaining a relationship with the Middle Kingdom. Many of these scholars applauded the Dalai Lama's willingness to accept less than total independence for Tibet, while the Chinese derided his efforts until the mid-1990s.

By 1993 the Dalai Lama had stated forthrightly that his goal was autonomy, not independence. "We are talking of a middle way—one country with two systems," he explained.[46] The Dalai Lama has also suggested that he might be the last Dalai Lama, or if others succeed him, they should be elected and even subject to impeachment. In spite of these statements, or perhaps because of the ones implying the need for democracy, the Chinese have continued to belittle the Dalai Lama and his supporters.

Nonetheless Tibetan academics such as Tashi Tsering have shown how and where cooperation can occur between Chinese and Tibetans. Tashi has persuaded the Chinese government to allow him to use profits from his businesses in Lhasa to build Tibetan schools in his native village. His goal in this tiny, remote community is simple. As he says, it is "nothing fancy, just to combat illiteracy."[47] The teachers at his school are high-school graduates who did not pass their college entrance exams. Tashi believes that only when people become literate can they break their unending cycle of poverty and gain power for themselves. He hopes his school will foster many such efforts.

As Tashi's story illustrates, the Chinese occupation of Tibet, however unwanted and oppressive, has given well-educated Tibetans with whom the Chinese feel comfortable the opportunity to work within the system to help their people and themselves. But it is a limited effort. Tashi's cooperation with the Chinese government has been resented in some circles. Tibetan students gutted his apartment during the 1989 demonstrations, though the Dalai Lama told me that he approved of what Tashi had been doing.[48] Moreover, Tashi has had to pay personally for the schools the government has failed to establish. People such as Tashi are an exception to the rule as few Tibetans have the resources, education, and temperament to accomplish what he has.

By mid-1995 it appeared that efforts at compromise might be breaking down. The Dalai Lama announced that his search teams had found a new child incarnation for the Panchen Lama in Tibet. The Chinese government refused to recognize the choice and angrily denounced the Dalai Lama, leading to the very real possibility that in the future there might be two rival candidates for this office and a further fracturing of Tibetan unity.

No kind of compromise can really work as long as the leaders of China justify their power with the myth that they have created a "Greater China." They have encouraged China's still largely peasant population to look back to the time of their grandparents, when they believe China under the Qing was a vast world empire. Chinese officials console themselves amid disruptive and confusing change by evoking a mythical past (which they claim they are reestablishing) when their countrymen marched across the continent fighting heroic battles and conquering strange lands. As Tibet's borderland yields to Han culture, the Chinese believe it proves the superiority of their society and justifies the changes that upset people's lives. As a result, China's leaders cling to the idea of controlling Tibet. They fear that if they relinquish the region, it will shatter the myth that they deserve power because they are making their country great. Yet Tibet is not China. Building a nation on the premise of restoring a fictitious great state and culture is building a nation on a fragile foundation.

Yet the question remains whether Tibet's fate should differ from those of other independent central Asian and Himalayan states that in the past two centuries have been overtaken by their larger and more powerful neighbors. While before 1950 Tibet was an independent state, it was not a modern state. The Chinese made their conquest just as other imperialist states have been making theirs for hundreds of years.

Nevertheless, Tibet has a longer and certainly grander history than those of most of these other states. The ferocity with which Tibetans have continued to proclaim their independence and the way Tibet has caught the imagination of the world demonstrate that Tibet should and probably will be independent some day. For if the history of the twentieth century is the story of small states being absorbed by large ones, then the history of the 1990s seems to be the story of these small states again becoming independent—to the surprise of a world that had forgotten them. China does not need Tibet, and if the Tibetans are lucky the Chinese will finally acknowledge that Tibet has become a huge and nonessential economic drain on China.

Perhaps then Tibet's economy will produce its destiny. Throughout history the Tibetan government united when the trade routes through central Asia provided the possibility of unified economic activity. When these routes were disrupted or blocked by the Chinese, Tibetans were at their mercy. China occupied Tibet when travel through central Asia was essentially closed. In the 1990s the Soviet Union has disintegrated and central Asia has reopened.

As of 1995 plans are under way for the construction of a new central Asian railroad. Already rumors suggest that a future struggle for power in Beijing may undermine the pretense to power that has held the Chinese state together, and may lead to calls for more provincial autonomy. Under these circumstances, Tibet could split off from China in combination with a massive uprising in Xinjiang, China's largely Muslim northwestern province that might receive aid from its central Asian relatives. Many of the Chinese who have emigrated to Tibet in such large numbers are Muslim Chinese, not Han Chinese. Their brethren have long been marching out of central Asia to join the Tibetans, and might merge again. Should this occur, relationships that have long been assumed dead might revive and help to restore Tibet.

If Tibet remains part of China, it will be overwhelmed. The Tibetan population will be reduced to a historical minority whose past is put on display solely for the benefit of tourists or students. This has already happened in much of Qinghai province and even in the Chinese hotels in Lhasa. Unless the large influx of Han immigrants stops soon, it will erase the remaining traces of Tibetan life.

At the turn of the century the Japanese Buddhist Ekai Kawaguchi spent two years in Tibet disguised as a Chinese monk. "The Chinese government," he noted, "appears mortified to see Tibet endeavoring to break off her traditional relation with China and to attach herself to Russia."[49] Kawaguchi also observed that the Chinese were anxious that the Nepalese "seem to cast their longing glances towards Tibet as the best field for their superfluous population; for

Tibet, while possessing an area about twelve-fold that of Nepal, is far more thinly populated."[50]

In the 1990s the Chinese are carrying out precisely what they worried the Nepalese would. They have flooded Tibet with their own people, who threaten to reduce the Tibetans to a colorful but submissive minority in their own land. But it is not inevitable that the Chinese will succeed. By the end of the next century the idea that the Chinese could dominate Tibet may seem as absurd as Kawaguchi's claim a hundred years ago that the Nepalese might do the same. Then both Tibet and China will be free to proceed along their own paths in their own ways.

Notes

FOREWORD

1. *New York Times* readers were similarly enthralled. His story, which was later made into a book, ran in the magazine section every Sunday for more than two months.

1. IMAGES AND REALITIES

1. See Peter Bishop, *The Myth of Shangri-La: Tibet, Travel Writing and the Western Creation of the Sacred Landscape* (Berkeley, 1989) for a discussion.

2. Melvyn C. Goldstein and Cynthia M. Beall, *Nomads of Western Tibet: The Survival of a Way of Life* (Berkeley, 1990), p. 46.

3. *Ibid.,* p. 46.

4. Schuyler Cammann, *Trade Through the Himalayas: The Early British Attempts to Open Tibet* (Princeton, 1951), p. 3.

5. For a cogent discussion, see Peter Molnar, "The Geologic History and Structure of the Himalayas," *American Scientist* 74, no. 2 (April 1986), 144–154.

6. Nigel Harris, "Tibet: Continents in Collision," *New Scientist,* December 9, 1989.

7. The Andes have also been rising rapidly and are said to have contributed to this phenomenon. See Maureen E. Raymo, William F. Ruddiman, and Philip N. Froelich, "Influence of Late Cenozoic Mountain Building on Ocean Geochemical Cycles," *Geology* 16, July 1988, 649–653.

8. Part of this argument was summarized in "Theory on a Plateau and the Climate Gains," *New York Times,* November 3, 1992, p. C4.

9. For a discussion of this, see M. E. Raymo, "Geochemical Evidence Supporting T. C. Chamberlin's Theory of Glaciation," *Geology* 19, April 1991, 344–347.

10. B. Dey, S. N. Kaythuria, and Osru Bhanu Kumar, "Himalayan Summer Snow Cover and Withdrawal of the Indian Summer Monsoon," *Journal of Climate and Applied Meteorology* 24, August 1985, 865–868.

11. Many other writers have used similar images to describe the medley of Tibetan types that crowd into Lhasa. See especially John F. Avedon, *In Exile from the Land of Snows* (New York, 1979), Chapter 1. See pp. 17–18 in the 1968 edition. A similar description can be found in Michael Buckley and Robert Strauss, *Tibet: A Survival Kit* (Berkeley, 1986), p. 29.

12. Christopher Beckwith, *The Tibetan Empire in Central Asia* (Princeton, 1987), p. 6.

13. Clements R. Markham, ed., *Narratives of the Mission of George Bogle to Tibet and of the Journey of Thomas Manning to Lhasa* (New Delhi, 1971), p. 69.

14. Rosemary Jones Tung, *A Portrait of Lost Tibet* (New York, 1980), p. 24. The photo is still on display at Taliesin, Wright's former winter residence.

15. Joseph Wolff, *Travels and Adventures* (London, 1860).

16. Thomas Torrance, "The Basic Spiritual Conceptions of the Religion of the Chiang," *Journal of the North China Branch of the Royal Asiatic Society* 6 (1933), 31. Thomas Torrance was a Christian missionary who began to work with the Qiang around 1915. His argument is made in his book, *China's First Missionaries* (London, 1937), and in earlier articles.

17. Rabbi E. Avichail and his Amishav Institute are preparing a book to support his case. However absurd some of these ideas seem, it is undoubtedly true that Jewish traders have long had contact with both China and Tibet. No doubt descendants and influences from some of these people remain in the area.

18. The Nazis even made a propaganda movie about one of these expeditions to Tibet, "The Enigma of Tibet." Mosse reports incorrectly that the expedition never got off the ground. George L. Mosse, *Towards the Final Solution: A History of European Racism* (Madison, 1978), p. 43. A few eccentric references to the Nazi interest and association with Tibet are found in Louis Paumels and Jacques Bergres, *The Morning of the Magicians* (New York, 1964), pp. 197–198.

19. Marco Polo, *The Travels of Marco Polo* (New York, n.d.), p. 97.

20. John MacGregor, *Tibet: A Chronicle of Exploration* (New York, 1970), p. 15.

21. *Ibid.*, p. 43.

22. G. W. Houston, "Jesus and His Missionaries in Tibet," *Tibet Journal* 16, no. 4 (Winter 1991), 9.

23. *Ibid.*, p. 14.

24. See Bishop, *Myth of Shangri-La*, for a discussion of this.

25. Harold Isaacs first discussed this dualism in his book *Scratches on Our Minds* (New York, 1958). For a more recent exposition, see Steven W. Mosher, *China Misperceived* (New York, 1990), especially Chapter 1.

26. Bishop, *Myth of Shangri-La*, p. 63.

27. G. Rawlinson, *The History of Herodotus* (New York, 1889), II, 407–410.

28. Father Fracensco Orazio Della Penna Di Billi, "Brief Account of the Kingdom of Tibet," in Markham, *Narratives*, p. 316.

29. George Bogle in Markham, *Narratives*, p. 165.

30. Cited in Alastair Lamb, *British India and Tibet, 1766–1910* (New York, 1986), p. 28.

31. Bishop, *Myth of Shangri-La*, p. 143.

32. Arthur Conan Doyle, "The Adventure of the Empty House," in Christopher Morley, ed., *Sherlock Holmes and Dr. Watson* (New York, 1944), p. 294.

33. *Ibid.*, p. 239.

34. Chanakya Sen, ed., *Tibet Disappears: A Documentary History of Tibet's International Status* (New York, 1960), p. 361.

2. THE FIRST TIBETAN DOMINION

1. William McGovern, *To Lhasa in Disguise* (New York, 1924), pp. 230–231.

2. *Ibid.*, p. 231.

3. See Beckwith's fascinating essay discussing this in *Tibetan Empire*, epilogue, pp. 173–202.

4. *Ibid.*

5. *Ibid.*

6. See the bibliographical essay in Beckwith, *Tibetan Empire*, pp. 229–243.

7. See, for instance, John K. Fairbanks, Edwin O. Reischauer, and Altert Craig, *East Asia: Tradition and Transformation* (Boston, 1989), p. 98.

8. For the dramatic story of the rescue of the rescuer of these documents, see Jeannette Mirsky, *Sir Aurel Stein: Archaeological Explorer* (Chicago, 1977), especially pp. 265–280.

9. Lately, as part of their efforts to prove that Tibet belongs to China, the Chinese have acknowledged their links to the Qiang. They have even begun to use DNA samplings to prove that they and the Tibetan people are biologically related and therefore that Tibet is part of China. It is a ridiculous leap in logic. If all groups with similar DNA samplings were part of the same nation, China could claim to control much of East Asia and the Europeans would still have a share of the Americas.

10. See the discussion in Beckwith, *Tibetan Empire*, p. 6. An interesting discussion of Tibetan origins, particularly the relationship between the Tibetans and various Central Asian groups, can be found in P. T. Tukla, "The Origins of Relations Between Tibet and Other Countries in Central Asia, 1," *Common Voice: Journal of the Allied Committee of the Peoples of Eastern Turkestan, Mongolia, Manchuria and Tibet Presently Under China 1,* 1986.

11. *Ancient Tibet: Research Materials from the Yeshe De Project* (Berkeley, 1986), p. 282.

12. *Ibid.,* p. 111–112, especially notes 6 and 7.

13. As quoted in Michel Peissel, *Cavaliers of Kham: The Secret War in Tibet* (London, 1972), p. 4.

14. For a discussion of the traditional Chinese view of Songtsen Gampo, especially his marriage to the Chinese princess, see Ren Naiqiang, "Srong-Btsan Sgam-po: A Chronology," *Tibet Studies* 2, 1989, 1–28. This article, based on Tang sources and originally published in 1981, notes that Songtsen Gampo was quite old when his bride finally arrived, and that she may not have been intended for him in the first place. A second more recent article in the same journal disputes many of the findings of this piece. See Pasang Wangdu, "Doubts on 'Srong-btsan sgam-po: A Chronology,' " pp. 28–37.

15. This argument has been advanced by Giuseppe Tucci in "The Wives of Srong btsan sgam po," *Oriens Extremus* 9, 1962, 121–130. Some sources say the brides were initially given to Songtsen Gampo's son and that it was only after the son died that the father himself wedded the two women. There is also some dispute about whether the Nepali wife actually existed, though few non-Chinese sources support this contention, which doesn't make much difference in any case.

16. Namkhai Norbu, *The Necklace of gZi: A Cultural History of Tibet* (Dharamsala, 1981), pp. 8–12.

17. For a description of the manufacturing process, see Paul J. Smith, *Taxing Heaven's Storehouse: Horses, Bureaucrats, and the Destruction of the Sichuan Tea Industry, 1074–1224* (Cambridge, Mass., 1991), pp. 60–63.

18. F. Spencer Chapman, *Lhasa: The Holy City* (London, 1938), p. 52.

19. *Ibid.*

20. McGovern, *To Lhasa in Disguise*, p. 207.

21. *Ibid.,* p. 208.

22. *Ancient Tibet*, p. 232.

23. *Ibid.*

24. Helmut Hoffman, "Early and Medieval Tibet," in Denis Sinor, ed., *The Cambridge History of Early Inner Asia* (Cambridge, England, 1990), pp. 383–384.

25. Erik Haarh, "The Identity of Tsu-chih-chien, the Tibetan 'King' Who Died in 804 AD," *Acta Orientalia* 25, no. 1–2 (1963), 121–170.

26. Charles Allen, *A Mountain in Tibet* (London, 1982), p. 14.

27. Ekai Kawaguchi, *Three Years in Tibet* (London, 1909), pp. 140–141.

28. This is described in Buckley and Strauss, *Tibet,* p. 248.

29. As quoted in Allen, *Mountain in Tibet,* p. 27.

30. *Ibid.,* pp. 29–30.

31. Beckwith, *Tibetan Empire,* pp. 182–183.

32. *Ibid.,* p. 183.

33. McGovern, *To Lhasa in Disguise,* p. 114.

34. David Snellgrove and Hugh Richardson, *A Cultural History of Tibet* (New York, 1968), p. 93.

35. Chapman, *Lhasa,* p. 307.

36. See Morris Rossabi, "Introduction," in Rossabi, ed., *China Among Equals: The Middle Kingdom and Its Neighbors, 10th–14th Centuries* (Berkeley, 1983), p. 9.

37. Chapman, *Lhasa,* p. 195.

38. Luciano Petech, "Tibetan Relations with Sung China and with the Mongols," in Rossabi, *China Among Equals,* p. 177.

39. Stephen Batchelor, *The Jewel in the Lotus* (London, 1987), p. 58.

40. Chapman, *Lhasa,* pp. 196–197.

41. *Ibid.*

3. TIBETANS, MONGOLS, AND MANCHUS

1. Giuseppe Tucci, *Tibet* (New York, 1967), p. 33.

2. Petech, "Tibetan Relations," pp. 179–181.

3. Tsepon W. D. Shakabpa, *Tibet: A Political History* (New Haven, 1967), p. 62.

4. *Ibid.*

5. C. W. Cassinelli and Robert B. Ekvall, *A Tibetan Principality: The Political System of Sa sKya* (Ithaca, 1969), p. 191.

6. *Ibid.,* pp. 16, 41.

7. H. Franke, "Tibetans in Yuan China," in J. Langlois, ed., *China Under Mongol Rule* (Princeton, 1981), pp. 306–310.

8. Jeffrey Shoening, "The Religious Structure at Sa-skya," in Lawrence Epstein and Richard Sherburne, eds., *Reflections on Tibetan Culture: Essays in Memory of Turrell V. Wylie* (Lewiston, N.Y., 1990), p. 11.

9. Wang Yao, "Fragments from Historical Records About the Life of Emperor Gongdi of the Song Dynasty," *Tibet Studies* 1, 1989, 24–39. This article tries to examine the story from both the Chinese and Tibetan sides.

10. Ray Huang, *China: A Macro History* (Armonk, N.Y., 1990), p. 145.

11. Franke, "Tibetans," p. 303.

12. Morris Rossabi, *Khubilai Khan: His Life and Times* (Berkeley, 1988), pp. 154–160.

13. Nicholas Poppe, *The Mongolian Monuments in Hp'ags-pa Script* (Wiesbaden, 1957).

14. Franke, "Tibetans," p. 309.

15. There has been a question in the minds of some scholars as to whether Sangko was Tibetan or part Tibetan, but that seems to have been cleared up by Rin-chen Bkra in "Seng-ge—A Tibetan Prime Minister of the Yuan Dynasty," *Tibet Studies* 1, 1989, 50–61.

16. Luciano Petech, "Sang-ko: A Tibetan Statesman in Yuan China," *Acta Orientalia* 34, 1980, 193–208. See also Rossabi, *Khubilai Khan*, pp. 192–199.

17. Franke, "Tibetans," p. 313.

18. Sven Hedin, *Central Asia and Tibet: Towards the Holy City of Lassa* (New York, 1903), I, 33.

19. Buckley and Strauss, *Tibet*, p. 203.

20. *Ibid.*, p. 227.

21. *Ibid.*, p. 244.

22. Hugh Richardson, *Tibet and Its History* (Boston, 1984), p. 37.

23. McGovern, *To Lhasa in Disguise*, p. 141.

24. Fosco Mariani, *Secret Tibet* (New York, 1952), p. 204.

25. W. W. Rockhill, *The Land of the Lamas* (New York, 1891), p. 217.

26. Chapman, *Lhasa*, pp. 294–295.

27. Richardson, *Tibet and Its History*, p. 37.

28. For a translation and comparison of the two basic stories of Tsongkhapa's life, see Marion H. Duncan, *Customs and Superstitions of Tibet* (London, 1964), pp. 251–256.

29. Chapman, *Lhasa*, p. 195.

30. Tucci, *Tibet*, pp. 33–34.

31. Vincent Chan, *Tibet: A Handbook* (Chico, Calif., 1994), p. 822.

32. Snellgrove and Richardson, *Cultural History of Tibet*, p. 182.

33. Shakabpa, *Tibet*, p. 95.

34. Chapman, *Lhasa*, p. 171.

35. Kawaguchi, *Three Years*, p. 286.

36. Chapman, *Lhasa*, p. 171.

37. Chapman, *Lhasa*, pp. 174–175.

38. Duncan, *Customs and Superstitions*, pp. 15–16.

39. Heinrich Harrier, *Seven Years in Tibet* (London, 1953), p. 164.

40. *Ibid.*, p. 126.

41. See Shakabpa, *Tibet,* pp. 114–117.

42. *Ibid.,* p. 114.

43. Richardson, *Tibet and Its History,* p. 47.

44. Rossabi, " 'Decline' of the Central Asian Caravan Trade," in James D. Tracy, ed., *The Rise of Merchant Empires* (Cambridge, England, 1990), p. 366.

45. Clifford Foust, *Muscovite and Mandarin: Russia's Trade with China and Its Setting, 1727–1805* (Chapel Hill, 1969), p. 5.

46. Luciano Petech, *China and Tibet in the Early Eighteenth Century: History of the Establishment of the Chinese Protectorate in Tibet* (Leiden, 1972), pp. 11–13.

47. Sir Charles Bell, *The People of Tibet* (Oxford, 1938), p. 147.

48. McGovern, *To Lhasa in Disguise,* p. 42.

49. Chapman, *Lhasa,* p. 241.

50. Harrier, *Seven Years,* p. 137.

51. Petech, *China and Tibet,* p. 11.

52. Clifford Foust, *Rhubarb: The Wondrous Drug* (Princeton, 1992), discusses all aspects of the rhubarb trade.

53. "Rhubarb," *Encyclopaedia Britannica,* 9th ed. (Chicago, 1892), XX, 529.

54. Petech, *China and Tibet,* p. 368.

55. Joseph Fletcher, "Ch'ing Inner Asia c. 1800," *Cambridge History of China,* vol. 10 (Cambridge, England, 1978), 94.

56. See, for instance, Rockhill, *Land of the Lamas,* pp. 51–53, 221–222.

57. Captain Hamilton Bower, *A Journey Across Tibet* (New York, 1894), p. 284.

58. Rockhill, *Land of the Lamas,* p. 120.

59. Petech, *China and Tibet,* pp. 149–151.

60. The issue of Manchu identity is a complex one. See Pamela Crossley, *The Orphan Warriors: Three Manchu Generations and the End of the Qing World* (Princeton, 1990).

61. Rockhill, *Land of the Lamas,* p. 54.

62. *Ibid.,* pp. 52–54.

63. Bower, *Journey Across Tibet,* p. 97.

64. Pedro Carrasco, *Land and Polity in Tibet* (Seattle, 1959), p. 25.

65. Fletcher, "Ch'ing Inner Asia," p. 101.

66. Crossley, *Orphan Warriors,* p. 17.

67. Bower, *Journey Across Tibet,* p. 281.

68. *Ibid.,* p. 22.

69. Fletcher, "Ch'ing Inner Asia," p. 35.

4. THE CLOSING OF TIBET

1. Snellgrove and Richardson, *Cultural History of Tibet*, p. 224.
2. As quoted in MacGregor, *Tibet*, p. 107.
3. *Ibid.*
4. Captain Samuel Turner, *An Account of an Embassy to the Court of the Teshoo Lama in Tibet: Containing a Narrative of a Journey Through Bootan, and Part of Tibet* (New Delhi, 1971), p. xiii.
5. McGovern, *To Lhasa in Disguise*, pp. 417–418.
6. Richardson, *Tibet and Its History*, p. 65.
7. Markham, *Narratives*, p. 58.
8. Turner, *Account of an Embassy*, p. xiii.
9. Cammann, *Trade Through the Himalayas*, pp. 115–120.
10. *Ibid.*, pp. 123–124.
11. Snellgrove and Richardson, *Cultural History of Tibet*, p. 231.
12. Bell, *People of Tibet*, p. 100.
13. Snellgrove and Richardson, *Cultural History of Tibet*, p. 170.
14. Richardson, *Tibet and Its History*, p. 71; Shakabpa, *Tibet*, p. 176.
15. Richardson, *Tibet and Its History*, p. 59.
16. Bell, *People of Tibet*, p. 66.
17. *Ibid.*, p. 85.
18. Joseph Fletcher, "The Heyday of the Ch'ing Order in Mongolia, Sinkiang and Tibet," in Sinor, *Cambridge History of Early Inner Asia*, p. 402.
19. *Ibid.* Also Shakabpa, *Tibet*, p. 175.
20. Bell, *People of Tibet*, pp. 140–147.
21. Shakabpa, *Tibet*, p. 179.
22. The most definitive account of the Tibetan trade during this period is available in Alastair Lamb, *Britain and Chinese Central Asia* (London, 1960), pp. 336–359, which has an appendix devoted solely to this subject. Lamb provides lists of goods and figures (which he admits are necessarily unreliable) for this trade in the late nineteenth century. He argues that new south Asian routes opened during this period were due to British and Nepalese expansion into the area around Tibet. He also shows the extent to which a desire for Tibetan shawl wool and a belief that Tibet might constitute a good market for south Asian tea helped push the British into repeated attempts to contact Tibet. He even notes that attempts by the British to bring this wool out by way of China failed, leaving south Asia as the only possible route. Finally he describes an interesting though ultimately unsuccessful project by the Rothschilds to develop Tibet as a source of gold. These schemes show the excitement generated by supposed commercial possibilities that Tibet offered to the interests that appeared on Tibet's borders.
23. Kawaguchi, *Three Years*, p. 448.
24. Fletcher, "Heyday of the Ch'ing Order," p. 406.

25. *Ibid.*, pp. 399–401.

26. Foust, *Muscovite and Mandarin*, pp. 46–95.

27. *Ibid.*, p. 197.

28. *Ibid.*, p. 198.

29. Peter Hopkirk, *Trespassers to the Roof of the World* (London, 1982). Cammann, *Trade Through the Himalayas*; MacGregor, *Tibet*; Graham Sandberg, *The Exploration of Tibet: History and Particulars* (New Delhi, 1973); George Woodcock, *Into Tibet: The Early British Explorers* (London, 1971). For a discussion of the whole genre, see Bishop, *Myth of Shangri-La.*

30. Fletcher, "Heyday of the Ch'ing Order," p. 396.

31. Thomas Manning, in Markham, *Narratives.*

32. Richardson, *Tibet and Its History*, p. 72.

33. See Derek Waller, *The Pundits: British Exploration of Tibet and Central Asia* (Lexington, Ky., 1990).

34. *Ibid.*; also MacGregor, *Tibet*, pp. 263–266.

35. McGovern, *To Lhasa in Disguise*, pp. 20–21.

36. Shakabpa, *Tibet*, p. 198.

37. Glenn Mullin, *Path of the Bodhisattva Warrior* (Ithaca, 1988), p. 56. Mullin elaborated on this affair in a message he posted on the Internet in October 1994.

38. Shakabpa, *Tibet*, p. 192.

39. Melvyn Goldstein, *A History of Modern Tibet, 1913–1951: The Demise of the Lamaist State* (Berkeley, 1989), p.42.

40. *Ibid.*, pp. 42–43.

41. *Ibid.*, p. 43.

42. Alexandra David-Neel, *Magic and Mystery in Tibet* (New York, 1971), a republication of the English translation by Claude Kendall.

43. Wilhelm Filchner, *Sturn uber Asien* (Berlin, 1926), as discussed in Mehra, *The Younghusband Expedition* (London, 1968), p. 137.

44. Mehra, *Younghusband Expedition.*

45. Richardson, *Tibet and Its History*, p. 82.

46. *Ibid.*

47. *Ibid.*

48. Kawaguchi, *Three Years*, p. 506.

49. Mehra, *Younghusband Expedition*, pp. 86–87.

50. Bell, *People of Tibet*, p. 68.

51. McGovern, *To Lhasa in Disguise*, p. 34.

52. *Ibid.*, pp. 46–47.

53. Paul A. Varg, *The Making of a Myth: The United States and China, 1897–1912* (East Lansing, 1968), pp. 149–150.

54. Peter Fleming, *Bayonets to Lhasa* (New York, 1986), p. 60.

55. Alastair Lamb, *The China-India Border: The Origins of the Disputed Boundaries* (New York, 1964), p. 134.

56. Alastair Lamb, *The McMahon Line: A Study in the Relations Between India, China and Tibet, 1904 to 1914* (London, 1966), I, 12. One scholar has even speculated that news of the Anglo-Chinese agreement abrogating the Tibetan-British treaty persuaded the Dalai Lama to leave Mongolia and begin the return to Tibet. See Parshotam Mehra, *The McMahon Line and After: A Study of the Triangular Contest on India's North-East Frontier Between Britain, China, and Tibet, 1904–47* (New York, 1974), p. 27.

57. This statement in the British foreign office files is quoted in Michael C. van Walt van Praag, *The Status of Tibet: History Rights, and Prospects in International Law* (Boulder, Colo., 1987), p. 38.

58. Li Tieh-tseng, *The Historical Status of Tibet* (New York, 1956), pp. 63–65.

59. Lamb, *McMahon Line*, I, 170.

60. *Ibid.*, pp. 187–191.

61. Bower, *Journey Across Tibet*, p. 224.

62. Jamyang Norbu, *Warriors of Tibet: The Story of Aten and the Khampas' Fight for the Freedom of their Country* (London, 1979), p. 28.

63. Lamb, *McMahon Line*, pp. 108, 251–257.

64. *Ibid.*, p. 28. Other sources, however, say he only went down on one knee at this time.

65. Bell, *People of Tibet*, p. 204.

66. Mehra, *Younghusband Expedition*, p. 147.

67. Liang Qichao, "Zhengzhixue dajia bolunzhili zhi xueshuo" ("The theory of the great political scientist Bluntchli"), *Yinpingshi heshi wenji (Collected Works and Essays from the Ice-Drinker's Studio)* (Shanghai, 1936), 5, 13:74–77.

68. Yang Shouren, *Xin Hunan* (New Hunan, 1903), as quoted in Harold Z. Schiffrin, *Sun Yat-sen and the Origins of the Chinese Revolution* (Berkeley, 1968), p. 295.

69. Dru Gladney, *Muslim Chinese: Ethnic Nationalism in the People's Republic* (Cambridge, Mass., 1991), p. 83.

70. Sun Yat-sen, as quoted in June Dreyer, *China's Forty Millions* (Cambridge, Mass., 1976), p. 16.

71. *Ibid.*, p. 17.

72. *Ibid.*

73. David Yen-ho Wu, "The Construction of Chinese and Non-Chinese Identities," *Daedalus* 120, no. 2 (Spring 1991), 167.

74. Shakabpa, *Tibet*, p. 248.

75. *Ibid.*

76. Lamb, *China-India Border*, p. 143.

77. Lamb, *McMahon Line*, II, 488–492.

78. Tom Grunfeld, *The Making of Modern Tibet* (Armonk, N.Y., 1987), pp. 64–66.

79. Bell, *People of Tibet*, pp. 119–120.
80. McGovern, *To Lhasa in Disguise*, p. 420.
81. *Ibid.*, p. 421.
82. Bell, *People of Tibet*, p. 249.
83. *Ibid.*, pp. 86–87.
84. *Ibid.*, p. 144.
85. Interview in Dharamsala, June 1992.
86. Bell, *People of Tibet*, p. 307.
87. Goldstein, *History of Modern Tibet*, p. 135.

5. THE "LIBERATION" OF TIBET

1. David-Neel, *Magic and Mystery in Tibet*, p. 2.
2. The Thirteenth Dalai Lama, in Mullin, *Path of the Bodhisattva Warrior*, p. 112.
3. Goldstein, *History of Modern Tibet*, pp. 152–156. Goldstein quotes a street song making fun of the regiment's rules and regulations (p. 154).
4. Bell, *People of Tibet*, p. 130.
5. Goldstein, *History of Modern Tibet*, p. 204.
6. *Ibid*, pp. 208–209.
7. Li Tieh-tseng, *Historical Status of Tibet*, p. 167.
8. Chapman, *Lhasa*, pp. 236–237.
9. Goldstein, *History of Modern Tibet*, p. 245.
10. Extract from the Chinese newspaper *Yung Bao*, March 27, 1937, as reproduced in Parshotam Mehra, *Tibetan Polity, 1904–37* (Wiesbaden, 1976), p. 75.
11. Dalai Lama, *Freedom in Exile: The Autobiography of the Dalai Lama* (New York, 1991), p. 12.
12. Thubten Jigme Norbu, Foreword, in Mullin, *Path of the Bodhisattva Warrior*, p. 12.
13. Goldstein, *History of Modern Tibet*, pp. 321–322.
14. Harrier, *Seven Years*, p. 192.
15. Dalai Lama, *Freedom in Exile*, p. 14.
16. Edgar Snow, *Red Star Over China* (New York, 1961), pp. 213–216.
17. Dick Wilson, *The Long March* (New York, 1971), p. 221.
18. Goldstein, *History of Modern Tibet*, p. 441.
19. As quoted in Lea Terhune, *Far Eastern Economic Review*, March 24, 1994.
20. John Ward Anderson and Molly Moore, " 'Ethnic Cleansing' Charges Echo in Himalayan Bhutan; Bhutan Determined to Preserve its Culture," *Washington Post*, April 4, 1994.

21. Chiang Kai-shek, *China's Destiny* (New York, 1947), pp. 12–13.

22. Lowell Thomas, Jr., *Out of This World: Across the Himalayas to Forbidden Tibet* (New York, 1950), p. 236.

23. Grunfeld, *Making of Modern Tibet*, pp. 85–86.

24. This is discussed in detail in Goldstein, *History of Modern Tibet*, pp. 570–588.

25. *Ibid.*, p. 586.

26. *Ibid.*, pp. 598–607.

27. *Ibid.*, p. 607.

28. Thomas, *Out of This World*, p. 240.

29. Mao Zedong, "We Are Not Going to Turn the Country over to Moscow," in Stuart Schram, *The Political Thought of Mao Tse-tung* (New York, 1972), p. 420.

30. As reported in Dreyer, *China's Forty Millions*, p. 67.

31. *Ibid.*, p. 87.

32. Goldstein, *History of Modern Tibet*, p. 684.

33. "Military Communiqué on Entry of Chinese Army into Tibet," New China News Agency, November 8, 1950, as translated in Union Research Institute, *Tibet: 1950–1967* (Hong Kong, 1968), p. 2.

34. Goldstein, *History of Modern Tibet*, pp. 690–698.

35. Union Research Institute, *Tibet: 1950–1967*, p. 2.

36. See Goldstein, *History of Modern Tibet*, pp. 690–698.

37. John Avedon, *In Exile from the Land of Snows* (London, 1984), pp. 31–32.

38. Dalai Lama, *Freedom in Exile*, pp. 51–52.

39. Richardson, *Tibet and Its History*, pp. 183–184.

40. "Agreement for the Peaceful Liberation of Tibet" (17-point Agreement of May 23, 1951), in *ibid.*, p. 290.

41. *Ibid.*, p. 291.

42. Dalai Lama, *Freedom in Exile*, p. 63.

43. George Patterson, *Tibet in Revolt* (London, 1960), pp. 80–85.

44. Dalai Lama, *Freedom in Exile*, p. 65.

45. *Ibid.*, p. 66.

46. Goldstein, *History of Modern Tibet*, p. 13.

47. Dalai Lama, *Freedom in Exile*, p. 64.

48. "On the Policies for Our Work in Tibet—Directive of the Central Committee of the Communist Party of China," April 6, 1952, in *Selected Works of Mao Tse-tung*, V (Peking, 1977), 73–76.

49. Dalai Lama as quoted in the *Statesman* (New Delhi), March 15, 1952, reprinted in Ramakant, *Nepal, China and India* (New Delhi, 1976), p. 79.

50. Ramakant, *Nepal, China and India*, p. 100.

51. Dalai Lama, *Freedom in Exile*, p. 78.

52. Fan Ming, "Another Major Accomplishment in the Reconstruc-

tion of Tibet," NCNA, Lhasa, as translated in Union Research Institute, *Tibet, 1950–1967*, p. 56.

53. Dreyer, *China's Forty Millions*, p. 133.

54. Dalai Lama, *Freedom in Exile*, p. 90.

55. *Ibid.*, p. 104.

56. Jamyang Norbu, *Warriors of Tibet: The Story of Aten, and the Khampas' Fight for the Freedom of Their Country* (London, 1986), p. 106.

57. Patterson, *Tibet in Revolt*.

58. The best account is Chris Mullin, "The CIA: Tibetan Conspiracy," *Far Eastern Economic Review* 89, no. 36, p. 31.

59. Grunfeld, *Making of Modern Tibet*, pp. 147–160.

60. Dalai Lama, *Freedom in Exile*, pp. 140–141.

61. *Ibid.*, p. 127.

62. Mao Zedong, "On the Correct Handling of Contradictions Among the People," *Selected Works of Mao Tsetung* (Beijing, 1977), p. 406.

63. Richardson, *Tibet and Its History*, p. 205.

64. Grunfeld, *Making of Modern Tibet*, pp. 129–134.

65. Dalai Lama, *Freedom in Exile*, pp. 131–132.

66. Dalai Lama, March 19, 1959, in Union Research Institute, *Tibet, 1950–1967*, p. 371.

67. Shakabpa, *Tibet*, p. 319.

68. Grunfeld, *Making of Modern Tibet*, pp. 129–134.

69. "Commentary on the So-called Statement of the Dalai Lama," NCNA, Beijing, April 20, 1959, in Union Research Institute, *Tibet, 1950–1967*, p. 382.

70. "Communiqué on the Revolt Issued by the New China News Agency," NCNA, March 28, 1959, in Union Research Institute, *Tibet, 1950–1967*, p. 348.

71. For a good description of press distortions of his flight, see Grunfeld, *Making of Modern Tibet*, pp. 138–146.

6. THE DELUGE

1. "To Strengthen the Organizational Structure of Various Departments Under the Preparatory Committee for the Tibet Autonomous Region," *Renmin Ribao (People's Daily)*, April 11, 1959, as reprinted in Union Research Institute, *Tibet: 1950–1967*, p. 387.

2. "Resolution on the Question of Tibet," *Renmin Ribao (People's Daily)*, April 29, 1959, *ibid.*, p. 390.

3. *Ibid.*

4. Kawaguchi, *Three Years*, p. 265.

5. Dreyer, *China's Forty Millions*, p. 184.

6. "Democratic Reforms to be Carried Out in Tibet, NCNA, July 2, 1959, as reprinted in Union Research Institute, *Tibet: 1950–1967*, p. 392–393.

7. *Ibid.*

8. Dreyer, *China's Forty Millions*, p. 185.

9. "Compensation Arrangements in Tibet," NCNA, Lhasa, November 2, from *Renmin Ribao (People's Daily)*, November 2, 1960, as reprinted in Union Research Institute, *Tibet: 1950–1967*, pp. 405–406.

10. "Tibet in 1960," *Renmin Ribao (People's Daily)*, December 15, 1960, *ibid.*, p. 412.

11. *Ibid.*, p. 417.

12. Chang Chingwu, "Correctly Implement the Party's Guideline and Policy on Democratic Reform in Tibet," *Renmin Ribao (People's Daily)*, May 25, 1962, *ibid.*, p. 428.

13. *Ibid.*, p. 516.

14. Alastair Lamb, *The Sino-Indian Border in Ladakh* (Canberra, 1973), pp. 66–73.

15. *Ibid.*, p. 73.

16. Roderick MacFarquhar, *The Origins of the Cultural Revolution 2: The Great Leap Forward 1958–1960* (New York, 1983), pp. 256–257.

17. Lamb, *Sino-Indian Border*, p. 74.

18. Avedon, *In Exile*, p. 121.

19 *Ibid.*, pp. 271–272.

20. Dreyer, *China's Forty Millions*, p. 217.

21. Liu Guokai, *A Brief Analysis of the Cultural Revolution* (New York, 1987), pp. 45–46.

22. Avedon, *In Exile*, pp. 302–303.

23. Tseten Wangchuk Sharlho, "China's Reforms in Tibet: Issues and Dilemmas," *Journal of Contemporary China* 1, no. 1 (Fall 1992), p. 36.

24. Dreyer, *China's Forty Millions*, pp. 240–241.

25. "How the Revolt in Tibet Broke Out—Exposing Teng Hsiao-p'ing, Chief Culprit Responsible for the Tibet Rebellion," *SCMP*, no. 4086, October 27, 1967, from *Chih-tien Chiang-shan*, Canton, October 27, 1967, as reprinted in Union Research Institute, *Tibet: 1950–1967*, pp. 689–700.

7. THE UNCOMFORTABLE DECADE

1. Tseten Sandrup, "Chinese Population—Threat to Tibetan Identity," paper distributed by the Tibet Information Office, 1992, p. 3.

2. Dalai Lama, *Tibet, China and the World* (New Delhi, 1989), p. 35.

3. *Ibid.*, pp. 352–353.

4. Report of the National United Front Work Conference, January 23, 1982, in *Minzu zhengce wenxuan (Selected Documents of Nationality Policy)*, (Urumqi, 1985), p. 10.

5. Planning Bureau of the Tibetan Autonomous Region, "Xizang jingji jianshe de weide chengjiu" ("The Great Achievements of Tibetan Economic Development"), *Xizang yanjiu*, no. 3 (1985), p. 15.

6. Li Rongxia, "Tibet in Stride with Current Reform," *Beijing Review*, April 29–May 5, 1991, p. 22.

7. As cited in Dawa Norbu, "China's Dialogue with the Dalai Lama" *Pacific Affairs* 64, no. 3 (Fall 1991), p. 358.

8. Zhao Zhen-yin, "Xizang shehui de juda bianhua" ("The Great Changes in Tibetan Society"), *Zhongguo zangxue*, no. 2 (1989), p. 9, as quoted in Sharlho, "China's Reforms," p. 40.

9. Interview in Dharamsala, June 1992.

10. Yin Fatang, "Yiqie cong xizang de shiji chufa" ("All Things Should Start from Tibet's Own Conditions"), *Xizang minzu wenli lunwen xuan (A Collection of Writings on the Tibetan People)* (Lhasa), p. 25. As quoted in Sharlho, "China's Reforms," p. 44.

11. Sharlho, "China's Reforms," p. 44.

12. Interview with the Dalai Lama in Dharamsala, June 1992.

13. Avedon, *In Exile*, p. 324. The two were imprisoned near each other.

14. "Xiang Official Talks About Central Government Aid," *Xinhua*, March 13, 1983, translated in *Foreign Broadcast Information Service* (hereafter *F.B.I.S.*), March 16, 1983, p. Q1.

15. Reprinted in *Renmin Ribao (People's Daily)*, June 4, 1984, and translated in *F.B.I.S.*, June 14, 1984, p. K3–13.

16. An explicit discussion of this occurred in Min Yan, "On Actual Inequality Among Nationalities Left Over by History," *Renmin Ribao (People's Daily)*, March 26, 1984, p. 5, translated in *F.B.I.S.*, April 3, 1984, p. K1–6.

17. Sharlho, "China's Reforms," p. 55.

18. Blake Kerr and John Ackerly, "Witness to Repression," *Utne Reader*, March/April 1989, p. 41.

19. Dalai Lama, "Address to Members of European Parliament," *Tibetan Bulletin* 19, no. 2 (May–July 1988).

20. At least one Tibetan writer alleged that it was foreign pressure and advisers (among others, President Jimmy Carter and the British Foreign Office) that convinced the Dalai Lama to propose his compromise. See Jamyang Norbu, "In Deng's Grave New World an Illusion Dies," *Tibetan Review*, August 1989. This provoked two letters from foreign supporters of the Tibet cause in the November 1989 issue of the same magazine, one (from Patricia Simmons) agreeing that the British Foreign Office had too much influence on the Dalai Lama, and the other from Michael C. Van

2

2 2 *Notes*

Walt defending his own role in helping formulate policies. A human rights report first published under the auspices of the UN and more recently revised by the Tibetan Young Buddhist Association in Dharamsala has suggested that although the Dalai Lama appeared to compromise with the Chinese, in fact he did not. The report points out that the Dalai Lama said the Tibetan people would have the final say and hence could override any agreement with the Chinese that might appear to compromise Tibet's independence. *Tibet: The Facts* (Dharamsala, 1990), p. 158.

21. For her account, see Christa Meindersma, "Massacre in the Forbidden Kingdom," *Reader's Digest*, October 1989, pp. 126–132.

22. "China's White Paper Distorts Tibetan Calls for Negotiations Without Preconditions," *Official Tibetan Response of "Opening of Tibet" and China's White Paper on Tibet*, September 24, 1992.

23. Jonathan Mirsky, "The Secret Massacre," (London) *Observer*, August 12, 1991.

24. See, for example, "A Bow to Tibet," *Time*, October 14, 1989.

25. *Present Conditions in Tibet* (Dharamsala, 1990), p. 95.

26. *Ibid.*, p. 89.

27. Dalai Lama, "Five-Point Peace Plan," September 21, 1987.

28. Dalai Lama and Galen Rowell, *My Tibet* (Berkeley, 1990), p. 11.

29. Dalai Lama, "Universal Responsibility and Our Global Environment," *Tibet Press Watch* 4, no. 3 (July 1992), 8.

30. "Tibet to Establish World's No. 1 Preserve," *Beijing Review*, April 9–15, 1990, pp. 11–12.

31. See Goldstein and Beall, *Nomads*, esp. pp. 58–71, 174–181.

32. Jackie Sam and Yao Shing-mu, *Hong Kong Standard* feature on Tibet, reprinted in *F.B.I.S.*, February 23, 1989, p. 65.

33. Rong Ma, "Han and Tibetan Residential Patterns in Lhasa," *China Quarterly*, December 1991, pp. 814–835.

34. Sandrup, "Chinese Population," see *Beijing Review*, February 24, 1984, p. 8.

35. *Ibid.*

36. "Claims of Han Emigration to Tibet Said Groundless," *Xinhua*, April 12, 1991, translated in *F.B.I.S.*, April 15, 1991, p. 67. These figures are constantly repeated in Chinese articles on Tibet. See, for example, "Babang Luobu," as reported in *F.B.I.S.*, June 29, 1993, p. 58. Interestingly, at about the same time Gyaincain Norbu, chair of the TAR government, in a speech reprinted in the *Tibetan Daily*, claimed there were 2,252,600 people in Tibet, of whom 2,260,000 or 98 percent were Tibetans. See *F.B.I.S.*, June 28, 1993, p. 29.

37. Jasper Becker, " 'Secret' Report Says 'Far Fewer Troops' in Tibet," *South China Morning Post*, June 8, 1992, *F.B.I.S.*, June 9, 1992, pp. 28–29.

38. Interview in Dharamsala, 1992.

39. *Present Conditions,* p. 47.

40. "Human Rights Desk, Official Document Reveals Coercive Birth Control Policy in Tibet; Policy Covers Even Farmers and Nomads in Eastern Tibet," Central Tibetan Administration, Dharamsala, as reprinted in *CTN News,* August 21, 1993.

41. Judith Banister, *China's Changing Population* (Stanford, 1987), pp. 249–250.

42. Susan Greenhaigh, "Shifts in China's Population Policy, 1984–86; Views from the Central, Provincial, and Local Levels," *Population and Development Review* 12, no. 3, 499–500.

43. Melvyn Goldstein and Cynthia M. Beall, "China's Birth Control Policy in the Tibet Autonomous Region," *Asian Survey* 21, no. 3 (March 1991), 285–303.

44. Tim McGirk, (London) *Independent,* May 11, 1994.

45. Dalai Lama, "The Importance of Indian Initiative on Tibet," *Tibetan Bulletin,* July–August 1993, translation of an address given in Dharamsala on May 30, 1993.

46. Jawed Naqvi, "Dalai Lama Says Autonomy, Not Independence Is Goal," Reuters, August 12, 1993.

47. Interview with Tashi Tsering, Lhasa, 1992.

48. Interview in Dharamsala, 1992.

49. Kawaguchi, *Three Years,* pp. 506–507.

50. *Ibid.,* p. 522.

Index

A NOTE ON THE AUTHOR

Lee Feigon chairs the East Asian Studies department and is professor of history at Colby College. He grew up in Chicago and studied at the University of California, Berkeley, the University of Chicago, and the University of Wisconsin, Madison. Mr. Feigon has written extensively on Asian and particularly Chinese history and politics, including the book *Chen Duxiu: Founder of the Chinese Communist Party* and articles in the *Atlantic*, the *Wall Street Journal*, the *Nation*, *Barron's*, and the *Chicago Tribune* as well as the *Journal of Asian Studies* and the *American Historical Review*. His most recent book, *China Rising: The Meaning of Tiananmen*, was widely praised.